Attributes of America
Understanding Our Constitutional Republic

Cynthia Noland Dunbar

Cover image courtesy of Brennon Dunbar.

Kendall Hunt
publishing company

www.kendallhunt.com
Send all inquiries to:
4050 Westmark Drive
Dubuque, IA 52004-1840

Copyright © 2015 by Cynthia Noland Dunbar

ISBN 978-1-4652-7639-1

Kendall Hunt Publishing Company has the exclusive rights to reproduce this work,
to publicly distribute this work, to publicly perform this work and to publicly display this work.

All rights reserved. No part of this publication may be reproduced,
stored in a retrieval system, or transmitted, in any form or by any
means, electronic, mechanical, photocopying, recording, or otherwise,
without the prior written permission of the copyright owner.

Printed in the United States of America

Contents

Introduction	v
Chapter One: The Three Branches of Government	1
Chapter Two: Fundamental Documents that Underpin Our Government	31
Chapter Three: How Laws are Enacted	53
Chapter Four: Ways Citizens Shape and Influence the Government	59
Chapter Five: American Exceptionalism	69
Chapter Six: Declaration of Independence	77
Chapter Seven: The Constitution	89
Chapter Eight: The Declaration, Constitution, and Bill of Rights	109
Chapter Nine: Constitutional Republic	125
Glossary of Terms	135

Introduction

It is important for everyone to possess a firm grasp of the governmental structure of the society in which they live. Such knowledge is especially necessary and productive when citizens are accountable for how their government uses its authority. This is the case for every U.S. Citizen. Our elected officials are called to serve the people; the people are not called to serve our elected officials.

> We hold these truths to be self-evident, that all men are created equal, that they are endowed by their Creator with certain unalienable Rights, that among these are Life, Liberty and the pursuit of Happiness.— That to secure these rights, Governments are instituted among Men, deriving their just powers from the consent of the governed,—That whenever any Form of Government becomes destructive of these ends, it is the Right of the People to alter or to abolish it, and to institute new Government, laying its foundation on such principles and organizing its powers in such form, as to them shall seem most likely to effect their Safety and Happiness.
>
> *Excerpt from Declaration of Independence,*
> *2nd Paragraph*

Our Founding Fathers established us as a Republic and placed the preservation of our nation firmly within our hands. While "We the People" are entrusted with preserving our Republic, let us not confuse this with actually being in complete control, as if we were a Democracy; we are not. However, the preservation of our Constitutional Republic, as it always has been, still rests within our hands.

At the close of the Constitutional Convention Mrs. Powel of Philadelphia asked Benjamin Franklin,

> "Well Doctor, what have we got, a republic or a monarchy?"

Benjamin Franklin's famous response to Mrs. Powel's question was simply,

> "A republic, if YOU can keep it."
> *Conversation between Mrs. Powel and Dr. Franklin*
> *Documented by James McHenry*
> *Included in the 1906 American Historical Review*

In short, our Constitutional Republic is entirely dependent upon those of us within it for its continued existence. Such dependence anticipates that we as citizens are knowledgeable, informed, and engaged. Without such involvement, we are ill-equipped to vigilantly guard and preserve our Republic, as well as the liberties and freedoms it affords us. The goal of ***The Attributes of America*** is to provide U.S. citizens with a basic overview of our Constitutional Republic, sufficient to equip us with an appreciation of, and tools to preserve, the underlying principles that make our Nation exceptional.

Chapter 1: THE THREE BRANCHES OF GOVERNMENT

Original Sources:
1. Constitution: Articles I, II, and III
2. Federalist Papers 47, 78, and 81
3. Commentaries on the Constitution, Book III, Chapter VII, and Chapter XXXVIII

The three branches of the U.S. Government are the Executive, Legislative, and Judicial. The U.S. Constitution lays out the power and authority of each of these separate branches. It is important to note that the powers given to each branch are unique and separate and do not overlap or invade the authority of the other two.

Article I details the powers of the Legislative branch, which for the Federal Government is called Congress. All **legislative power**—the ability to make law—of the Federal government is given to Congress, and Congress is made up of both the Senate and the House of Representatives. Many people only refer to U.S. Representatives, or House members, as Congressmen. However, both U.S. Representatives and U.S. Senators are technically Congressmen.

Because there are two different chambers in Congress it is known as a **bicameral legislature.** This shows an important aspect of our Federal system of divided powers. The Senators, prior to Constitutional Amendment 17, were elected by their respective State legislatures. Today, the voters of their state directly elect their U.S. Senators. However, the Senate chamber still represents State Rights, as each and every state, regardless of its size or population, is given an equal voice in Congress through their two Senators. Voters of each state also directly elect their members of the House of Representatives. This chamber gives equal voice to the people, which can have the effect of either diminishing or increasing the power of a particular state, since the total number of Representatives in Congress from a given state varies based upon that state's population.

U.S. Capitol © Orhan Cam/Shutterstock.com

This bicameral system reflects our principles of Federalism. **Federalism** exists where authority coexists and is placed within separate governing sovereigns. Federalism in the United States places authority within both the national government, often referred to as the federal government, and the state governments. This principle of Federalism is also reflected within our electoral system. Allowing the people the right of an individual vote reflects the national face of our government. Allowing the states the ability to cast their electoral votes reflects the coexisting sovereignty between the states and the federal government. Should these principles of Federalism that were important to our Founding Fathers be replaced with a desire for a strong national government, then neither a bicameral legislature nor the Electoral College would remain necessary methods for displacing centralized control. Advocating majority vote over the Electoral College is an example of embracing a strong centralized government over maintaining principles of federalism.

Article II details the powers of the Executive branch, specifically the office of the President. In short, the **Executive branch** executes—meaning the Executive branch is responsible for putting into force the laws that are enacted by the Legislative branch. This is why the President has the authority to either sign into law, or veto, a bill passed by Congress. If the President signs the legislation into law, it makes the President, and by extension the entire Executive branch, ultimately responsible for seeing that the law is enforced. While the Presidential office is frequently viewed as the most powerful position, it does not actively possess legislative authority. Since the Constitution gives the legislative authority within Article I, the President is constrained to the function of carrying out the laws passed by Congress. Consequently, Congress as a whole arguably holds even more power than does the President of the United States. However, Congressmen individually do not.

White House © Vacclav/Shutterstock.com

Article III grants authority to the **Judiciary**, more specifically the Supreme Court and all Federal Courts. This is the shortest of the first three Articles of the Constitution, and for good reason. The Founders intended the judiciary to be the weakest branch of the three. The judiciary is responsible to take the laws as passed by Congress and apply them to a given set of facts, otherwise known as a **case or controversy**. Other than in very specific cases, the Supreme Court generally possesses only **appellate jurisdiction**. What this means is simply that cases cannot be filed or arise in the Supreme Court. Instead, they must be tried in lower courts and be appealed to the Supreme Court for review of the lower court's decision. Additionally, cases heard in lower courts do not have an automatic right of appeal to the Supreme Court. The Supreme Court must grant an appellant a **Writ of Certiorari**, a process that allows the Supreme Court the ability to select which cases it will accept for review, allowing a case to be heard.

There is a debate as to whether or not the Supreme Court is the only branch responsible for determining the **Constitutionality** of a Law. This debate highlights the importance of understanding the different roles and authorities of the three branches. The Constitution in Article VI, Clause 3 requires all three branches to swear or affirm to uphold the Constitution.

The Senators and Representatives before mentioned, and the members of the several state legislatures, and all executive and judicial officers, both of the United States and of the several states, shall be bound by oath or affirmation, to support this Constitution; but no religious test shall ever be required as a qualification to any office or public trust under the United States.

This affirmation places a burden upon every elected official to determine the Constitutionality of any action prior to taking it. The only remaining question would be, "Does the opinion of the Supreme Court take precedence over the other two branches as to what is, or is not, constitutional?"

Supreme Court © Dave Newman/Shutterstock.com

The **Doctrine of Nonacquiescence** allows the three branches, each vested with the responsibility to uphold the constitution, the freedom to ignore the determinations of the other two branches. If one branch does not agree with another branch, no single branch has the authority to mandate the compliance of the other. This tension between the branches underscores the need to understand checks and balances. It is helpful to study what the Founders anticipated would be the role of each of the three branches, as well as how each branch was to hold in check the other two branches. For example, the intended check on the judiciary for creating law was impeachment by Congress. This was viewed as appropriate since it would be punishing the Art. III branch for attempting to utilize Art. I power.

Three branches were created, and checks and balances were put in place as protective barriers from **despotic or tyrannical rule**. The belief of the Founding Fathers was that keeping power and authority widely distributed was a necessary safeguard to the protection of the people from the government itself. The more the power could be dispersed, the better. That was the same idea behind the principle of Federalism. Federalism acted as a **vertical distribution of power** between the Federal and State governments. Checks and balances were implemented as a **horizontal distribution of power** between the three federal branches. The urgency of the Founders to limit power, rather than expand it, was grounded in the belief that to accumulate all authority in one place would be to place the governed at the mercy of tyranny.

At the time of our nation's founding there was a general distrust of large or powerful government, especially government that was far removed from local control and accountability. The United States became one nation and one people in 1776 by our Declaration of Independence. **Articles of Confederation**, created November 15, 1777 and finally ratified March 1, 1781, served to loosely govern this one nation. However, it soon became apparent that these Articles of Confederation were a little too loosely configured to be able to effectively govern. It was in this climate that the **Constitutional Convention** convened between May 25, 1787 and September 17, 1787. The initial goal of the Convention was to amend the Articles of Confederation to be more effective. While there were parties who continued to support this strategy, almost from its inception, the Convention set out to draft a new document that could serve as the Supreme Law of the Land.

The Federalist Papers were published in an effort to inform and educate Americans about the need, purpose and, functionality of the proposed Constitution. These Federalist Papers consisted of a series of writings authored by Alexander Hamilton, James Madison, and John Jay; each wrote articles on

Federalist Paper No. 50 © Everett Historical/Shutterstock.com

various aspects of the proposed Constitution. Each of these three men were credible sources, capable of articulating the goals and objectives of the new Constitution should it be ratified.

Alexander Hamilton wrote 52 of the 85 compiled papers. He became the first Secretary of the Treasury and was an articulate spokesman for the justification of the Constitution. While he was the primary contributor to the Federalist Papers, these papers garnered significant credibility through the addition of two other authors. **John Jay**, the first Chief Justice of the Supreme Court, could hardly be viewed as a novice concerning the legal philosophies and intentions injected within the four corners of the Constitution. Finally, **James Madison**, our 4th President, was such a chief architect of the Constitution and Bill of Rights as to later be known as the **Father of our Constitution**. The clear and concise documentation of Hamilton, coupled with the credibility and station of Jay and Madison, make the Federalist Papers an indispensible resource in determining the goals and intentions of the Founding Fathers expressed within the Constitution.

Alexander Hamilton © Kovalchuk Oleksandr/Shutterstock.com

Documents that were written during the era prior to the ratification of our Constitution, such as the Federalist Papers, are invaluable to gaining a proper understanding of the goals established within our Constitution. Additionally, writings made shortly after the ratification—adoption of the Constitution—can also be very helpful, as it was during this time that the implementation of the new Constitution began to shed light on the balance of power between the three branches. James Madison nominated Joseph Story to the Supreme Court; Story was a legal scholar who would later draft a complete treatise on the document he had been asked to repeatedly interpret. **Justice Joseph Story** served on the U.S. Supreme Court from 1811 to 1845. He wrote his Commentaries on the Constitution of the United States in 1833 and dedicated them to Chief Justice Marshall with whom he had served on the Supreme Court. His **Commentaries on the Constitution of the United States** are still viewed today as a crucial review of our Constitutional Republic and the legal philosophy underlying it. Reading treatises such as these provide us with enormous insight into how our Republic is to function.

Constitution of the United States

Article I

Section. 1

All legislative Powers herein granted shall be vested in a Congress of the United States, which shall consist of a Senate and House of Representatives.

Section. 2

The House of Representatives shall be composed of Members chosen every second Year by the People of the several States, and the Electors in each State shall have the Qualifications requisite for Electors of the most numerous Branch of the State Legislature.

No Person shall be a Representative who shall not have attained to the Age of twenty five Years, and been seven Years a Citizen of the United States, and who shall not, when elected, be an Inhabitant of that State in which he shall be chosen.

Representatives and direct Taxes shall be apportioned among the several States which may be included within this Union, according to their respective Numbers, which shall be determined by adding to the whole Number of free Persons, including those bound to Service for a Term of Years, and excluding Indians not taxed, three fifths of all other Persons. The actual Enumeration shall be made within three Years after the first Meeting of the Congress of the United States, and within every subsequent Term of ten Years, in such Manner as they shall by Law direct. The Number of Representatives shall not exceed one for every thirty Thousand, but each State shall have at Least one Representative; and until such enumeration shall be made, the State of New Hampshire shall be entitled to chuse three, Massachusetts eight, Rhode-Island and Providence Plantations one, Connecticut five, New-York six, New Jersey four, Pennsylvania eight, Delaware one, Maryland six, Virginia ten, North Carolina five, South Carolina five, and Georgia three.

When vacancies happen in the Representation from any State, the Executive Authority thereof shall issue Writs of Election to fill such Vacancies.

The House of Representatives shall chuse their Speaker and other Officers; and shall have the sole Power of Impeachment.

Section. 3

The Senate of the United States shall be composed of two Senators from each State, chosen by the Legislature thereof, for six Years; and each Senator shall have one Vote.

Immediately after they shall be assembled in Consequence of the first Election, they shall be divided as equally as may be into three Classes. The Seats of the Senators of the first Class shall be vacated at the Expiration of the second Year, of the second Class at the Expiration of the fourth Year, and of the third Class at the Expiration of the sixth Year, so that one third may be chosen every second Year; and if Vacancies happen by Resignation, or otherwise, during the Recess of the Legislature of any State, the Executive thereof may make temporary Appointments until the next Meeting of the Legislature, which shall then fill such Vacancies.

No Person shall be a Senator who shall not have attained to the Age of thirty Years, and been nine Years a Citizen of the United States, and who shall not, when elected, be an Inhabitant of that State for which he shall be chosen.

The Vice President of the United States shall be President of the Senate, but shall have no Vote, unless they be equally divided.

The Senate shall chuse their other Officers, and also a President pro tempore, in the Absence of the Vice President, or when he shall exercise the Office of President of the United States.

The Senate shall have the sole Power to try all Impeachments. When sitting for that Purpose, they shall be on Oath or Affirmation. When the President of the United States is tried, the Chief Justice shall preside: And no Person shall be convicted without the Concurrence of two thirds of the Members present.

Judgment in Cases of Impeachment shall not extend further than to removal from Office, and disqualification to hold and enjoy any Office of honor, Trust or Profit under the United States: but the Party convicted shall nevertheless be liable and subject to Indictment, Trial, Judgment and Punishment, according to Law.

Section. 4

The Times, Places and Manner of holding Elections for Senators and Representatives, shall be prescribed in each State by the Legislature thereof; but the Congress may at any time by Law make or alter such Regulations, except as to the Places of chusing Senators.

The Congress shall assemble at least once in every Year, and such Meeting shall be on the first Monday in December, unless they shall by Law appoint a different Day.

Section. 5

Each House shall be the Judge of the Elections, Returns and Qualifications of its own Members, and a Majority of each shall constitute a Quorum to do Business; but a smaller Number may adjourn from day to day, and may be authorized to compel the Attendance of absent Members, in such Manner, and under such Penalties as each House may provide.

Each House may determine the Rules of its Proceedings, punish its Members for disorderly Behaviour, and, with the Concurrence of two thirds, expel a Member.

Each House shall keep a Journal of its Proceedings, and from time to time publish the same, excepting such Parts as may in their Judgment require Secrecy; and the Yeas and Nays of the Members of either House on any question shall, at the Desire of one fifth of those Present, be entered on the Journal.

Neither House, during the Session of Congress, shall, without the Consent of the other, adjourn for more than three days, nor to any other Place than that in which the two Houses shall be sitting.

Section. 6

The Senators and Representatives shall receive a Compensation for their Services, to be ascertained by Law, and paid out of the Treasury of the United States. They shall in all Cases, except Treason, Felony and Breach of the Peace, be privileged from Arrest during their Attendance at the Session of their respective Houses, and in going to and returning from the same; and for any Speech or Debate in either House, they shall not be questioned in any other Place.

No Senator or Representative shall, during the Time for which he was elected, be appointed to any civil Office under the Authority of the United States, which shall have been created, or the Emoluments whereof shall have been encreased during such time; and no Person holding any Office under the United States, shall be a Member of either House during his Continuance in Office.

Section. 7

All Bills for raising Revenue shall originate in the House of Representatives; but the Senate may propose or concur with Amendments as on other Bills.

Every Bill which shall have passed the House of Representatives and the Senate, shall, before it become a Law, be presented to the President of the United States; If he approve he shall sign it, but if not he shall return it, with his Objections to that House in which it shall have originated, who shall enter the Objections at large on their Journal, and proceed to reconsider it. If after such Reconsideration two thirds of that House shall agree to pass the Bill, it shall be sent, together with the Objections, to the other House, by which it shall likewise be reconsidered, and if approved by two thirds of that House, it shall become a Law. But in all such Cases the Votes of both Houses shall be determined by yeas and Nays, and the Names of the Persons voting for and against the Bill shall be entered on the Journal of each House respectively. If any Bill shall not be returned by the President within ten Days (Sundays excepted) after it shall have been presented to him, the Same shall be a Law, in like Manner as if he had signed it, unless the Congress by their Adjournment prevent its Return, in which Case it shall not be a Law.

Every Order, Resolution, or Vote to which the Concurrence of the Senate and House of Representatives may be necessary (except on a question of Adjournment) shall be presented to the President of the United States; and before the Same shall take Effect, shall be approved by him, or being disapproved by him, shall be repassed by two thirds of the Senate and House of Representatives, according to the Rules and Limitations prescribed in the Case of a Bill.

Section. 8

The Congress shall have Power To lay and collect Taxes, Duties, Imposts and Excises, **to pay the Debts** and **provide for the common Defence and general Welfare of the United States;** but all Duties, Imposts and Excises shall be uniform throughout the United States;

To borrow Money on the credit of the United States;

To regulate Commerce with foreign Nations, and among the several States, and with the Indian Tribes;

To establish an uniform Rule of Naturalization, and **uniform Laws on the subject of Bankruptcies** throughout the United States;

To coin Money, regulate the Value thereof, and of foreign Coin, and fix the Standard of Weights and Measures;

To provide for the Punishment of counterfeiting the Securities and current Coin of the United States;

To establish Post Offices and post Roads;

To promote the Progress of Science and useful Arts, by securing for limited Times to Authors and Inventors the exclusive Right to their respective Writings and Discoveries;

To constitute Tribunals inferior to the supreme Court;

To define and punish Piracies and Felonies committed on the high Seas, and Offences against the Law of Nations;

To declare War, grant Letters of Marque and Reprisal, and make Rules concerning Captures on Land and Water;

To raise and support Armies, but no Appropriation of Money to that Use shall be for a longer Term than two Years;

To provide and maintain a Navy;

To make Rules for the Government and **Regulation of the land and naval Forces;**

To provide for calling forth the Militia to execute the Laws of the Union, suppress Insurrections and repel Invasions;

To provide for organizing, arming, and disciplining, the Militia, and for governing such Part of them as may be employed in the Service of the United States, reserving to the States respectively, the Appointment of the Officers, and the Authority of training the Militia according to the discipline prescribed by Congress;

To exercise exclusive Legislation in all Cases whatsoever, over such District (not exceeding ten Miles square) **as may**, by Cession of particular States, and the Acceptance of Congress, **become the Seat of the Government of the United States**, and to exercise like Authority over all Places purchased by the Consent of the Legislature of the State in which the Same shall be, for the Erection of Forts, Magazines, Arsenals, dock-Yards, and other needful Buildings;—And

To make all Laws which shall be necessary and proper for carrying into Execution the foregoing Powers, and all other Powers vested by this Constitution in the Government of the United States, or in any Department or Officer thereof.

Section. 9

The Migration or Importation of such Persons as any of the States now existing shall think proper to admit, shall not be prohibited by the Congress prior to the Year one thousand eight hundred and eight, but a Tax or duty may be imposed on such Importation, not exceeding ten dollars for each Person.

The Privilege of the Writ of Habeas Corpus shall not be suspended, unless when in Cases of Rebellion or Invasion the public Safety may require it.

No Bill of Attainder or ex post facto Law shall be passed.

No Capitation, or other direct, Tax shall be laid, unless in Proportion to the Census or enumeration herein before directed to be taken.

No Tax or Duty shall be laid on Articles exported from any State.

No Preference shall be given by any Regulation of Commerce or Revenue to the Ports of one State over those of another: nor shall Vessels bound to, or from, one State, be obliged to enter, clear, or pay Duties in another.

No Money shall be drawn from the Treasury, but in Consequence of Appropriations made by Law; and a regular Statement and Account of the Receipts and Expenditures of all public Money shall be published from time to time.

No Title of Nobility shall be granted by the United States: And no Person holding any Office of Profit or Trust under them, shall, without the Consent of the Congress, accept of any present, Emolument, Office, or Title, of any kind whatever, from any King, Prince, or foreign State.

Section. 10

No State shall enter into any Treaty, Alliance, or Confederation; grant Letters of Marque and Reprisal; coin Money; emit Bills of Credit; make any Thing but gold and silver Coin a Tender in Payment of Debts; pass any Bill of Attainder, ex post facto Law, or Law impairing the Obligation of Contracts, or grant any Title of Nobility.

No State shall, without the Consent of the Congress, lay any Imposts or Duties on Imports or Exports, except what may be absolutely necessary for executing it's inspection Laws: and the net Produce of all Duties and Imposts, laid by any State on Imports or Exports, shall be for the Use of the Treasury of the United States; and all such Laws shall be subject to the Revision and Controul of the Congress.

No State shall, without the Consent of Congress, lay any Duty of Tonnage, keep Troops, or Ships of War in time of Peace, enter into any Agreement or Compact with another State, or with a foreign Power, or engage in War, unless actually invaded, or in such imminent Danger as will not admit of delay.

Constitution of the United States
Article II

Section. 1

The executive Power shall be vested in a President of the United States of America. He shall hold his Office during the Term of four Years, and, together with the Vice President, chosen for the same Term, be elected, as follows

Each State shall appoint, in such Manner as the Legislature thereof may direct, a Number of Electors, equal to the whole Number of Senators and Representatives to which the State may be entitled in the Congress: but no Senator or Representative, or Person holding an Office of Trust or Profit under the United States, shall be appointed an Elector.

The Electors shall meet in their respective States, and vote by Ballot for two Persons, of whom one at least shall not be an Inhabitant of the same State with themselves. And they shall make a List of all the Persons voted for, and of the Number of Votes for each; which List they shall sign and certify, and transmit sealed to the Seat of the Government of the United States, directed to the President of the Senate. The President of the Senate shall, in the Presence of the Senate and House of Representatives, open all the Certificates, and the Votes shall then be counted. The Person having the greatest Number of Votes shall be the President, if such Number be a Majority of the whole Number of Electors appointed; and if there be more than one who have such Majority, and have an equal Number of Votes, then the House of Representatives shall immediately chuse by Ballot one of them for President; and if no Person have a Majority, then from the five highest on the List the said House shall in like Manner chuse the President. But in chusing the President, the Votes shall be taken by States, the Representation from each State having one Vote; A quorum for this Purpose shall consist of a Member or Members from two thirds of the States, and a Majority of all the States shall be necessary to a Choice. In every Case, after the Choice of the President, the Person having the greatest Number of Votes of the Electors shall be the Vice President. But if there should remain two or more who have equal Votes, the Senate shall chuse from them by Ballot the Vice President.

The Congress may determine the Time of chusing the Electors, and the Day on which they shall give their Votes; which Day shall be the same throughout the United States.

No Person except a natural born Citizen, or a Citizen of the United States, at the time of the Adoption of this Constitution, shall be eligible to the Office of President; neither shall any Person be eligible to that Office who shall not have attained to the Age of thirty five Years, and been fourteen Years a Resident within the United States.

In Case of the Removal of the President from Office, or of his Death, Resignation, or Inability to discharge the Powers and Duties of the said Office, the Same shall devolve on the Vice President, and the Congress may by Law provide for the Case of Removal, Death, Resignation or Inability, both of the President and Vice President, declaring what Officer shall then act as President, and such Officer shall act accordingly, until the Disability be removed, or a President shall be elected.

The President shall, at stated Times, receive for his Services, a Compensation, which shall neither be encreased nor diminished during the Period for which he shall have been elected, and he shall not receive within that Period any other Emolument from the United States, or any of them.

Before he enter on the Execution of his Office, he shall take the following Oath or Affirmation:—"I do solemnly swear (or affirm) that I will faithfully execute the Office of President of the United States, and will to the best of my Ability, preserve, protect and defend the Constitution of the United States."

Section. 2

The President shall be Commander in Chief of the Army and Navy of the United States, and of the Militia of the several States, when called into the actual Service of the United States; he may require the Opinion, in writing, of the principal Officer in each of the executive Departments, upon any Subject relating to the Duties of their respective Offices, and he shall have Power to grant Reprieves and Pardons for Offences against the United States, except in Cases of Impeachment.

He shall have Power, by and with the Advice and Consent of the Senate, to make Treaties, provided two thirds of the Senators present concur; and he shall nominate, and by and with the Advice and Consent of the Senate, shall appoint Ambassadors, other public Ministers and Consuls, **Judges of the supreme Court**, and all other Officers of the United States, whose Appointments are not herein otherwise provided for, and which shall be established by Law: but the Congress may by Law vest the Appointment of such inferior Officers, as they think proper, in the President alone, in the Courts of Law, or in the Heads of Departments.

The President shall have Power to fill up all Vacancies that may happen during the Recess of the Senate, by granting Commissions which shall expire at the End of their next Session.

Section. 3

He shall from time to time give to the Congress Information of the State of the Union, and recommend to their Consideration such Measures as he shall judge necessary and expedient; he may, on extraordinary Occasions, convene both Houses, or either of them, and in Case of Disagreement between them, with Respect to the Time of Adjournment, he may adjourn them to such Time as he shall think proper; he shall receive Ambassadors and other public Ministers; he shall take Care that the Laws be faithfully executed, and shall Commission all the Officers of the United States.

Section. 4

The President, Vice President and all civil Officers of the United States, shall be removed from Office on Impeachment for, and Conviction of, Treason, Bribery, or other high Crimes and Misdemeanors.

Constitution of the United States
Article III

Section. 1

The judicial Power of the United States, shall be vested in one supreme Court, and in such inferior Courts as the Congress may from time to time ordain and establish. The Judges, both of the supreme and inferior Courts, shall hold their Offices during good Behaviour, and shall, at stated Times, receive for their Services, a Compensation, which shall not be diminished during their Continuance in Office.

Section. 2

The judicial Power shall extend to all Cases, in Law and Equity, arising under this Constitution, the Laws of the United States, and Treaties made, or which shall be made, under their Authority;—to all Cases affecting Ambassadors, other public Ministers and Consuls;—to all Cases of admiralty and maritime Jurisdiction;—to Controversies to which the United States shall be a Party;—**to Controversies** between two or more States;—between a State and Citizens of another State,—between Citizens of different States,—between Citizens of the same State claiming Lands under Grants of different States, and between a State, or the Citizens thereof, and foreign States, Citizens or Subjects.

In all Cases affecting Ambassadors, other public Ministers and Consuls, and those in which a State shall be Party, the supreme Court shall have original Jurisdiction. In all the other Cases before mentioned, the supreme Court shall have appellate Jurisdiction, both as to Law and Fact, with such Exceptions, and under such Regulations as the Congress shall make.

The Trial of all Crimes, except in Cases of Impeachment, shall be by Jury; and such Trial shall be held in the State where the said Crimes shall have been committed; but when not committed within any State, the Trial shall be at such Place or Places as the Congress may by Law have directed.

Section. 3

Treason against the United States, shall consist only in levying War against them, or **in adhering to their Enemies, giving them Aid and Comfort.** No Person shall be convicted of Treason unless on the Testimony of two Witnesses to the same overt Act, or on Confession in open Court.

The Congress shall have Power to declare the Punishment of Treason, but no Attainder of Treason shall work Corruption of Blood, or Forfeiture except during the Life of the Person attainted.

Federalist No. 47
The Particular Structure of the New Government and the Distribution of Power Among Its Different Parts

From the New York Packet. Friday, February 1, 1788.

Author: James Madison

To the People of the State of New York:

HAVING reviewed the general form of the proposed government and the general mass of power allotted to it, I proceed to examine the particular structure of this government, and the distribution of this mass of power among its constituent parts. One of the principal objections inculcated by the more respectable adversaries to the Constitution, is its supposed violation of the political maxim, that the legislative, executive, and judiciary departments ought to be separate and distinct. In the structure of the federal government, no regard, it is said, seems to have been paid to this essential precaution in favor of liberty. The several departments of power are distributed and blended in such a manner as at once to destroy all symmetry and beauty of form, and to expose some of the essential parts of the edifice to the danger of being crushed by the disproportionate weight of other parts. No political truth is certainly of greater intrinsic value, or is stamped with the authority of more enlightened patrons of liberty, than that on which the objection is founded.

The accumulation of all powers, legislative, executive, and judiciary, in the same hands, whether of one, a few, or many, and whether hereditary, selfappointed, or elective, may justly be pronounced the very definition of tyranny. Were the federal Constitution, therefore, really chargeable with the accumulation of power, or with a mixture of powers, having a dangerous tendency to such an accumulation, no further arguments would be necessary to inspire a universal reprobation of the system. I persuade myself, however, that it will be made apparent to every one, that the charge cannot be supported, and that the maxim on which it relies has been totally misconceived and misapplied. In order to form correct ideas on this important subject, it will be proper to investigate the sense in which the preservation of liberty requires that the three great departments of power should be separate and distinct. The oracle who is always consulted and cited on this subject is the celebrated Montesquieu. If he be not the author of this invaluable precept in the science of politics, he has the merit at least of displaying and recommending it most effectually to the attention of mankind. Let us endeavor, in the first place, to ascertain his meaning on this point. The British Constitution was to Montesquieu what Homer has been to the didactic writers on epic poetry. As the latter have considered the work of the immortal bard as the perfect model from which the principles and rules of the epic art were to be drawn, and by which all similar works were to be judged, so this great political critic appears to have viewed the Constitution of England as the standard, or to use his own expression, as the mirror of political liberty; and to have delivered, in the form of elementary truths, the several characteristic principles of that particular system. That we may be sure, then, not to mistake his meaning in this case, let us recur to the source from which the maxim was drawn. On the slightest view of the British Constitution, we must perceive that the legislative, executive, and judiciary departments are by no means totally separate and distinct from each other. The executive magistrate forms an integral part of the legislative authority. He alone has the prerogative of making treaties with foreign sovereigns, which, when made, have, under certain limitations, the force of legislative acts. All the members of the judiciary department are appointed by him, can be removed by him on the address of the two Houses of Parliament, and form, when he pleases to consult them, one of his constitutional councils. One branch of the legislative department forms also a great constitutional council to the executive chief, as, on another hand, it is the sole depositary of judicial power in cases of impeachment, and is invested with the supreme appellate jurisdiction in all other cases. The judges, again, are so far connected with the legislative department as often to attend and participate in its deliberations, though not admitted to a legislative vote. From these facts, by which Montesquieu was guided, it may clearly be inferred that, in saying **"There can be no liberty where the legislative and executive powers are united in the same person, or body of magistrates," or, "if the power of judging be not separated from the legislative and executive powers,"** he did not mean that these departments ought to have no partial agency in, or no control over, the acts of each other. His meaning, as his own words import, and still more conclusively as illustrated by the example in his eye, can amount to no more than this, that where the whole power of one department is exercised by the same hands which possess the WHOLE power of another department, the fundamental principles of a free constitution are subverted. This would have been the case in the constitution examined by him, if the king, who is the sole executive magistrate, had possessed also the complete legislative power, or the supreme administration of justice; or if the entire legislative body had possessed the supreme judiciary, or the supreme executive authority. This, however, is not among the vices of that constitution. The magistrate in whom the whole executive power resides cannot of himself make a law, though he can put a negative on every law; nor administer justice in person, though he has the appointment of those who do administer it. The judges can exercise no executive prerogative, though they are shoots from the executive stock; nor any legislative function, though they may be advised with by the legislative councils. The entire legislature can perform no judiciary act, though by the joint act of two of its branches the judges may be removed from their offices, and though one of its branches is possessed of the judicial power in the last resort. The entire legislature, again, can exercise no executive prerogative, though one of its branches constitutes the supreme executive magistracy, and another, on the impeachment of a third, can try and condemn all the subordinate officers in the executive department. The reasons on which Montesquieu grounds his maxim are a further demonstration of his meaning. **"When the legislative and executive powers are united in the same person or body,"** says he, **"there can be no liberty, because apprehensions may arise lest the same monarch or senate should enact tyrannical laws to execute them in a tyrannical manner." Again: "Were the power of judging joined with the legislative, the life and liberty of the subject would be exposed to arbitrary control, for THE JUDGE would then be THE LEGISLATOR.**

Were it joined to the executive power, the judge might behave with all the violence of an oppressor. "Some of these reasons are more fully explained in other passages;" but briefly stated as they are here, they sufficiently establish the meaning which we have put on this celebrated maxim of this celebrated author.

If we look into the constitutions of the several States, we find that, notwithstanding the emphatical and, in some instances, the unqualified terms in which this axiom has been laid down, there is not a single instance in which the several departments of power have been kept absolutely separate and distinct. New Hampshire, whose constitution was the last formed, seems to have been fully aware of the impossibility and inexpediency of avoiding any mixture whatever of these departments, and has qualified the doctrine by declaring "that the legislative, executive, and judiciary powers ought to be kept as separate from, and independent of, each other as the nature of a free government will admit; or as is consistent with that chain of connection that binds the whole fabric of the constitution in one indissoluble bond of unity and amity." Her constitution accordingly mixes these departments in several respects. The Senate, which is a branch of the legislative department, is also a judicial tribunal for the trial of impeachments. The President, who is the head of the executive department, is the presiding member also of the Senate; and, besides an equal vote in all cases, has a casting vote in case of a tie. The executive head is himself eventually elective every year by the legislative department, and his council is every year chosen by and from the members of the same department. Several of the officers of state are also appointed by the legislature. And the members of the judiciary department are appointed by the executive department. The constitution of Massachusetts has observed a sufficient though less pointed caution, in expressing this fundamental article of liberty. It declares "that the legislative department shall never exercise the executive and judicial powers, or either of them; the executive shall never exercise the legislative and judicial powers, or either of them; the judicial shall never exercise the legislative and executive powers, or either of them. "This declaration corresponds precisely with the doctrine of Montesquieu, as it has been explained, and is not in a single point violated by the plan of the convention. It goes no farther than to prohibit any one of the entire departments from exercising the powers of another department. In the very Constitution to which it is prefixed, a partial mixture of powers has been admitted. The executive magistrate has a qualified negative on the legislative body, and the Senate, which is a part of the legislature, is a court of impeachment for members both of the executive and judiciary departments. The members of the judiciary department, again, are appointable by the executive department, and removable by the same authority on the address of the two legislative branches.

Lastly, a number of the officers of government are annually appointed by the legislative department. As the appointment to offices, particularly executive offices, is in its nature an executive function, the compilers of the Constitution have, in this last point at least, violated the rule established by themselves. I pass over the constitutions of Rhode Island and Connecticut, because they were formed prior to the Revolution, and even before the principle under examination had become an object of political attention. The constitution of New York contains no declaration on this subject; but appears very clearly to have been framed with an eye to the danger of improperly blending the different departments. It gives, nevertheless, to the executive magistrate, a partial control over the legislative department; and, what is more, gives a like control to the judiciary department; and even blends the executive and judiciary departments in the exercise of this control. In its council of appointment members of the legislative are associated with the executive authority, in the appointment of officers, both executive and judiciary. And its court for the trial of impeachments and correction of errors is to consist of one branch of the legislature and the principal members of the judiciary department. The constitution of New Jersey has blended the different powers of government more than any of the preceding. The governor, who is the executive magistrate, is appointed by the legislature; is chancellor and ordinary, or surrogate of the State; is a member of the Supreme Court of Appeals, and president, with a casting vote, of one of the legislative branches. The same legislative branch acts again as executive council of the governor, and with him constitutes the Court of Appeals. The members of the judiciary department are appointed by the legislative department and removable by one branch of it, on the impeachment of the other. According to the constitution of Pennsylvania, the president, who is the head of the executive department, is annually elected by a vote in which the legislative department predominates. In conjunction with an executive council, he appoints the members of the judiciary department, and forms a court of impeachment for trial of all officers, judiciary as well as executive. The judges of the Supreme Court and justices of the peace seem also to be removable by the legislature; and the executive power of pardoning in certain cases, to be referred to the same department. The members of the executive counoil are made ex-officio justices of peace throughout the State. In Delaware, the chief executive magistrate is annually elected by the legislative department. The speakers of the two legislative branches are vice-presidents in the executive department. The executive chief, with six others, appointed, three by each of the legislative branches constitutes the Supreme Court of Appeals; he is joined with the legislative department in the appointment of the other judges. Throughout the States, it appears that the members of the legislature may at the same time be justices of the peace; in this State, the members of one branch of it are ex-officio justices of the peace; as are also the members of the executive council. The principal officers of the executive department are appointed by the legislative; and one branch of the latter forms a court of impeachments. All officers may be removed on address of the legislature. Maryland has adopted the maxim in the most unqualified terms; declaring that the legislative, executive, and judicial powers of government ought to be forever separate and distinct from each other. Her constitution, notwithstanding, makes the executive magistrate appointable by the legislative department; and the members of the judiciary by the executive department. The language of Virginia is still more pointed on this subject. Her constitution declares, "that the legislative, executive, and judiciary departments shall be separate and distinct; so that neither exercise the powers properly belonging to the other; nor shall any person exercise the powers of more than one of them at the same time, except that the justices of county courts shall be eligible to either House of Assembly." Yet we find not only this express exception, with respect to the members of the irferior courts, but that the chief magistrate, with his executive council, are appointable by the legislature; that two members of the latter are triennially displaced at the pleasure of the legislature; and that all the principal offices, both executive and judiciary, are filled by the same department. The executive prerogative of pardon, also, is in one case vested in the legislative department. The constitution of North Carolina, which declares "that the legislative, executive, and supreme judicial powers of government ought to be forever separate and distinct from each other," refers, at the same time, to the legislative department, the appointment not only of the executive chief, but all the principal officers within both that and the judiciary department. In South Carolina, the constitution makes the executive magistracy eligible by the legislative department.

It gives to the latter, also, the appointment of the members of the judiciary department, including even justices of the peace and sheriffs; and the appointment of officers in the executive department, down to captains in the army and navy of the State.

In the constitution of Georgia, where it is declared "that the legislative, executive, and judiciary departments shall be separate and distinct, so that neither exercise the powers properly belonging to the other," we find that the executive department is to be filled by appointments of the legislature; and the executive prerogative of pardon to be finally exercised by the same authority. Even justices of the peace are to be appointed by the legislature. In citing these cases, in which the legislative, executive, and judiciary departments have not been kept totally separate and distinct, I wish not to be regarded as an advocate for the particular organizations of the several State governments. I am fully aware that among the many excellent principles which they exemplify, they carry strong marks of the haste, and still stronger of the inexperience, under which they were framed. It is but too obvious that in some instances the fundamental principle under consideration has been violated by too great a mixture, and even an actual consolidation, of the different powers; and that in no instance has a competent provision been made for maintaining in practice the separation delineated on paper. What I have wished to evince is, that the charge brought against the proposed Constitution, of violating the sacred maxim of free government, is warranted neither by the real meaning annexed to that maxim by its author, nor by the sense in which it has hitherto been understood in America. This interesting subject will be resumed in the ensuing paper.

Publius.

Federalist No. 78
The Judiciary Department

From McLEAN'S Edition, New York.

Author: Alexander Hamilton

To the People of the State of New York:

WE PROCEED now to an examination of the judiciary department of the proposed government.

In unfolding the defects of the existing Confederation, the utility and necessity of a federal judicature have been clearly pointed out. It is the less necessary to recapitulate the considerations there urged, as the propriety of the institution in the abstract is not disputed; the only questions which have been raised being relative to the manner of constituting it, and to its extent. To these points, therefore, our observations shall be confined.

The manner of constituting it seems to embrace these several objects: 1st. The mode of appointing the judges. 2d. The tenure by which they are to hold their places. 3d. The partition of the judiciary authority between different courts, and their relations to each other.

First. As to the mode of appointing the judges; this is the same with that of appointing the officers of the Union in general, and has been so fully discussed in the two last numbers, that nothing can be said here which would not be useless repetition.

Second. As to the tenure by which the judges are to hold their places; this chiefly concerns their duration in office; the provisions for their support; the precautions for their responsibility.

According to the plan of the convention, all judges who may be appointed by the United States are to hold their offices DURING GOOD BEHAVIOR; which is conformable to the most approved of the State constitutions and among the rest, to that of this State. Its propriety having been drawn into question by the adversaries of that plan, is no light symptom of the rage for objection, which disorders their imaginations and judgments. The standard of good behavior for the continuance in office of the judicial magistracy, is certainly one of the most valuable of the modern improvements in the practice of government. In a monarchy it is an excellent barrier to the despotism of the prince; in a republic it is a no less excellent barrier to the encroachments and oppressions of the representative body. And it is the best expedient which can be devised in any government, to secure a steady, upright, and impartial administration of the laws.

Whoever attentively considers the different departments of power must perceive, that, in a government in which they are separated from each other, the judiciary, from the nature of its functions, will always be the least dangerous to the political rights of the Constitution; because it will be least in a capacity to annoy or injure them. The Executive not only dispenses the honors, but holds the sword of the community. The legislature not only commands the purse, but prescribes the rules by which the duties and rights of every citizen are to be regulated. The judiciary, on the contrary, has no influence over either the sword or the purse; no direction either of the strength or of the wealth of the society; and can take no active resolution whatever. It may truly be said to have neither force nor will, but merely judgment; and must ultimately depend upon the aid of the executive arm even for the efficacy of its judgments.

This simple view of the matter suggests several important consequences. It proves incontestably, that the judiciary is beyond comparison the weakest of the three departments of power1; that it can never attack with success either of the other two; and that all possible care is requisite to enable it to defend itself against their attacks. It equally proves, that though individual oppression may now and then proceed from the courts of justice, the general liberty of the people can never be endangered from that quarter; I mean so long as the judiciary remains truly distinct from both the legislature and the Executive. For I agree, that "there is no liberty, if the power of judging be not separated from the legislative and executive powers." 2 And it proves, in the last place, that as liberty can have nothing to fear from the judiciary alone, but would have every thing to fear from its union with either of the other departments; that as all the effects of such a union must ensue from a dependence of the former on the latter, notwithstanding a nominal and apparent separation; that as, from the natural feebleness of the judiciary, it is in continual jeopardy of being overpowered, awed, or influenced by its co-ordinate branches; and that as nothing can contribute so much to its firmness and independence as permanency in office, this quality may therefore be justly regarded as an indispensable ingredient in its constitution, and, in a great measure, as the citadel of the public justice and the public security.

The complete independence of the courts of justice is peculiarly essential in a limited Constitution. By a limited Constitution, I understand one which contains certain specified exceptions to the legislative authority; such, for instance, as that it shall pass no bills of attainder, no ex-post-facto laws, and the like. Limitations of this kind can be preserved in practice no other way than through the medium of courts of justice, whose duty it must be to declare all acts contrary to the manifest tenor of the Constitution void. Without this, all the reservations of particular rights or privileges would amount to nothing.

Some perplexity respecting the rights of the courts to pronounce legislative acts void, because contrary to the Constitution, has arisen from an imagination that the doctrine would imply a superiority of the judiciary to the legislative power. It is urged that the authority which can declare the acts of another void, must necessarily be superior to the one whose acts may be declared void. As this doctrine is of great importance in all the American constitutions, a brief discussion of the ground on which it rests cannot be unacceptable.

There is no position which depends on clearer principles, than that every act of a delegated authority, contrary to the tenor of the commission under which it is exercised, is void. No legislative act, therefore, contrary to the Constitution, can be valid. To deny this, would be to affirm, that the deputy is greater than his principal; that the servant is above his master; that the representatives of the people are superior to the people themselves; that men acting by virtue of powers, may do not only what their powers do not authorize, but what they forbid.

If it be said that the legislative body are themselves the constitutional judges of their own powers, and that the construction they put upon them is conclusive upon the other departments, it may be answered, that this cannot be the natural presumption, where it is not to be collected from any particular provisions in the Constitution. It is not otherwise to be supposed, that the Constitution could intend to enable the representatives of the people to substitute their WILL to that of their constituents. It is far more rational to suppose, that the courts were designed to be an intermediate body between the people and the legislature, in order, among other things, to keep the latter within the limits assigned to their authority. The interpretation of the laws is the proper and peculiar province of the courts. A constitution is, in fact, and must be regarded by the judges, as a fundamental law. It therefore belongs to them to ascertain its meaning, as well as the meaning of any particular act proceeding from the legislative body. If there should happen to be an irreconcilable variance between the two, that which has the superior obligation and validity ought, of course, to be preferred; or, in other words, the Constitution ought to be preferred to the statute, the intention of the people to the intention of their agents.

Nor does this conclusion by any means suppose a superiority of the judicial to the legislative power. It only supposes that the power of the people is superior to both; and that where the will of the legislature, declared in its statutes, stands in opposition to that of the people, declared in the Constitution, the judges ought to be governed by the latter rather than the former. They ought to regulate their decisions by the fundamental laws, rather than by those which are not fundamental.

This exercise of judicial discretion, in determining between two contradictory laws, is exemplified in a familiar instance. It not uncommonly happens, that there are two statutes existing at one time, clashing in whole or in part with each other, and neither of them containing any repealing clause or expression. In such a case, it is the province of the courts to liquidate and fix their meaning and operation. So far as they can, by any fair construction, be reconciled to each other, reason and law conspire to dictate that this should be done; where this is impracticable, it becomes a matter of necessity to give effect to one, in exclusion of the other. The rule which has obtained in the courts for determining their relative validity is, that the last in order of time shall be preferred to the first. But this is a mere rule of construction, not derived from any positive law, but from the nature and reason of the thing. It is a rule not enjoined upon the courts by legislative provision, but adopted by themselves, as consonant to truth and propriety, for the direction of their conduct as interpreters of the law. They thought it reasonable, that between the interfering acts of an equal authority, that which was the last indication of its will should have the preference.

But in regard to the interfering acts of a superior and subordinate authority, of an original and derivative power, the nature and reason of the thing indicate the converse of that rule as proper to be followed. They teach us that the prior act of a superior ought to be preferred to the subsequent act of an inferior and subordinate authority; and that accordingly, whenever a particular statute contravenes the Constitution, it will be the duty of the judicial tribunals to adhere to the latter and disregard the former.

It can be of no weight to say that the courts, on the pretense of a repugnancy, may substitute their own pleasure to the constitutional intentions of the legislature. This might as well happen in the case of two contradictory statutes; or it might as well happen in every adjudication upon any single statute. The courts must declare the sense of the law; and if they should be disposed to exercise will instead of judgment, the consequence would equally be the substitution of their pleasure to that of the legislative body. The observation, if it prove any thing, would prove that there ought to be no judges distinct from that body.

If, then, the courts of justice are to be considered as the bulwarks of a limited Constitution against legislative encroachments, this consideration will afford a strong argument for the permanent tenure of judicial offices, since nothing will contribute so much as this to that independent spirit in the judges which must be essential to the faithful performance of so arduous a duty.

This independence of the judges is equally requisite to guard the Constitution and the rights of individuals from the effects of those ill humors, which the arts of designing men, or the influence of particular conjunctures, sometimes disseminate among the people themselves, and which, though they speedily give place to better information, and more deliberate reflection, have a tendency, in the meantime, to occasion dangerous innovations in the government, and serious oppressions of the minor party in the community. Though I trust the friends of the proposed Constitution will never concur with its enemies, 3 in questioning that fundamental principle of republican government, which admits the right of the people to alter or abolish the established Constitution, whenever they find it inconsistent with their happiness, yet it is not to be inferred from this principle, that the representatives of the people, whenever a momentary inclination happens to lay hold of a majority of their constituents, incompatible with the provisions in the existing Constitution, would, on that account, be justifiable in a violation of those provisions; or that the courts would be under a greater obligation to connive at infractions in this shape, than when they had proceeded wholly from the cabals of the representative body. Until the people have, by some solemn and authoritative act, annulled or changed the established form, it is binding upon themselves collectively, as well as individually; and no presumption, or even knowledge, of their sentiments, can warrant their representatives in a departure from it, prior to such an act. But it is easy to see, that it would require an uncommon portion of fortitude in the judges to do their duty as faithful guardians of the Constitution, where legislative invasions of it had been instigated by the major voice of the community.

But it is not with a view to infractions of the Constitution only, that the independence of the judges may be an essential safeguard against the effects of occasional ill humors in the society. These sometimes extend no farther than to the injury of the private rights of particular classes of citizens, by unjust and partial laws. Here also the firmness of the judicial magistracy is of vast importance in mitigating the severity and confining the operation of such laws. It not only serves to moderate the immediate mischiefs of those which may have been passed, but it operates as a check upon the legislative body in passing them; who, perceiving that obstacles to the success of iniquitous intention are to be expected from the scruples of the courts, are in a manner compelled, by the very motives of the injustice they meditate, to qualify their attempts. This is a circumstance calculated to have more influence upon the character of our governments, than but few may be aware of. The benefits of the integrity and moderation of the judiciary have already been felt in more States than one; and though they may have displeased those whose sinister expectations they may have disappointed, they must have commanded the esteem and applause of all the virtuous and disinterested. Considerate men, of every description, ought to prize whatever will tend to beget or fortify that temper in the courts: as no man can be sure that he may not be to-morrow the victim of a spirit of injustice, by which he may be a gainer to-day. And every man must now feel, that the inevitable tendency of such a spirit is to sap the foundations of public and private confidence, and to introduce in its stead universal distrust and distress.

That inflexible and uniform adherence to the rights of the Constitution, and of individuals, which we perceive to be indispensable in the courts of justice, can certainly not be expected from judges who hold their offices by a temporary commission. Periodical appointments, however regulated, or by whomsoever made, would, in some way or other, be fatal to their necessary independence. If the power of making them was committed either to the Executive or legislature, there would be danger of an improper complaisance to the branch which possessed it; if to both, there would be an unwillingness to hazard the displeasure of either; if to the people, or to persons chosen by them for the special purpose, there would be too great a disposition to consult popularity, to justify a reliance that nothing would be consulted but the Constitution and the laws.

There is yet a further and a weightier reason for the permanency of the judicial offices, which is deducible from the nature of the qualifications they require. It has been frequently remarked, with great propriety, that a voluminous code of laws is one of the inconveniences necessarily connected with the advantages of a free government. To avoid an arbitrary discretion in the courts, it is indispensable that they should be bound down by strict rules and precedents, which serve to define and point out their duty in every particular case that comes before them; and it will readily be conceived from the variety of controversies which grow out of the folly and wickedness of mankind, that the records of those precedents must unavoidably swell to a very considerable bulk, and must demand long and laborious study to acquire a competent knowledge of them. Hence it is, that there can be but few men in the society who will have sufficient skill in the laws to qualify them for the stations of judges. And making the proper deductions for the ordinary depravity of human nature, the number must be still smaller of those who unite the requisite integrity with the requisite knowledge. These considerations apprise us, that the government can have no great option between fit character; and that a temporary duration in office, which would naturally discourage such characters from quitting a lucrative line of practice to accept a seat on the bench, would have a tendency to throw the administration of justice into hands less able, and less well qualified, to conduct it with utility and dignity. In the present circumstances of this country, and in those in which it is likely to be for a long time to come, the disadvantages on this score would be greater than they may at first sight appear; but it must be confessed, that they are far inferior to those which present themselves under the other aspects of the subject.

Upon the whole, there can be no room to doubt that the convention acted wisely in copying from the models of those constitutions which have established GOOD BEHAVIOR as the tenure of their judicial offices, in point of duration; and that so far from being blamable on this account, their plan would have been inexcusably defective, if it had wanted this important feature of good government. The experience of Great Britain affords an illustrious comment on the excellence of the institution.

Publius

1. The celebrated Montesquieu, speaking of them, says: "Of the three powers above mentioned, the judiciary is next to nothing." "Spirit of Laws." vol. i., page 186.

2. Idem, page 181.

3. Vide "Protest of the Minority of the Convention of Pennsylvania," Martin's Speech, etc.

Federalist No. 81
The Judiciary Continued, and the Distribution of the Judicial Authority
From McLEAN'S Edition, New York.
Author: Alexander Hamilton

To the People of the State of New York:

LET US now return to the partition of the judiciary authority between different courts, and their relations to each other, "The judicial power of the United States is" (by the plan of the convention) "to be vested in one Supreme Court, and in such inferior courts as the Congress may, from time to time, ordain and establish." [1]

That there ought to be one court of supreme and final jurisdiction, is a proposition which is not likely to be contested. The reasons for it have been assigned in another place, and are too obvious to need repetition. The only question that seems to have been raised concerning it, is, whether it ought to be a distinct body or a branch of the legislature. The same contradiction is observable in regard to this matter which has been remarked in several other cases. The very men who object to the Senate as a court of impeachments, on the ground of an improper intermixture of powers, advocate, by implication at least, the propriety of vesting the ultimate decision of all causes, in the whole or in a part of the legislative body.

The arguments, or rather suggestions, upon which this charge is founded, are to this effect: "The authority of the proposed Supreme Court of the United States, which is to be a separate and independent body, will be superior to that of the legislature. The power of construing the laws according to the spirit of the Constitution, will enable that court to mould them into whatever shape it may think proper; especially as its decisions will not be in any manner subject to the revision or correction of the legislative body. This is as unprecedented as it is dangerous. In Britain, the judicial power, in the last resort, resides in the House of Lords, which is a branch of the legislature; and this part of the British government has been imitated in the State constitutions in general. The Parliament of Great Britain, and the legislatures of the several States, can at any time rectify, by law, the exceptionable decisions of their respective courts. But the errors and usurpations of the Supreme Court of the United States will be uncontrollable and remediless." This, upon examination, will be found to be made up altogether of false reasoning upon misconceived fact.

In the first place, there is not a syllable in the plan under consideration which directly empowers the national courts to construe the laws according to the spirit of the Constitution, or which gives them any greater latitude in this respect than may be claimed by the courts of every State. I admit, however, that the Constitution ought to be the standard of construction for the laws, and that wherever there is an evident opposition, the laws ought to give place to the Constitution. But this doctrine is not deducible from any circumstance peculiar to the plan of the convention, but from the general theory of a limited Constitution; and as far as it is true, is equally applicable to most, if not to all the State governments. There can be no objection, therefore, on this account, to the federal judicature which will not lie against the local judicatures in general, and which will not serve to condemn every constitution that attempts to set bounds to legislative discretion.

But perhaps the force of the objection may be thought to consist in the particular organization of the Supreme Court; in its being composed of a distinct body of magistrates, instead of being one of the branches of the legislature, as in the government of Great Britain and that of the State. To insist upon this point, the authors of the objection must renounce the meaning they have labored to annex to the celebrated maxim, requiring a separation of the departments of power. It shall, nevertheless, be conceded to them, agreeably to the interpretation given to that maxim in the course of these papers, that it is not violated by vesting the ultimate power of judging in a part of the legislative body. But though this be not an absolute violation of that excellent rule, yet it verges so nearly upon it, as on this account alone to be less eligible than the mode preferred by the convention. From a body which had even a partial agency in passing bad laws, we could rarely expect a disposition to temper and moderate them in the application. The same spirit which had operated in making them, would be too apt in interpreting them; still less could it be expected that men who had infringed the Constitution in the character of legislators, would be disposed to repair the breach in the character of judges. Nor is this all. Every reason which recommends the tenure of good behavior for judicial offices, militates against placing the judiciary power, in the last resort, in a body composed of men chosen for a limited period. There is an absurdity in referring the determination of causes, in the first instance, to judges of permanent standing; in the last, to those of a temporary and mutable constitution. And there is a still greater absurdity in subjecting the decisions of men, selected for their knowledge of the laws, acquired by long and laborious study, to the revision and control of men who, for want of the same advantage, cannot but be deficient in that knowledge. The members of the legislature will rarely be chosen with a view to those qualifications which fit men for the stations of judges; and as, on this account, there will be great reason to apprehend all the ill consequences of defective information, so, on account of the natural propensity of such bodies to party divisions, there will be no less reason to fear that the pestilential breath of faction may poison the fountains of justice. The habit of being continually marshalled on opposite sides will be too apt to stifle the voice both of law and of equity.

These considerations teach us to applaud the wisdom of those States who have committed the judicial power, in the last resort, not to a part of the legislature, but to distinct and independent bodies of men. Contrary to the supposition of those who have represented the plan of the convention, in this respect, as novel and unprecedented, it is but a copy of the constitutions of New Hampshire, Massachusetts, Pennsylvania, Delaware, Maryland, Virginia, North Carolina, South Carolina, and Georgia; and the preference which has been given to those models is highly to be commended.

It is not true, in the second place, that the Parliament of Great Britain, or the legislatures of the particular States, can rectify the exceptionable decisions of their respective courts, in any other sense than might be done by a future legislature of the United States. The theory, neither of the British, nor the State constitutions, authorizes the revisal of a judicial sentence by a legislative act. Nor is there any thing in the proposed Constitution, more than in either of them, by which it is forbidden. In the former, as well as in the latter, the impropriety of the thing, on the general principles of law and reason, is the sole obstacle. A legislature, without exceeding its province, cannot reverse a determination once made in a particular case; though it may prescribe a new rule for future cases. This is the principle, and it applies in all its consequences, exactly in the same manner and extent, to the State governments, as to the national government now under consideration. Not the least difference can be pointed out in any view of the subject.

It may in the last place be observed that the supposed danger of judiciary encroachments on the legislative authority, which has been upon many occasions reiterated, is in reality a phantom. Particular misconstructions and contraventions of the will of the legislature may now and then happen; but they can never be so extensive as to amount to an inconvenience, or in any sensible degree to affect the order of the political system. This may be inferred with certainty, from the general nature of the judicial power, from the objects to which it relates, from the manner in which it is exercised, from its comparative weakness, and from its total incapacity to support its usurpations by force. And the inference is greatly fortified by the consideration of the important constitutional check which the power of instituting impeachments in one part of the legislative body, and of determining upon them in the other, would give to that body upon the members of the judicial department. This is alone a complete security. There never can be danger that the judges, by a series of deliberate usurpations on the authority of the legislature, would hazard the united resentment of the body intrusted with it, while this body was possessed of the means of punishing their presumption, by degrading them from their stations. While this ought to remove all apprehensions on the subject, it affords, at the same time, a cogent argument for constituting the Senate a court for the trial of impeachments.

Having now examined, and, I trust, removed the objections to the distinct and independent organization of the Supreme Court, I proceed to consider the propriety of the power of constituting inferior courts, [2] and the relations which will subsist between these and the former.

The power of constituting inferior courts is evidently calculated to obviate the necessity of having recourse to the Supreme Court in every case of federal cognizance. It is intended to enable the national government to institute or authorize, in each State or district of the United States, a tribunal competent to the determination of matters of national jurisdiction within its limits.

But why, it is asked, might not the same purpose have been accomplished by the instrumentality of the State courts? This admits of different answers. Though the fitness and competency of those courts should be allowed in the utmost latitude, yet the substance of the power in question may still be regarded as a necessary part of the plan, if it were only to empower the national legislature to commit to them the cognizance of causes arising out of the national Constitution. To confer the power of determining such causes upon the existing courts of the several States, would perhaps be as much "to constitute tribunals," as to create new courts with the like power. But ought not a more direct and explicit provision to have been made in favor of the State courts? There are, in my opinion, substantial reasons against such a provision: the most discerning cannot foresee how far the prevalency of a local spirit may be found to disqualify the local tribunals for the jurisdiction of national causes whilst every man may discover, that courts constituted like those of some of the States would be improper channels of the judicial authority of the Union. State judges, holding their offices during pleasure, or from year to year, will be too little independent to be relied upon for an inflexible execution of the national laws. And if there was a necessity for confiding the original cognizance of causes arising under those laws to them there would be a correspondent necessity for leaving the door of appeal as wide as possible. In proportion to the grounds of confidence in, or distrust of, the subordinate tribunals, ought to be the facility or difficulty of appeals. And well satisfied as I am of the propriety of the appellate jurisdiction, in the several classes of causes to which it is extended by the plan of the convention. I should consider every thing calculated to give, in practice, an unrestrained course to appeals, as a source of public and private inconvenience.

I am not sure, but that it will be found highly expedient and useful, to divide the United States into four or five or half a dozen districts; and to institute a federal court in each district, in lieu of one in every State. The judges of these courts, with the aid of the State judges, may hold circuits for the trial of causes in the several parts of the respective districts. Justice through them may be administered with ease and despatch; and appeals may be safely circumscribed within a narrow compass. This plan appears to me at present the most eligible of any that could be adopted; and in order to it, it is necessary that the power of constituting inferior courts should exist in the full extent in which it is to be found in the proposed Constitution.

These reasons seem sufficient to satisfy a candid mind, that the want of such a power would have been a great defect in the plan. Let us now examine in what manner the judicial authority is to be distributed between the supreme and the inferior courts of the Union. The Supreme Court is to be invested with original jurisdiction, only "in cases affecting ambassadors, other public ministers, and consuls, and those in which a state shall be a party." Public ministers of every class are the immediate representatives of their sovereigns. All questions in which they are concerned are so directly connected with the public peace, that, as well for the preservation of this, as out of respect to the sovereignties they represent, it is both expedient and proper that such questions should be submitted in the first instance to the highest judicatory of the nation. Though consuls have not in strictness a diplomatic character, yet as they are the public agents of the nations to which they belong, the same observation is in a great measure applicable to them. In cases in which a State might happen to be a party, it would ill suit its dignity to be turned over to an inferior tribunal. Though it may rather be a digression from the immediate subject of this paper, I shall take occasion to mention here a supposition which has excited some alarm upon very mistaken grounds. It has been suggested that an assignment of the public securities of one State to the citizens of another, would enable them to prosecute that State in the federal courts for the amount of those securities; a suggestion which the following considerations prove to be without foundation.

It is inherent in the nature of sovereignty not to be amenable to the suit of an individual without its consent. This is the general sense, and the general practice of mankind; and the exemption, as one of the attributes of sovereignty, is now enjoyed by the government of every State in the Union. Unless, therefore, there is a surrender of this immunity in the plan of the convention, it will remain with the States, and the danger intimated must be merely ideal. The circumstances which are necessary to produce an alienation of State sovereignty were discussed in considering the article of taxation, and need not be repeated here. A recurrence to the principles there established will satisfy us, that there is no color to pretend that the State governments would, by the adoption of that plan, be divested of the privilege of paying their own debts in their own way, free from every constraint but that which flows from the obligations of good faith. The contracts between a nation and individuals are only binding on the conscience of the sovereign, and have no pretensions to a compulsive force. They confer no right of action, independent of the sovereign will. To what purpose would it be to authorize suits against States for the debts they owe? How could recoveries be enforced? It is evident, it could not be done without waging war against the contracting State; and to ascribe to the federal courts, by mere implication, and in destruction of a preexisting right of the State governments, a power which would involve such a consequence, would be altogether forced and unwarrantable.

Let us resume the train of our observations. We have seen that the original jurisdiction of the Supreme Court would be confined to two classes of causes, and those of a nature rarely to occur. In all other cases of federal cognizance, the original jurisdiction would appertain to the inferior tribunals; and the Supreme Court would have nothing more than an appellate jurisdiction, "with such exceptions and under such regulations as the Congress shall make."

The propriety of this appellate jurisdiction has been scarcely called in question in regard to matters of law; but the clamors have been loud against it as applied to matters of fact. Some wellintentioned men in this State, deriving their notions from the language and forms which obtain in our courts, have been induced to consider it as an implied supersedure of the trial by jury, in favor of the civillaw mode of trial, which prevails in our courts of admiralty, probate, and chancery. A technical sense has been affixed to the term "appellate," which, in our law parlance, is commonly used in reference to appeals in the course of the civil law. But if I am not misinformed, the same meaning would not be given to it in any part of New England. There an appeal from one jury to another, is familiar both in language and practice, and is even a matter of course, until there have been two verdicts on one side. The word "appellate," therefore, will not be understood in the same sense in New England as in New York, which shows the impropriety of a technical interpretation derived from the jurisprudence of any particular State. The expression, taken in the abstract, denotes nothing more than the power of one tribunal to review the proceedings of another, either as to the law or fact, or both. The mode of doing it may depend on ancient custom or legislative provision (in a new government it must depend on the latter), and may be with or without the aid of a jury, as may be judged advisable. If, therefore, the reexamination of a fact once determined by a jury, should in any case be admitted under the proposed Constitution, it may be so regulated as to be done by a second jury, either by remanding the cause to the court below for a second trial of the fact, or by directing an issue immediately out of the Supreme Court.

But it does not follow that the reexamination of a fact once ascertained by a jury, will be permitted in the Supreme Court. Why may not it be said, with the strictest propriety, when a writ of error is brought from an inferior to a superior court of law in this State, that the latter has jurisdiction of the fact as well as the law? It is true it cannot institute a new inquiry concerning the fact, but it takes cognizance of it as it appears upon the record, and pronounces the law arising upon it. [3] This is jurisdiction of both fact and law; nor is it even possible to separate them. Though the commonlaw courts of this State ascertain disputed facts by a jury, yet they unquestionably have jurisdiction of both fact and law; and accordingly when the former is agreed in the pleadings, they have no recourse to a jury, but proceed at once to judgment. I contend, therefore, on this ground, that the expressions, "appellate jurisdiction, both as to law and fact," do not necessarily imply a reexamination in the Supreme Court of facts decided by juries in the inferior courts.

The following train of ideas may well be imagined to have influenced the convention, in relation to this particular provision. The appellate jurisdiction of the Supreme Court (it may have been argued) will extend to causes determinable in different modes, some in the course of the common law, others in the course of the civil law. In the former, the revision of the law only will be, generally speaking, the proper province of the Supreme Court in the latter, the reexamination of the fact is agreeable to usage, and in some cases, of which prize causes are an example, might be essential to the preservation of the public peace. It is therefore necessary that the appellate jurisdiction should, in certain cases, extend in the broadest sense to matters of fact. It will not answer to make an express exception of cases which shall have been originally tried by a jury, because in the courts of some of the States all causes are tried in this mode [4] and such an exception would preclude the revision of matters of fact, as well where it might be proper, as where it might be improper. To avoid all inconveniences, it will be safest to declare generally, that the Supreme Court shall possess appellate jurisdiction both as to law and fact, and that this jurisdiction shall be subject to such exceptions and regulations as the national legislature may prescribe. This will enable the government to modify it in such a manner as will best answer the ends of public justice and security. This view of the matter, at any rate, puts it out of all doubt that the supposed abolition of the trial by jury, by the operation of this provision, is fallacious and untrue. The legislature of the United States would certainly have full power to provide, that in appeals to the Supreme Court there should be no reexamination of facts where they had been tried in the original causes by juries. This would certainly be an authorized exception but if, for the reason already intimated, it should be thought too extensive, it might be qualified with a limitation to such causes only as are determinable at common law in that mode of trial.

The amount of the observations hitherto made on the authority of the judicial department is this: that it has been carefully restricted to those causes which are manifestly proper for the cognizance of the national judicature that in the partition of this authority a very small portion of original jurisdiction has been preserved to the Supreme Court, and the rest consigned to the subordinate tribunals that the Supreme Court will possess an appellate jurisdiction, both as to law and fact, in all the cases referred to them, both subject to any exceptions and regulations which may be thought advisable that this appellate jurisdiction does, in no case, abolish the trial by jury and that an ordinary degree of prudence and integrity in the national councils will insure us solid advantages from the establishment of the proposed judiciary, without exposing us to any of the inconveniences which have been predicted from that source. PUBLIUS.

1. Article 3, sec. 1.

2. This power has been absurdly represented as intended to abolish all the county courts in the several States, which are commonly called inferior courts. But the expressions of the Constitution are, to constitute "tribunals INFERIOR TO THE SUPREME COURT; and the evident design of the provision is to enable the institution of local courts, subordinate to the Supreme, either in States or larger districts. It is ridiculous to imagine that county courts were in contemplation.

3. This word is composed of JUS and DICTIO, juris dictio or a speaking and pronouncing of the law.

4. I hold that the States will have concurrent jurisdiction with the subordinate federal judicatories, in many cases of federal cognizance, as will be explained in my next paper.

Commentaries on the Constitution of the United States

Book Three
Chapter 7

§ 517. IN surveying the general structure of the constitution of the United States, we are naturally led to an examination of the fundamental principles, on which it is organized, for the purpose of carrying into effect the objects disclosed in the preamble. Every government must include within its scope, at least if it is to possess suitable stability and energy, the exercise of the three great powers, upon which all governments are supposed to rest, viz. the executive, the legislative, and the judicial powers. The manner and extent, in which these powers are to be exercised, and the functionaries, in whom they are to be vested, constitute the great distinctions, which are known in the forms of government. In absolute governments the whole executive, legislative, and judicial powers are, at least in their final result, exclusively confined to a single individual; and such a form of government is denominated a despotism, as the whole sovereignty of the state is vested in him. If the same powers are exclusively confided to a few persons, constituting a permanent sovereign council, the government may be appropriately denominated an absolute or despotic Aristocracy. **If they are exercised by the people at large in their original sovereign assemblies, the government is a pure Democracy . . . But in a representative republic all power emanates from the people, and is exercised by their choice, and never extends beyond the lives of the individuals, to whom it is entrusted. It may be entrusted for any shorter period; and then it returns to them again, to be again delegated by a new choice.**

§ 518. In the convention, which framed the constitution of the United States, the first resolution adopted by that body was, that "a national government out to be established, consisting of a supreme legislative, judiciary, and executive." And from this fundamental proposition sprung the subsequent organization of the whole government of the United States. It is, then, our duty to examine and consider the grounds, on which this proposition rests, since it lies at the bottom of all our institutions, state, as well as national.

§ 519. In the establishment of a free government, the division of the three great powers of government, the executive, the legislative, and the judicial, among different functionaries, has been a favorite policy with patriots and statesmen. **It has by many been deemed a maxim of vital importance, that these powers should for ever be kept separate and distinct.** And accordingly we find it laid down with emphatic care in the bill of rights of several of the state constitutions. In the constitution of Massachusetts, for example, it is declared, that "in the government of this commonwealth, the legislative department shall never exercise the executive and judicial powers, or either of them; the executive shall never exercise the legislative and judicial powers, or either of them; the judicial shall never exercise the legislative and executive powers, or either of them; to the end it may be a government of laws and not of men"1 Other declarations of a similar character are to be found in other state constitutions. 2

§ 520. Montesquieu seems to have been the first, who, with a truly philosophical eye, surveyed the political truth involved in this maxim, in its full extent, and gave to it a paramount importance and value. As it is tacitly assumed, as a fundamental basis in the constitution of the United States, in the distribution of its powers, it may be worth inquiry, what is the true nature, object, and extent of the maxim, and of the reasoning, by which it is supported. **The remarks of Montesquieu on this subject will be found in a professed commentary upon the constitution of England.** 1 "When," says he, "the legislative and executive powers are united in the same person, or in the same body of magistrates, there can be no liberty, because apprehensions may arise, lest the same monarch or senate should enact tyrannical laws, to execute them in a tyrannical manner. Again; there is no liberty, if the judiciary power be not separated from the legislative and executive. Were it joined with the legislative, the life and liberty of the subject would be exposed to arbitrary control; for the judge would be the legislator. Were it joined to the executive power, the judge might behave with violence and oppression. There would be an end of every thing, were the same man, or the same body, whether of the nobles, or of the people, to exercise these three powers, that of enacting laws, that of executing the public resolutions, and of trying the causes of individuals." 2

§ 521. The same reasoning is adopted by Mr. Justice Blackstone, in his Commentaries. 3

"In all tyrannical governments," says he, "the supreme magistracy, or the right both of making and of enforcing laws, is vested in the same man, or one and the same body of men; and wherever these two powers are united together there can be no public liberty. The magistrate may enact tyrannical laws, and exeute them in a tyrannical manner, since he is possessed, in quality of dispenser of justice, with all power, which he, as legislator, things proper to give himself. But where the legislative and executive authority are in distinct hands, the former will take care not to entrust the latter with so large a power, as may tend to the subversion of its own independence, and therewith of the liberty of the subject." Again; "In this distinct and separate existence of the judicial power in a peculiar body of men, nominated, indeed, by, but not removable at, the pleasure of the crown, consists one main preservative of the public liberty; which cannot long subsist in any state, unless the administration of common justice be in some degree separated from the legislative, and also the executive power. Were it joined with the legislative, the life, liberty, and property of the subject would be in the hands of arbitrary judges, whose decisions would then be regulated only by their opinions, and not by any fundamental principles of law; which, though legislators may depart from, yet judges are bound to observe. Were it joined with the executive, this union might soon be an overbalance for the legislative."

§ 522. And the Federalist has, with equal point and brevity, remarked, that "the accumulation of all powers legislative, executive, and judiciary, in the same hands, whether of one, a few, or many, and whether hereditary, self-appointed, or elective, may be justly pronounced the very definition of tyranny."

Justice Joseph Story, 1833

Justice Story on Federal Common Law:

Book III.
The Constitution of The United States:
Chapter XXXxviii.
Judiciary—Organization And Powers

§ 855. It is observable, that the language is, that "the judicial power shall extend to all cases *in law* and *equity*," arising under the constitution, laws, and treaties of the United States. What is to be understood by "cases in law and equity," in this clause? Plainly, cases at the common law, as contradistinguished from cases in equity, according to the known distinction in the jurisprudence of England, which our ancestors brought with them upon their emigration, and with which all the American states were familiarly acquainted. Here, then, at least, the constitution of the United States appeals to, and adopts, the common law to the extent of making it a rule in the pursuit of remedial justice in the courts of the Union. If the remedy must be in law, or in equity, according to the course of proceedings at the common law, in cases arising under the constitution, laws, and treaties, of the United States, it would seem irresistibly to follow, that the principles of decision, by which these remedies must be administered, must be derived from the same source. Hitherto, such has been the uniform interpretation and mode of administering justice in the courts of the United States in this class of civil cases.

Two Treatises of Government

John Locke

of Civil Government
Chap. VII. of Political or Civil Society

§. 91. For he being supposed to have all, both legislative and executive power in himself alone, there is no judge to be found, no appeal lies open to any one, who may fairly, and indifferently, and with authority decide, and from whose decision relief and redress may be expected of any injury or inconviency, that may be suffered from the prince, or by his order: so that such a man, however intitled, Czar, or Grand Seignior, or how you please, is as much in the state of nature, with all under his dominion, as he is with the rest of mankind: for where-ever any two men are, who have no standing rule, and common judge to appeal to on earth, for the determination of controversies of right betwixt them, there they are still in the state of * nature, and under all the inconveniencies of it, with only this woful difference to the subject, or rather slave of an absolute prince: that whereas, in the ordinary state of nature, he has a liberty to judge of his right, and according to the best of his power, to maintain it; now, whenever his property is invaded by the will and order of his monarch, he has not only no appeal, as those in society ought to have, but as if he were degraded from the common state of rational creatures, is denied a liberty to judge of, or to defend his right; and so is exposed to all the misery and inconveniencies, that a man can fear from one, who being in the unrestrained state of nature, is yet corrupted with flattery, and armed with power.

QUESTIONS

1. According to Story, based upon Montesquieu and Blackstone, the accumulation of legislative, executive, and judicial powers into one person or branch was viewed as the very definition of what?

2. Which, according to Hamilton, was to be the weakest branch of the three? Why?

3. What is the constitutionally established tenure in office for members of the Supreme Court of the United States (SCOTUS)?

4. What was the check that was held over the judiciary by the legislative branch, should judges attempt in any way to assert legislative authority?

Chapter 2

FUNDAMENTAL DOCUMENTS THAT UNDERPIN OUR GOVERNMENT

Original Sources:
1. The Spirit of Laws, Montesquieu, Book I. Of Laws in General, 1748.
2. Commentaries on the Laws of England, Blackstone, Introduction, Section Second, Of the Nature of Laws in General, 1765–1769.
3. The Second Treatise of Civil Government, Locke, Chapter II, Of the State of Nature, 1690.
4. The Mayflower Compact, 1620.
5. The Fundamental Orders of Connecticut, 1639.
6. George Washington's Farewell Address, 1796.

The Founders of our **Constitutional Republic** were reading the writings of political philosophers in an effort to uncover and implement the principles of government that would tend to best preserve liberty. There were three men who were the most heavily read and cited from during the time of our Declaration of Independence in 1776 until the ratification of our Bill of Rights in 1791. Charles-Louis de Secondat, Baron de Montesquieu, who wrote the Spirit of the Laws, was the single most-quoted individual. Sir William Blackstone, who wrote the Commentaries on the Laws of England, was quoted the second most frequently. And John Locke, who wrote Two Treatises of Government, was quoted third most frequently.

In reading these men's writings, it becomes clear that many of the views expressed by the Founding Fathers in our charter documents originated with these political philosophers. For example, Montesquieu advocated three branches of government and the need for the powers to be separated amongst those branches. Besides the specifics of governmental formation, what stands out most clearly are the foundational principles all three of these men agreed were important.

Baron Montesquieu © Everett Historical/Shutterstock.com

One of the first principles was a belief that just laws exist prior to any law being positively enacted by man. Montesquieu in his Spirit of the Laws, Book I, Chapter I said it this way, "To say that there is nothing just or unjust, but what is commanded or forbidden by positive laws, is the same as saying that, before the describing of a circle, all the radii were not equal." His point is well made; obviously, all the radii in a circle are equal prior to the circle being described, as that is the very nature of a circle. Blackstone and Locke embraced this belief in the preexistence of law as well.

Blackstone spoke of the preexistence of law and tied it to another principle upon which all three authors agreed, the dependent state of man upon his

Creator. Blackstone in his Commentaries on the Laws of England was very expressive about this dependent state of man.

> *"'God is related to the universe as creator and preserver: the laws by which he created all things are those by which he preserves them. He acts according to these rules, because he knows them; he knows them, because he made them; and he made them, because they are relative to his wisdom and power. . . . if one intelligent being had created another intelligent being, the latter ought to continue in its original state of dependence;' this is how Montesquieu explained the relationship of dependency in which we as the creation have to our Creator."*

Another principle upon which the three authors agreed was the importance of reason in discovering the preexistent laws. While all three men believed in the ability of man to reason, they also believed that this reason could be skewed. Blackstone made clear man's complete dependence upon God, even including our very ability to reason.

> *Man, considered as a creature, must necessarily be subject to the laws of his creator, for he is entirely a dependent being. A being, independent of any other, has no rule to pursue, but such as he prescribes to himself; but a state of dependence will inevitably oblige the inferior to take the will of him, on whom he depends, as the rule of his conduct; not indeed in every particular, but in all those points wherein his dependence consists. This principle therefore has more or less extent and effect, in proportion as the superiority of the one and the dependence of the other is greater or less, absolute or limited. And consequently, as man depends absolutely upon his maker for everything, it is necessary that he should in all points conform to his maker's will.*

From this belief then follows the question as to how we are to discover the creator's will. Political philosophers, such as Voltaire, who would later influence the French Revolution, argued for the supremacy of man's ability to reason independently. However, the beliefs that fanned the flames of the American Revolution were different. Blackstone denied that reason alone, without revelation, was sufficient for us to fully grasp what laws should be put in place for the protection of our unalienable rights.

> *And if our reason were always, as in our first ancestor before his transgression, clear and perfect, unruffled by passions, unclouded by prejudice, unimpaired by disease or intemperance, the task would be pleasant and easy; we should need no other guide but this. But every man now finds the contrary in his own experience; that his reason is corrupt, and his understanding full of ignorance and error.*
>
> *But we are not from thence to conclude that the knowledge of these truths was attainable by reason, in its present corrupted state; since we find that, until they were revealed, they were hid from the wisdom of ages.*
>
> *Yet undoubtedly the revealed law is of infinitely more authenticity than that moral system which is framed by ethical writers, and denominated the natural law; because one is the law of nature, expressly declared so to be by God Himself; the other is only what, by the assistance of human reason, we imagine to be that law. If we could be as certain of the latter as we are of the former, both would have an equal authority; but, till then, they can never be put in any competition together.*

A third foundational principle that was similarly unquestionable to all three political philosophers was that liberty was not the freedom to do whatever the individual desired. True liberty was constrained not only by concerns for our fellow man, but also there existed no liberty to do those things that we knew we should not. Montesquieu in Book XI, Chapter III explained that,

> *"political liberty does not consist in an unlimited freedom. In governments, that is, in societies directed by laws, liberty can consist only in the power of doing what we ought to will, and in not being constrained to do what we ought not to will."*

Locke explained the same belief as follows:

> *"But though this be a state of liberty, yet it is not a state of licence: though man in that state have an uncontrollable liberty to dispose of his person or possessions, yet he has not liberty to destroy himself. . . ."*
>
> John Locke, The Two Treatises of Civil Government, Chapter II Of the State of Nature, §6.

John Locke © Georgios Kollidas/Shutterstock.com

Consequently, the belief that there are certain actions that man objectively ought not do-actions that would ultimately be detrimental or destructive to the individual were he free to choose them-was embraced by all three political philosophers: Montesquieu, Blackstone, and Locke.

Blackstone not only confirmed this understanding but linked the freewill, or liberty of man, inextricably to the pursuit of happiness. When Blackstone wrote in his Commentaries on the Laws of England, Book I, Part I, Section II that God,

". . . created man, and endued him with freewill to conduct himself in all parts of life, he laid down certain immutable laws of human nature, whereby that freewill is in some degree regulated and restrained,"

he tied those restraints to what tended to man's felicity. This felicity, or man's happiness, was not to be determined by man individually, but simply that his action was to conform to the laws of nature and nature's god.[1] Blackstone went on to explain,

". . . that this or that action tends to man's real happiness, and therefore very justly concluding that the performance of it is a part of the law of nature; or, on the other hand, that this or that action is destructive of man's real happiness, and therefore that the law of nature forbids it."

---

1 The law of nature and nature's god will be more fully explained in Chapter VI when we discuss the Declaration of Independence.

Consequently, Montesquieu, Blackstone, and Locke all believed that the definition of liberty was not synonymous with **licentiousness,** or the freedom of man to do whatever he desired. Liberty instead was the freedom to do what was right, and the freedom to refrain from having to do what was wrong. Liberty was constrained by the need to take into consideration those with whom we lived in community, and was to only allow us the freedom to do those things that tended to our "real happiness." This definition of liberty was interwoven with the **pursuit of happiness,** and the pursuit of happiness possessed an objective definition; it was not an ambiguous term to be subjectively determined by the individual. Only those pursuits that aligned with the law of nature and nature's god were pursuits that truly tended to our happiness. All other pursuits were deemed harmful, and were, therefore, not protected as unalienable rights.

These beliefs in the preexistence of law with unalienable rights established by a creator provided the framework for the U.S. government to be instituted. Such principles were clearly shown within the charter documents of our nation's earliest years. It was this supremacy of a governing law that would tend toward guiding man in proper moral conduct that was seen as the best means of preservation of society as a whole. The fear was that no form of government could successfully govern a community of citizens who were not sufficiently self-governed in their moral choices.

[N]either the wisest constitution nor the wisest laws will secure the liberty and happiness of a people whose manners are universally corrupt.

Samuel Adams,
essay in The Public Advertiser, Circa 1749

It was this pursuit of morality that was to serve as the strongest basis for the preservation of our Constitution, as the document itself was so loosely constructed to have such limited, non-dictatorial control, as to be ineffective to the task of governance over those the Founders would deem licentious in their behavior. John Adams, our second President, declared our Constitution to be drafted solely for the governance of a moral and religious people.

While our country remains untainted with the principles and manners which are now producing desolation in so many parts of the world; while she

continues sincere, and incapable of insidious and impious policy, we shall have the strongest reason to rejoice in the local destination assigned us by Providence. But should the people of America once become capable of that deep simulation towards one another, and towards foreign nations, which assumes the language of justice and moderation while it is practising iniquity and extravagance, and . . . while it is rioting in rapine and insolence, this country will be the most miserable habitation in the Nvorld [sic]; because we have no government armed with power capable of contending with human passions unbridled by morality and religion. Avarice, ambition, revenge, or gallantry, would break the strongest cords of our Constitution as a whale goes through a net. Our Constitution was made only for a moral and religious people. It is wholly inadequate to the government of any other.

John Adams, October 11, 1798
Letter to Officers of the 1st Brigade,
3rd Division, Militia of Mass.

The Founders perceived that when society as a whole consisted of people who were morally self-governing, then the government did not need to be heavy-handed and dictatorial. The further away from this state of self-governance, the more licentious the society, the more restrictive the government would need to become to maintain order. However, the Constitutional Republic they had instituted was not built with the capacity to impose such dictatorial control. It was for this reason that the Founders believed the Constitution to be wholly incapable of governing any society other than one that was inherently moral, and the only way such morality could be assured would be through the people maintaining a commitment to religion. George Washington, in his *Farewell Address*, referred to religion and morality as the two indispensible pillars of our society, with religion being essential to the presence of morality.

George Washington © Victorian Traditions/Shutterstock.com

The Spirit of the Laws

Charles de Secondat, Baron de Montesquieu

Book XI.:
of the Laws which Establish Political Liberty, with Regard to the Constitution.

CHAP. I.: A general Idea. I make a distinction between the laws that establish political liberty, as it relates to the constitution, and those by which it is established, as it relates to the citizen. The former shall be the subject of this book; the latter I shall examine in the next.

CHAP. II.: Different Significations of the Word, Liberty. THERE is no word that admits of more various significations, and has made more different impressions on the human mind, than that of liberty. Some have taken it for a facility of deposing a person on whom they had conferred a tyrannical authority: others, for the power of choosing a superior whom they are obliged to obey; others, for the right of bearing arms, and of being thereby enabled to use violence: others, in fine, for the privilege of being governed by a native of their own country, or by their own laws. * A certain nation, for a long time, thought liberty consisted in the privilege of wearing a long beard. Some have annexed this name to one form of government exclusive of others: those who had a republican taste applied it to this species of polity: those who liked a monarchical state gave it to monarchy. Thus they have all applied the name of liberty to the government most suitable to their own customs and inclinations; and as, in republics, the people have not so constant and so present a view of the causes of their misery, and as the magistrates seem to act only in conformity to the laws, hence liberty is generally said to reside in republics, and to be banished from monarchies. In fine, as in democracies the people seem to act almost as they please, this sort of government has been deemed the most free, and the power of the people has been confounded with their liberty.

CHAP. III.: In what Liberty consists. IT is true that, in democracies, the people seem to act as they please; but political liberty does not consist in an unlimited freedom. In governments, that is, in societies directed by laws, liberty can consist only in the power of doing what we ought to will, and in not being constrained to do what we ought not to will. We must have continually present to our minds the difference between independence and liberty. Liberty is a right of doing whatever the laws permit; and, if a citizen could do what they forbid, he would be no longer possessed of liberty, because all his fellow-citizens would have the same power.

Blackstone's Commentaries on the Laws of England
Book I
Part I
Section The Second.
of the Nature of Laws In General.

LAW, in it's most general and comprehensive sense, signifies a rule of action; and is applied indiscriminately to all kinds of action, whether animate or inanimate, rational or irrational. Thus we say, the laws of motion, of gravitation, of optics, or mechanics, as well as the laws of nature and of nations. And it is that rule of action, which is prescribed by some superior, and which the inferior is bound to obey.

Thus when the supreme being formed the universe, and created matter out of nothing, he impressed certain principles upon that matter, from which it can never depart, and without which it would cease to be. When he put that matter into motion, he established certain laws of motion, to which all moveable bodies must conform. And, to descend from the greatest operations to the smallest, when a workman forms a clock, or other piece of mechanism, he establishes at his own pleasure certain arbitrary laws for it's direction; as that the hand shall describe a given space in a given time; to which law as long as the work conforms, so long it continues in perfection, and answers the end of it's formation.

If we farther advance, from mere inactive matter to vegetable and animal life, we shall find them still governed by laws; more numerous indeed, but equally fixed and invariable. The whole progress of plants, from the seed to the root, and from thence to the seed again; . . . the method of animal nutrition, digestion, secretion, and all other branches of vital economy; . . . are not left to chance, or the will of the creature itself, but are performed in a wondrous involuntary manner, and guided by unerring rules laid down by the great creator.

This then is the general signification of law, a rule of action dictated by some superior being: and, in those creatures that have neither the power to think, nor to will, such laws must be invariably obeyed, so long as the creature itself subsists, for it's existence depends on that obedience. But laws, in their more confined sense, and in which it is our present business to consider them, denote the rules, not of action in general, but of human action or conduct: that is, the precepts by which man, the noblest of all sublunary beings, a creature endowed with both reason and freewill, is commanded to make use of those faculties in the general regulation of his behaviour.

Man, considered as a creature, must necessarily be subject to the laws of his creator, for he is entirely a dependent being. A being, independent of any other, has no rule to pursue, but such as he prescribes to himself; but a state of dependence will inevitably oblige the inferior to take the will of him, on whom he depends, as the rule of his conduct: not indeed in every particular, but in all those points wherein his dependence consists. This principle therefore has more or less extent and effect, in proportion as the superiority of the one and the dependence of the other is greater or less, absolute or limited. And consequently, as man depends absolutely upon his maker for every thing, it is necessary that he should in all points conform to his maker's will.

This will of his maker is called the law of nature. For as God, when he created matter, and endued it with a principle of mobility, established certain rules for the perpetual direction of that motion; so, when he created man, and endued him with freewill to conduct himself in all parts of life, he laid down certain immutable laws of human nature, whereby that freewill is in some degree regulated and restrained, and gave him also the faculty of reason to discover the purport of those laws.

Considering the creator only as a being of infinite power, he was able unquestionably to have prescribed whatever laws he pleased to his creature, man, however unjust or severe. But as be is also a being of infinite wisdom, he has laid down only such laws as were founded in those relations of justice, that existed in the nature of things antecedent to any positive precept. These are the eternal, immutable laws of good and evil, to which the creator himself in all his dispensations conforms; and which he has enabled human reason to discover, so far as they are necessary for the conduct of human actions. Such among others are these principles: that we should live honestly, should hurt nobody, and should render to every one his due; to which three general precepts Justinian[1] has reduced the whole doctrine of law.

But if the discovery of these first principles of the law of nature depended only upon the due exertion of right reason, and could not otherwise be obtained than by a chain of metaphysical disquisitions, mankind would have wanted some inducement to have quickened their inquiries, and the greater part of the world would have rested content in mental indolence, and ignorance it's inseparable companion. As therefore the creator is a being, not only of infinite power, and wisdom, but also of infinite goodness, he has been pleased so to contrive the constitution and frame of humanity, that we should want no other prompter to inquire after and pursue the rule of right, but only our own self-love, that universal principle of action. For he has so intimately connected, so inseparably interwoven the laws of eternal justice with the happiness of each individual, that the latter cannot be attained but by observing the former; and, if the former be punctually obeyed, it cannot but induce the latter. In consequence of which mutual connection of justice and human felicity, he has not perplexed the law of nature with a multitude of abstracted rules and precepts, referring merely to the fitness or unfitness of things, as some have vainly surmised; but has graciously reduced the rule of obedience to this one paternal precept, "that man should pursue his own true and substantial happiness." This is the foundation of what we call ethics, or natural law. For the several articles into which it is branched in our systems, amount to no more than demonstrating, that this or that action tends to man's real happiness, and therefore very justly concluding that the performance of it is a part of the law of nature; or, on the other hand, that this or that action is destructive of man's real happiness, and therefore that the law of nature forbids it.

This law of nature, being coeval with mankind and dictated by God himself, is of course superior in obligation to any other-It is binding over all the globe in all countries, and at all times; no human laws are of any validity, if contrary to this: and such of them as are valid derive all their force, and all their authority, mediately or immediately, from this original.

But in order to apply this to the particular exigencies of each individual, it is still necessary to have recourse to reason; whose office it is to discover, as was before observed, what the law of nature directs in every circumstance of life: by considering, what method will tend the most effectually to our own substantial happiness. And if our reason were always, as in our first ancestor before his transgression, clear and perfect, unruffled by passions, unclouded by prejudice, unimpaired by disease or intemperance, the task would be pleasant and easy; we should need no other guide but this. But every man now finds the contrary in his own experience; that his reason is corrupt, and his understanding full of ignorance and error.

This has given manifold occasion for the benign interposition of divine providence; which, in compassion to the frailty, the imperfection, and the blindness of human reason, hath been pleased, at sundry times and in divers manners, to discover and enforce it's laws by an immediate and direct revelation. The doctrines thus delivered we call the revealed or divine law, and they are to be found only in the holy scriptures. These precepts, when revealed, are found upon comparison to be really a part of the original law of nature, as they tend in all their consequences to man's felicity. But we are not from thence to conclude that the knowledge of these truths was attainable by reason, in it's present corrupted state; since we find that, until they were revealed, they were hid from the wisdom of ages. As then the moral precepts of this law are indeed of the same original with those of the law of nature, so their Intrinsic obligation is of equal strength and perpetuity. Yet undoubtedly the revealed law is of infinitely more authenticity than that moral system, which is framed by ethical writers, and denominated the natural law. Because one is the law of nature, expressly declared so to be by God himself; the other is only what, by the assistance of human reason, we imagine to be that law. If we could be as certain of the latter as we are of the former, both would have an equal authority; but, till then, they can never be put in any competition together.

Upon these two foundations, the law of nature and the law of revelation, depend all human laws; that is to say, no human laws should be suffered to contradict these. There are, it is true a great number of indifferent points, in which both the divine law and the natural leave a man at his own liberty; but which are found necessary for the benefit of society to be restrained within certain limits. And herein it is that human laws have their greatest force and efficacy; for, with regard to such points as are not indifferent, human laws are only declaratory of, and act in subordination to, the former. To instance in the case of murder; this is expressly forbidden by the divine, and demonstrably by the natural law; and from these prohibitions arises the true unlawfulness of this crime. Those human laws that annex a punishment to it, do not at all increase its moral guilt, or superadd any fresh obligation in foroconscientiae to abstain from it's perpetration. Nay, if any human law should allow or enjoin us to commit it, we are bound to transgress that human law, or else we must offend both the natural and the divine. But with regard to matters that are in themselves indifferent, and are not commanded or forbidden by those superior laws; such, for instance, as exporting of wool into foreign countries; here the inferior legislature has scope and opportunity to interpose, and to make that action unlawful which before was not so.

The Two Treatises of Civil Government

John Locke

Book II
of Civil Government

CHAP. II. of the State of Nature.

§. 4.

TO understand political power right, and derive it from its original, we must consider, what state all men are naturally in, and that is, a state of perfect freedom to order their actions, and dispose of their possessions and persons, as they think fit, within the bounds of the law of nature, without asking leave, or depending upon the will of any other man.

A state also of equality, wherein all the power and jurisdiction is reciprocal, no one [196] having more than another; there being nothing more evident, than that creatures of the same species and rank, promiscuously born to all the same advantages of nature, and the use of the same faculties, should also be equal one amongst another without subordination or subjection, unless the lord and master of them all should, by any manifest declaration of his will, set one above another, and confer on him, by an evident and clear appointment, an undoubted right to dominion and sovereignty.

§. 5.

This equality of men by nature, the judicious Hooker looks upon as so evident in itself, and beyond all question, that he makes it the foundation of that obligation to mutual love amongst men, on which he builds the duties they owe one another, and from whence he derives the great maxims of justice and charity. His words are,

The like natural inducement hath brought men to know that it is no less their duty, to love others than themselves; for seeing those things which are equal, must needs all have one measure; if I cannot but wish to receive good, even as much at every man's hands, as any man can wish unto his own soul, how should I look to have any part of my desire herein satisfied, unless myself be careful to satisfy the like desire, which is undoubtedly in other men, being of one and the same nature? To have any thing offered them repugnant to this desire, must needs in all [197] respects grieve them as much as me; so that if I do harm, I must look to suffer, there being no reason that others should shew greater measure of love to me, than they have by me shewed unto them: my desire therefore to be loved of my equals in nature, as much as possible may be, imposeth upon me a natural duty of bearing to them-ward fully the like affection; from which relation of equality between ourselves and them that are as ourselves, what several rules and canons natural reason hath drawn, for direction of life, no man is ignorant. Eccl. Pol. Lib. I.

§. 6.

But though this be a state of liberty, yet it is not a state of licence: though man in that state have an uncontroulable liberty to dispose of his person or possessions, yet he has not liberty to destroy himself, or so much as any creature in his possession, but where some nobler use than its bare preservation calls for it. The state of nature has a law of nature to govern it, which obliges every one: and reason, which is that law, teaches all mankind, who will but consult it, that being all equal and independent, no one ought to harm another in his life, health, liberty, or possessions: for men being all the workmanship of one omnipotent, and infinitely wise maker; all the servants of one sovereign master, sent into the world by his order, and about his business; they are his property, whose workmanship they are, made to last [198] during his, not one another's pleasure: and being furnished with like faculties, sharing all in one community of nature, there cannot be supposed any such subordination among us, that may authorize us to destroy one another, as if we were made for one another's uses, as the inferior ranks of creatures are for our's. Every one, as he is bound to preserve himself, and not to quit his station wilfully, so by the like reason, when his own preservation comes not in competition, ought he, as much as he can, to preserve the rest of mankind, and may not, unless it be to do justice on an offender, take away, or impair the life, or what tends to the preservation of the life, the liberty, health, limb, or goods of another.
in other men's.

Mayflower Compact

November 11, 1620
(1st Governing Document of Plymouth Colony)

In the name of God, Amen. We, whose names are underwritten, the loyal subjects of our dread Sovereigne Lord, King James, by the grace of God, of Great Britaine, France and Ireland king, defender of the faith, etc. having undertaken, for the glory of God, and advancement of the Christian faith, and honour of our king and country, a voyage to plant the first colony in the Northerne parts of Virginia, doe by these presents solemnly and mutually in the presence of God and one of another, covenant and combine ourselves together into a civill body politick, for our better ordering and preservation, and furtherance of the ends aforesaid; and by virtue hereof to enacte, constitute, and frame such just and equall laws, ordinances, acts, constitutions and offices, from time to time, as shall be thought most meete and convenient for the generall good of the Colonie unto which we promise all due submission and obedience. In witness whereof we have hereunder subscribed our names at Cape-Codd the 11. of November, in the year of the raigne of our sovereigne lord, King James, of England, France and Ireland, the eighteenth, and of Scotland the fiftie-fourth. Anno Dom. 1620.

John Carver	Edward Tilley	Degory Priest
William Bradford	John Tilley	Thomas Williams
Edward Winslow	Francis Cooke	Gilbert Winslow
William Brewster	Thomas Rogers	Edmund Margeson
Issac Allerton	Thomas Tinker	Peter Browne
Myles Standish	John Rigdale	Richard Britteridge
John Alden	Edward Fuller	George Soule
Samuel Fuller	John Turner	Richard Clarke
Christopher Martin	Francis Eaton	Richard Gardiner
William Mullins	James Chilton	John Allerton
William White	John Crackston	Thomas English
Richard Warren	John Billington	Edward Dotey
John Howland	Moses Fletcher	Edward Leister
Stephen Hopkins	John Goodman	

(This document is believed by some historians to be the 1st document of self-governance.)

Fundamental Orders of Connecticut

Adopted by the Connecticut
Colony Council, 1639

For as much as it hath pleased Almighty God by the wise disposition of his divine providence so to order and dispose of things that we the Inhabitants and Residents of Windsor, Hartford and Wethersfield are now cohabiting and dwelling in and upon the River of Connectecotte and the lands thereunto adjoining; and well knowing where a people are gathered together the word of God requires that to maintain the peace and union of such a people there should be an orderly and decent Government established according to God, to order and dispose of the affairs of the people at all seasons as occasion shall require; do therefore associate and conjoin ourselves to be as one Public State or Commonwealth; and do for ourselves and our successors and such as shall be adjoined to us at any time hereafter, enter into Combination and Confederation together, to maintain and preserve the liberty and purity of the Gospel of our Lord Jesus which we now profess, as also, the discipline of the Churches, which according to the truth of the said Gospel is now practiced amongst us; as also in our civil affairs to be guided and governed according to such Laws, Rules, Orders and Decrees as shall be made, ordered, and decreed as followeth:

1. It is Ordered, sentenced, and decreed, that there shall be yearly two General Assemblies or Courts, the one the second Thursday in April, the other the second Thursday in September following; the first shall be called the Court of Election, wherein shall be yearly chosen from time to time, so many Magistrates and other public Officers as shall be found requisite: Whereof one to be chosen Governor for the year ensuing and until another be chosen, and no other Magistrate to be chosen for more than one year: provided always there be six chosen besides the Governor, which being chosen and sworn according to an Oath recorded for that purpose, shall have the power to administer justice according to the Laws here established, and for want thereof, according to the Rule of the Word of God; which choice shall be made by all that are admitted freemen and have taken the Oath of Fidelity, and do cohabit within this Jurisdiction having been admitted Inhabitants by the major part of the Town wherein they live or the major part of such as shall be then present.

2. It is Ordered, sentenced, and decreed, that the election of the aforesaid Magistrates shall be in this manner: every person present and qualified for choice shall bring in (to the person deputed to receive them) one single paper with the name of him written in it whom he desires to have Governor, and he that hath the greatest number of papers shall be Governor for that year. And the rest of the Magistrates or public officers to be chosen in this manner: the Secretary for the time being shall first read the names of all that are to be put to choice and then shall severally nominate them distinctly, and every one that would have the person nominated to be chosen shall bring in one single paper written upon, and he that would not have him chosen shall bring in a blank; and every one that hath more written papers than blanks shall be a Magistrate for that year; which papers shall be received and told by one or more that shall be then chosen by the court and sworn to be faithful therein; but in case there should not be six chosen as aforesaid, besides the Governor, out of those which are nominated, than he or they which have the most writen papers shall be a Magistrate or Magistrates for the ensuing year, to make up the aforesaid number.

3. It is Ordered, sentenced, and decreed, that the Secretary shall not nominate any person, nor shall any person be chosen newly into the Magistracy which was not propounded in some General Court before, to be nominated the next election; and to that end it shall be lawful for each of the Towns aforesaid by their deputies to nominate any two whom they conceive fit to be put to election; and the Court may add so many more as they judge requisite.

4. It is Ordered, sentenced, and decreed, that no person be chosen Governor above once in two years, and that the Governor be always a member of some approved Congregation, and formerly of the Magistracy within this Jurisdiction; and that all the Magistrates, Freemen of this Commonwealth; and that no Magistrate or other public officer shall execute any part of his or their office before they are severally sworn, which shall be done in the face of the court if they be present, and in case of absence by some deputed for that purpose.

5. It is Ordered, sentenced, and decreed, that to the aforesaid Court of Election the several Towns shall send their deputies, and when the Elections are ended they may proceed in any public service as at other Courts. Also the other General Court in September shall be for making

of laws, and any other public occasion, which concerns the good of the Commonwealth.

6. It is Ordered, sentenced, and decreed, that the Governor shall, either by himself or by the Secretary, send out summons to the Constables of every Town for the calling of these two standing Courts one month at least before their several times: And also if the Governor and the greatest part of the Magistrates see cause upon any special occasion to call a General Court, they may give order to the Secretary so to do within fourteen days warning: And if urgent necessity so require, upon a shorter notice, giving sufficient grounds for it to the deputies when they meet, or else be questioned for the same; And if the Governor and major part of Magistrates shall either neglect or refuse to call the two General standing Courts or either of them, as also at other times when the occasions of the Commonwealth require, the Freemen thereof, or the major part of them, shall petition to them so to do; if then it be either denied or neglected, the said Freemen, or the major part of them, shall have the power to give order to the Constables of the several Towns to do the same, and so may meet together, and choose to themselves a Moderator, and may proceed to do any act of power which any other General Courts may.

7. It is Ordered, sentenced, and decreed, that after there are warrants given out for any of the said General Courts, the Constable or Constables of each Town, shall forthwith give notice distinctly to the inhabitants of the same, in some public assembly or by going or sending from house to house, that at a place and time by him or them limited and set, they meet and assemble themselves together to elect and choose certain deputies to be at the General Court then following to agitate the affairs of the Commonwealth; which said deputies shall be chosen by all that are admitted Inhabitants in the several Towns and have taken the oath of fidelity; provided that none be chosen a Deputy for any General Court which is not a Freeman of this Commonwealth. The aforesaid deputies shall be chosen in manner following: every person that is present and qualified as before expressed, shall bring the names of such, written in several papers, as they desire to have chosen for that employment, and these three or four, more or less, being the number agreed on to be chosen for that time, that have the greatest number of papers written for them shall be deputies for that Court; whose names shall be endorsed on the back side of the warrant and returned into the Court, with the Constable or Constables' hand unto the same.

8. It is Ordered, sentenced, and decreed, that Windsor, Hartford, and Wethersfield shall have power, each Town, to send four of their Freemen as their deputies to every General Court; and Whatsoever other Town shall be hereafter added to this Jurisdiction, they shall send so many deputies as the Court shall judge meet, a reasonable proportion to the number of Freemen that are in the said Towns being to be attended therein; which deputies shall have the power of the whole Town to give their votes and allowance to all such laws and orders as may be for the public good, and unto which the said Towns are to be bound.

9. It is Ordered, sentenced, and decreed, that the deputies thus chosen shall have power and liberty to appoint a time and a place of meeting together before any General Court, to advise and consult of all such things as may concern the good of the public, as also to examine their own Elections, whether according to the order, and if they or the greatest part of them find any election to be illegal they may seclude such for present from their meeting, and return the same and their reasons to the Court; and if it be proved true, the Court may fine the party or parties so intruding, and the Town, if they see cause, and give out a warrant to go to a new election in a legal way, either in part or in whole. Also the said deputies shall have power to fine any that shall be disorderly at their meetings, or for not coming in due time or place according to appointment; and they may return the said fines into the Court if it be refused to be paid, and the Treasurer to take notice of it, and to escheat or levy the same as he does other fines.

10. It is Ordered, sentenced, and decreed, that every General Court, except such as through neglect of the Governor and the greatest part of the Magistrates the Freemen themselves do call, shall consist of the Governor, or some one chosen to moderate the Court, and four other Magistrates at least, with the major part of the deputies of the several Towns legally chosen; and in case the Freemen, or major part of them, through neglect or refusal of the Governor and major part of the Magistrates, shall call a Court, it shall consist of the major part of Freemen that are present or their deputies, with a Moderator chosen by them: In which said General Courts shall consist the supreme power of the Commonwealth, and they only shall have power to make laws or repeal them, to grant levies, to admit of Freemen, dispose of lands undisposed of, to several Towns or persons, and also shall have power to call either Court or Magistrate or any other person whatsoever into question for any misdemeanor, and may for just causes displace or deal otherwise according to the nature of the offense; and also may deal in any other matter that concerns the good of this Commonwealth, except the election of Magistrates, which shall be done by the whole body of Freemen. In which Court the Governor or Moderator shall have power to order the Court, to give liberty of speech, and silence unseasonable and disorderly

speakings, to put all things to vote, and in case the vote be equal to have the casting voice. But none of these Courts shall be adjourned or dissolved without the consent of the major part of the Court.

11. It is Ordered, sentenced, and decreed, that when any General Court upon the occasions of the Commonwealth have agreed upon any sum, or sums of money to be levied upon the several Towns within this Jurisdiction, that a committee be chosen to set out and appoint what shall be the proportion of every Town to pay of the said levy, provided the committee be made up of an equal number out of each Town.

14th January, 1639, the 11 Orders above said are voted.

President George Washington's Farewell Address

(Sept. 19, 1796)

Friends and Fellow Citizens:

The period for a new election of a citizen to administer the executive government of the United States being not far distant, and the time actually arrived when your thoughts must be employed in designating the person who is to be clothed with that important trust, it appears to me proper, especially as it may conduce to a more distinct expression of the public voice, that I should now apprise you of the resolution I have formed, to decline being considered among the number of those out of whom a choice is to be made.

I beg you, at the same time, to do me the justice to be assured that this resolution has not been taken without a strict regard to all the considerations appertaining to the relation which binds a dutiful citizen to his country; and that in withdrawing the tender of service, which silence in my situation might imply, I am influenced by no diminution of zeal for your future interest, no deficiency of grateful respect for your past kindness, but am supported by a full conviction that the step is compatible with both.

The acceptance of, and continuance hitherto in, the office to which your suffrages have twice called me have been a uniform sacrifice of inclination to the opinion of duty and to a deference for what appeared to be your desire. I constantly hoped that it would have been much earlier in my power, consistently with motives which I was not at liberty to disregard, to return to that retirement from which I had been reluctantly drawn. The strength of my inclination to do this, previous to the last election, had even led to the preparation of an address to declare it to you; but mature reflection on the then perplexed and critical posture of our affairs with foreign nations, and the unanimous advice of persons entitled to my confidence, impelled me to abandon the idea.

I rejoice that the state of your concerns, external as well as internal, no longer renders the pursuit of inclination incompatible with the sentiment of duty or propriety, and am persuaded, whatever partiality may be retained for my services, that, in the present circumstances of our country, you will not disapprove my determination to retire.

The impressions with which I first undertook the arduous trust were explained on the proper occasion. In the discharge of this trust, I will only say that I have, with good intentions, contributed towards the organization and administration of the government the best exertions of which a very fallible judgment was capable. Not unconscious in the outset of the inferiority of my qualifications, experience in my own eyes, perhaps still more in the eyes of others, has strengthened the motives to diffidence of myself; and every day the increasing weight of years admonishes me more and more that the shade of retirement is as necessary to me as it will be welcome. Satisfied that if any circumstances have given peculiar value to my services, they were temporary, I have the consolation to believe that, while choice and prudence invite me to quit the political scene, patriotism does not forbid it.

In looking forward to the moment which is intended to terminate the career of my public life, my feelings do not permit me to suspend the deep acknowledgment of that debt of gratitude which I owe to my beloved country for the many honors it has conferred upon me; still more for the steadfast confidence with which it has supported me; and for the opportunities I have thence enjoyed of manifesting my inviolable attachment, by services faithful and persevering, though in usefulness unequal to my zeal. If benefits have resulted to our country from these services, let it always be remembered to your praise, and as an instructive example in our annals, that under circumstances in which the passions, agitated in every direction, were liable to mislead, amidst appearances sometimes dubious, vicissitudes of fortune often discouraging, in situations in which not unfrequently want of success has countenanced the spirit of criticism, the constancy of your support was the essential prop of the efforts, and a guarantee of the plans by which they were effected. Profoundly penetrated with this idea, I shall carry it with me to my grave, as a strong incitement to unceasing vows that heaven may continue to you the choicest tokens of its beneficence; that your union and brotherly affection may be perpetual; that the free Constitution, which is the work of your hands, may be sacredly maintained; that its administration in every department may be stamped with wisdom and virtue; that, in fine, the happiness of the people of these States, under the auspices of liberty, may be made complete by so careful a preservation and so prudent a use of this blessing as will acquire to them the glory of recommending it to the applause, the affection, and adoption of every nation which is yet a stranger to it.

Here, perhaps, I ought to stop. But a solicitude for your welfare, which cannot end but with my life, and the apprehension of danger, natural to that solicitude, urge me, on an occasion like the present, to offer to your solemn contemplation, and to recommend to your frequent review, some sentiments which are the result of much reflection, of no inconsiderable observation, and which appear to me all-important to the permanency of your felicity as a people. These will be offered to you with the more freedom, as you can only see in them the disinterested warnings of a parting friend, who can possibly have no personal motive to bias his counsel. Nor can I forget, as an encouragement to it, your indulgent reception of my sentiments on a former and not dissimilar occasion.

Interwoven as is the love of liberty with every ligament of your hearts, no recommendation of mine is necessary to fortify or confirm the attachment.

The unity of government which constitutes you one people is also now dear to you. It is justly so, for it is a main pillar in the edifice of your real independence, the support of your tranquility at home, your peace abroad; of your safety; of your prosperity; of that very liberty which you so highly prize. But as it is easy to foresee that, from different causes and from different quarters, much pains will be taken, many artifices employed to weaken in your minds the conviction of this truth; as this is the point in your political fortress against which the batteries of internal and external enemies will be most constantly and actively (though often covertly and insidiously) directed, it is of infinite moment that you should properly estimate the immense value of your national union to your collective and individual happiness; that you should cherish a cordial, habitual, and immovable attachment to it; accustoming yourselves to think and speak of it as of the palladium of your political safety and prosperity; watching for its preservation with jealous anxiety; discountenancing whatever may suggest even a suspicion that it can in any event be abandoned; and indignantly frowning upon the first dawning of every attempt to alienate any portion of our country from the rest, or to enfeeble the sacred ties which now link together the various parts.

For this you have every inducement of sympathy and interest. Citizens, by birth or choice, of a common country, that country has a right to concentrate your affections. The name of American, which belongs to you in your national capacity, must always exalt the just pride of patriotism more than any appellation derived from local discriminations. With slight shades of difference, you have the same religion, manners, habits, and political principles. You have in a common cause fought and triumphed together; the independence and liberty you possess are the work of joint counsels, and joint efforts of common dangers, sufferings, and successes.

But these considerations, however powerfully they address themselves to your sensibility, are greatly outweighed by those which apply more immediately to your interest. Here every portion of our country finds the most commanding motives for carefully guarding and preserving the union of the whole.

The North, in an unrestrained intercourse with the South, protected by the equal laws of a common government, finds in the productions of the latter great additional resources of maritime and commercial enterprise and precious materials of manufacturing industry. The South, in the same intercourse, benefiting by the agency of the North, sees its agriculture grow and its commerce expand. Turning partly into its own channels the seamen of the North, it finds its particular navigation invigorated; and, while it contributes, in different ways, to nourish and increase the general mass of the national navigation, it looks forward to the protection of a maritime strength, to which itself is unequally adapted. The East, in a like intercourse with the West, already finds, and in the progressive improvement of interior communications by land and water, will more and more find a valuable vent for the commodities which it brings from abroad, or manufactures at home. The West derives from the East supplies requisite to its growth and comfort, and, what is perhaps of still greater consequence, it must of necessity owe the secure enjoyment of indispensable outlets for its own productions to the weight, influence, and the future maritime strength of the Atlantic side of the Union, directed by an indissoluble community of interest as one nation. Any other tenure by which the West can hold this essential advantage, whether derived from its own separate strength, or from an apostate and unnatural connection with any foreign power, must be intrinsically precarious.

While, then, every part of our country thus feels an immediate and particular interest in union, all the parts combined cannot fail to find in the united mass of means and efforts greater strength, greater resource, proportionably greater security from external danger, a less frequent interruption of their peace by foreign nations; and, what is of inestimable value, they must derive from union an exemption from those broils and wars between themselves, which so frequently afflict neighboring countries not tied together by the same governments, which their own rival ships alone would be sufficient to produce, but which opposite foreign alliances, attachments, and intrigues would stimulate and embitter. Hence, likewise, they will avoid the necessity of those overgrown military establishments which, under any form of government, are inauspicious to liberty, and which are to be regarded as particularly hostile to republican liberty. In this sense it is that your union ought to be considered as a main prop of your liberty, and that the love of the one ought to endear to you the preservation of the other.

These considerations speak a persuasive language to every reflecting and virtuous mind, and exhibit the continuance of the Union as a primary object of patriotic desire. Is there a doubt whether a common government can embrace so large a sphere? Let experience solve it. To listen to mere speculation in such a case were criminal. We are authorized to hope that a proper organization of the whole with the auxiliary agency of governments for the respective subdivisions, will afford a happy issue to the experiment. It is well worth a fair and full experiment. With such powerful and obvious motives to union, affecting all parts of our country, while experience shall not have demonstrated its impracticability, there will always be reason to distrust the patriotism of those who in any quarter may endeavor to weaken its bands.

In contemplating the causes which may disturb our Union, it occurs as matter of serious concern that any ground should have been furnished for characterizing parties by geographical discriminations, Northern and Southern, Atlantic and Western; whence designing men may endeavor to excite a belief that there is a real difference of local interests and views. One of the expedients of party to acquire influence within particular districts is to misrepresent the opinions and aims of other districts. You cannot shield yourselves too much against the jealousies and heartburnings which spring from these misrepresentations; they tend to render alien to each other those who ought to be bound together by fraternal affection. The inhabitants of our Western country have lately had a useful lesson on this head; they have seen, in the negotiation by the Executive, and in the unanimous ratification by the Senate, of the treaty with Spain, and in the universal satisfaction at that event, throughout the United States, a decisive proof how unfounded were the suspicions propagated among them of a policy in the General Government and in the Atlantic States unfriendly to their interests in regard to the Mississippi; they have been witnesses to the formation of two treaties, that with Great Britain, and that with Spain, which secure to them everything they could desire, in respect to our foreign relations, towards confirming their prosperity. Will it not be their wisdom to rely for the preservation of these advantages on the Union by which they were procured ? Will they not henceforth be deaf to those advisers, if such there are, who would sever them from their brethren and connect them with aliens?

To the efficacy and permanency of your Union, a government for the whole is indispensable. No alliance, however strict, between the parts can be an adequate substitute; they must inevitably experience the infractions and interruptions which all alliances in all times have experienced. Sensible of this momentous truth, you have improved upon your first essay, by the adoption of a constitution of government better calculated than your former for an intimate union, and for the efficacious management of your common concerns. This government, the offspring of our own choice, uninfluenced and unawed, adopted upon full investigation and mature deliberation, completely free in its principles, in the distribution of its powers, uniting security with energy, and containing within itself a provision for its own amendment, has a just claim to your confidence and your support. Respect for its authority, compliance with its laws, acquiescence in its measures, are duties enjoined by the fundamental maxims of true liberty. The basis of our political systems is the right of the people to make and to alter their constitutions of government. But the Constitution which at any time exists, till changed by an explicit and authentic act of the whole people, is sacredly obligatory upon all. The very idea of the power and the right of the people to establish government presupposes the duty of every individual to obey the established government.

All obstructions to the execution of the laws, all combinations and associations, under whatever plausible character, with the real design to direct, control, counteract, or awe the regular deliberation and action of the constituted authorities, are destructive of this fundamental principle, and of fatal tendency. They serve to organize faction, to give it an artificial and extraordinary force; to put, in the place of the delegated will of the nation the will of a party, often a small but artful and enterprising minority of the community; and, according to the alternate triumphs of different parties, to make the public administration the mirror of the ill-concerted and incongruous projects of faction, rather than the organ of consistent and wholesome plans digested by common counsels and modified by mutual interests.

However combinations or associations of the above description may now and then answer popular ends, they are likely, in the course of time and things, to become potent engines, by which cunning, ambitious, and unprincipled men will be enabled to subvert the power of the people and to usurp for themselves the reins of government, destroying afterwards the very engines which have lifted them to unjust dominion.

Towards the preservation of your government, and the permanency of your present happy state, it is requisite, not only that you steadily discountenance irregular oppositions to its acknowledged authority, but also that you resist with care the spirit of innovation upon its principles, however specious the pretexts. One method of assault may be to effect, in the forms of the Constitution, alterations which will impair the energy of the system, and thus to undermine what cannot be directly overthrown. In all the changes to which you may be invited, remember that time and habit are at least as necessary to fix the true character of governments as of other human institutions; that experience is the surest standard by which to test the real tendency of the existing constitution of a country; that facility in changes, upon the credit of mere hypothesis and opinion, exposes to perpetual change, from the endless variety of hypothesis and opinion; and remember, especially, that for the efficient management of your common interests, in a country so extensive as ours, a government of as much vigor as is consistent with the perfect security of liberty is indispensable. Liberty itself will find in such a government, with powers properly distributed and adjusted, its surest guardian. It is, indeed, little else than a name, where the government is too feeble to withstand the enterprises of faction, to confine each member of the society within the limits prescribed by the laws, and to maintain all in the secure and tranquil enjoyment of the rights of person and property.

I have already intimated to you the danger of parties in the State, with particular reference to the founding of them on geographical discriminations. Let me now take a more comprehensive view, and warn you in the most solemn manner against the baneful effects of the spirit of party generally.

This spirit, unfortunately, is inseparable from our nature, having its root in the strongest passions of the human mind. It exists under different shapes in all governments, more or less stifled, controlled, or repressed; but, in those of the popular form, it is seen in its greatest rankness, and is truly their worst enemy.

The alternate domination of one faction over another, sharpened by the spirit of revenge, natural to party dissension, which in different ages and countries has perpetrated the most horrid enormities, is itself a frightful despotism. But this leads at length to a more formal and permanent despotism. The disorders and miseries which result gradually incline the minds of men to seek security and repose in the absolute power of an individual; and sooner or later the chief of some prevailing faction, more able or more fortunate than his competitors, turns this disposition to the purposes of his own elevation, on the ruins of public liberty.

Without looking forward to an extremity of this kind (which nevertheless ought not to be entirely out of sight), the common and continual mischiefs of the spirit of party are sufficient to make it the interest and duty of a wise people to discourage and restrain it.

It serves always to distract the public councils and enfeeble the public administration. It agitates the community with ill-founded jealousies and false alarms, kindles the animosity of one part against another, foments occasionally riot and insurrection. It opens the door to foreign influence and corruption, which finds a facilitated access to the government itself through the channels of party passions. Thus the policy and the will of one country are subjected to the policy and will of another.

There is an opinion that parties in free countries are useful checks upon the administration of the government and serve to keep alive the spirit of liberty. This within certain limits is probably true; and in governments of a monarchical cast, patriotism may look with indulgence, if not with favor, upon the spirit of party. But in those of the popular character, in governments purely elective, it is a spirit not to be encouraged. From their natural tendency, it is certain there will always be enough of that spirit for every salutary purpose. And there being constant danger of excess, the effort ought to be by force of public opinion, to mitigate and assuage it. A fire not to be quenched, it demands a uniform vigilance to prevent its bursting into a flame, lest, instead of warming, it should consume.

It is important, likewise, that the habits of thinking in a free country should inspire caution in those entrusted with its administration, to confine themselves within their respective constitutional spheres, avoiding in the exercise of the powers of one department to encroach upon another. The spirit of encroachment tends to consolidate the powers of all the departments in one, and thus to create, whatever the form of government, a real despotism. A just estimate of that love of power, and proneness to abuse it, which predominates in the human heart, is sufficient to satisfy us of the truth of this position. The necessity of reciprocal checks in the exercise of political power, by dividing and distributing it into different depositaries, and constituting each the guardian of the public weal against invasions by the others, has been evinced by experiments ancient and modern; some of them in our country and under our own eyes. To preserve them must be as necessary as to institute them. If, in the opinion of the people, the distribution or modification of the constitutional powers be in any particular wrong, let it be corrected by an amendment in the way which the Constitution designates. But let there be no change by usurpation; for though this, in one instance, may be the instrument of good, it is the customary weapon by which free governments are destroyed. The precedent must always greatly overbalance in permanent evil any partial or transient benefit, which the use can at any time yield.

Of all the dispositions and habits which lead to political prosperity, religion and morality are indispensable supports. In vain would that man claim the tribute of patriotism, who should labor to subvert these great pillars of human happiness, these firmest props of the duties of men and citizens. The mere politician, equally with the pious man, ought to respect and to cherish them. A volume could not trace all their connections with private and public felicity. Let it simply be asked: Where is the security for property, for reputation, for life, if the sense of religious obligation desert the oaths which are the instruments of investigation in courts of justice? And let us with caution indulge the supposition that morality can be maintained without religion. Whatever may be conceded to the influence of refined education on minds of peculiar structure, reason and experience both forbid us to expect that national morality can prevail in exclusion of religious principle.

It is substantially true that virtue or morality is a necessary spring of popular government. The rule, indeed, extends with more or less force to every species of free government. Who that is a sincere friend to it can look with indifference upon attempts to shake the foundation of the fabric?

Promote then, as an object of primary importance, institutions for the general diffusion of knowledge. In proportion as the structure of a government gives force to public opinion, it is essential that public opinion should be enlightened.

As a very important source of strength and security, cherish public credit. One method of preserving it is to use it as sparingly as possible, avoiding occasions of expense by cultivating peace, but remembering also that timely disbursements to prepare for danger frequently prevent much greater disbursements to repel it, avoiding likewise the accumulation of debt, not only by shunning occasions of expense, but by vigorous exertion in time of peace to discharge the debts which unavoidable wars may have occasioned, not ungenerously throwing upon posterity the burden which we ourselves ought to bear. The execution of these maxims belongs to your representatives, but it is necessary that public opinion should co-operate. To facilitate to them the performance of their duty, it is essential that you should practically bear in mind that towards the payment of debts there must be revenue; that to have revenue there must be taxes; that no taxes can be devised which are not more or less inconvenient and unpleasant; that the intrinsic embarrassment, inseparable from the selection of the proper objects (which is always a choice of difficulties), ought to be a decisive motive for a candid construction of the conduct of the government in making it, and for a spirit of acquiescence in the measures for obtaining revenue, which the public exigencies may at any time dictate.

Observe good faith and justice towards all nations; cultivate peace and harmony with all. Religion and morality enjoin this conduct; and can it be, that good policy does not equally enjoin it? It will be worthy of a free, enlightened, and at no distant period, a great nation, to give to mankind the magnanimous and too novel example of a people always guided by an exalted justice and benevolence. Who can doubt that, in the course of time and things, the fruits of such a plan would richly repay any temporary advantages which might be lost by a steady adherence to it? Can it be that Providence has not connected the permanent felicity of a nation with its virtue? The experiment, at least, is recommended by every sentiment which ennobles human nature. Alas! is it rendered impossible by its vices?

In the execution of such a plan, nothing is more essential than that permanent, inveterate antipathies against particular nations, and passionate attachments for others, should be excluded; and that, in place of them, just and amicable feelings towards all should be cultivated. The nation which indulges towards another a habitual hatred or a habitual fondness is in some degree a slave. It is a slave to its animosity or to its affection, either of which is sufficient to lead it astray from its duty and its interest. Antipathy in one nation against another disposes each more readily to offer insult and injury, to lay hold of slight causes of umbrage, and to be haughty and intractable, when accidental or trifling occasions of dispute occur. Hence, frequent collisions, obstinate, envenomed, and bloody contests. The nation, prompted by ill-will and resentment, sometimes impels to war the government, contrary to the best calculations of policy. The government sometimes participates in the national propensity, and adopts through passion what reason would reject; at other times it makes the animosity of the nation subservient to projects of hostility instigated by pride, ambition, and other sinister and pernicious motives. The peace often, sometimes perhaps the liberty, of nations, has been the victim.

So likewise, a passionate attachment of one nation for another produces a variety of evils. Sympathy for the favorite nation, facilitating the illusion of an imaginary common interest in cases where no real common interest exists, and infusing into one the enmities of the other, betrays the former into a participation in the quarrels and wars of the latter without adequate inducement or justification. It leads also to concessions to the favorite nation of privileges denied to others which is apt doubly to injure the nation making the concessions; by unnecessarily parting with what ought to have been retained, and by exciting jealousy, ill-will, and a disposition to retaliate, in the parties from whom equal privileges are withheld. And it gives to ambitious, corrupted, or deluded citizens (who devote themselves to the favorite nation), facility to betray or sacrifice the interests of their own country, without odium, sometimes even with popularity; gilding, with the appearances of a virtuous sense of obligation, a commendable deference for public opinion, or a laudable zeal for public good, the base or foolish compliances of ambition, corruption, or infatuation.

As avenues to foreign influence in innumerable ways, such attachments are particularly alarming to the truly enlightened and independent patriot. How many opportunities do they afford to tamper with domestic factions, to practice the arts of seduction, to mislead public opinion, to influence or awe the public councils? Such an attachment of a small or weak towards a great and powerful nation dooms the former to be the satellite of the latter.

Against the insidious wiles of foreign influence (I conjure you to believe me, fellow-citizens) the jealousy of a free people ought to be constantly awake, since history and experience prove that foreign influence is one of the most baneful foes of republican government. But that jealousy to be useful must be impartial; else it becomes the instrument of the very influence to be avoided, instead of a defense against it. Excessive partiality for one foreign nation and excessive dislike of another cause those whom they actuate to see danger only on one side, and serve to veil and even second the arts of influence on the other. Real patriots who may resist the intrigues of the favorite are liable to become suspected and odious, while its tools and dupes usurp the applause and confidence of the people, to surrender their interests.

The great rule of conduct for us in regard to foreign nations is in extending our commercial relations, to have with them as little political connection as possible. So far as we have already formed engagements, let them be fulfilled with perfect good faith. Here let us stop. Europe has a set of primary interests which to us have none; or a very remote relation. Hence she must be engaged in frequent controversies, the causes of which are essentially foreign to our concerns. Hence, therefore, it must be unwise in us to implicate ourselves by artificial ties in the ordinary vicissitudes of her politics, or the ordinary combinations and collisions of her friendships or enmities.

Our detached and distant situation invites and enables us to pursue a different course. If we remain one people under an efficient government. the period is not far off when we may defy material injury from external annoyance; when we may take such an attitude as will cause the neutrality we may at any time resolve upon to be scrupulously respected; when belligerent nations, under the impossibility of making acquisitions upon us, will not lightly hazard the giving us provocation; when we may choose peace or war, as our interest, guided by justice, shall counsel.

Why forego the advantages of so peculiar a situation? Why quit our own to stand upon foreign ground? Why, by interweaving our destiny with that of any part of Europe, entangle our peace and prosperity in the toils of European ambition, rivalship, interest, humor or caprice?

It is our true policy to steer clear of permanent alliances with any portion of the foreign world; so far, I mean, as we are now at liberty to do it; for let me not be understood as capable of patronizing infidelity to existing engagements. I hold the maxim no less applicable to public than to private affairs, that honesty is always the best policy. I repeat it, therefore, let those engagements be observed in their genuine sense. But, in my opinion, it is unnecessary and would be unwise to extend them.

Taking care always to keep ourselves by suitable establishments on a respectable defensive posture, we may safely trust to temporary alliances for extraordinary emergencies.

Harmony, liberal intercourse with all nations, are recommended by policy, humanity, and interest. But even our commercial policy should hold an equal and impartial hand; neither seeking nor granting exclusive favors or preferences; consulting the natural course of things; diffusing and diversifying by gentle means the streams of commerce, but forcing nothing; establishing (with powers so disposed, in order to give trade a stable course, to define the rights of our merchants, and to enable the government to support them) conventional rules of intercourse, the best that present circumstances and mutual opinion will permit, but temporary, and liable to be from time to time abandoned or varied, as experience and circumstances shall dictate; constantly keeping in view that it is folly in one nation to look for disinterested favors from another; that it must pay with a portion of its independence for whatever it may accept under that character; that, by such acceptance, it may place itself in the condition of having given equivalents for nominal favors, and yet of being reproached with ingratitude for not giving more. There can be no greater error than to expect or calculate upon real favors from nation to nation. It is an illusion, which experience must cure, which a just pride ought to discard.

In offering to you, my countrymen, these counsels of an old and affectionate friend, I dare not hope they will make the strong and lasting impression I could wish; that they will control the usual current of the passions, or prevent our nation from running the course which has hitherto marked the destiny of nations. But, if I may even flatter myself that they may be productive of some partial benefit, some occasional good; that they may now and then recur to moderate the fury of party spirit, to warn against the mischiefs of foreign intrigue, to guard against the impostures of pretended patriotism; this hope will be a full recompense for the solicitude for your welfare, by which they have been dictated.

How far in the discharge of my official duties I have been guided by the principles which have been delineated, the public records and other evidences of my conduct must witness to you and to the world. To myself, the assurance of my own conscience is, that I have at least believed myself to be guided by them.

In relation to the still subsisting war in Europe, my proclamation of the twenty-second of April, 1793, is the index of my plan. Sanctioned by your approving voice, and by that of your representatives in both houses of Congress, the spirit of that measure has continually governed me, uninfluenced by any attempts to deter or divert me from it.

After deliberate examination, with the aid of the best lights I could obtain, I was well satisfied that our country, under all the circumstances of the case, had a right to take, and was bound in duty and interest to take, a neutral position. Having taken it, I determined, as far as should depend upon me, to maintain it, with moderation, perseverance, and firmness.

The considerations which respect the right to hold this conduct, it is not necessary on this occasion to detail. I will only observe that, according to my understanding of the matter, that right, so far from being denied by any of the belligerent powers, has been virtually admitted by all.

The duty of holding a neutral conduct may be inferred, without anything more, from the obligation which justice and humanity impose on every nation, in cases in which it is free to act, to maintain inviolate the relations of peace and amity towards other nations.

The inducements of interest for observing that conduct will best be referred to your own reflections and experience. With me a predominant motive has been to endeavor to gain time to our country to settle and mature its yet recent institutions, and to progress without interruption to that degree of strength and consistency which is necessary to give it, humanly speaking, the command of its own fortunes.

Though, in reviewing the incidents of my administration, I am unconscious of intentional error, I am nevertheless too sensible of my defects not to think it probable that I may have committed many errors. Whatever they may be, I fervently beseech the Almighty to avert or mitigate the evils to which they may tend. I shall also carry with me the hope that my country will never cease to view them with indulgence; and that, after forty five years of my life dedicated to its service with an upright zeal, the faults of incompetent abilities will be consigned to oblivion, as myself must soon be to the mansions of rest.

Relying on its kindness in this as in other things, and actuated by that fervent love towards it, which is so natural to a man who views in it the native soil of himself and his progenitors for several generations, I anticipate with pleasing expectation that retreat in which I promise myself to realize, without alloy, the sweet enjoyment of partaking, in the midst of my fellow-citizens, the benign influence of good laws under a free government, the ever-favorite object of my heart, and the happy reward, as I trust, of our mutual cares, labors, and dangers.

(This document is believed by some historians to be the 1st written constitution.)

QUESTIONS

1. Who were the three most influential political philosophers that impacted America's founding, and what were their writings?

2. To what other unalienable right was our liberty tied, and how were both these rights to be objectively understood?

3. According to Blackstone, how could mankind ascertain the preexisting laws to which we should conform? What was the difference between *natural law* and the *laws of nature*?

4. What did George Washington perceive to be the two indispensible supports for political prosperity? Also, what type of government did he perceive resulted from the consolidation of powers of all the departments into one?

Chapter 3
HOW LAWS ARE ENACTED

Original Sources:
1. Article I, Section 5 of the Constitution (see page 18)
2. Article I, Section 7 of the Constitution (see page 19)
3. Article II, Section 2, Paragraph 2 of the Constitution (see page 24)
4. 20th Amendment to the Constitution

Article I, Section 5, of the Constitution states that: "Each House may determine the Rules of its Proceedings," and it is from this single clause that rules and regulations are adopted that govern how a law is to be enacted by Congress. Members of the House of Representatives have two-year terms. A new term begins each January of odd numbered years, following an election year in even numbered years. It is at this time that each House establishes its Rules. Senators are elected for six-year terms; therefore, the election cycle of Senators alternates, so there is no set term where all one hundred Senators are up for election. Because of this, the Senate arbitrarily amends its Rules from time-to-time, with no set date for amendment.

While a bill may originate in either chamber of Congress, most are introduced within the House of Representatives. It is important to note that the rules pertaining to the enactment of a law differ, depending upon which chamber the legislation originates. There are certain bills or actions that must start in a particular chamber. For example, bills that effect either revenue or **appropriations** must originate in the House of Representatives. This is one of the reasons so many bills start in the House. Meanwhile, the Senate has the authority to give advice and consent on treaties and on certain Presidential Nominations, such as Supreme Court nominees.

The reality is that it is a rather difficult process for a bill, which starts as an idea presented by one or more Congressmen, to actually make it into a law. This is a good thing. It means that there is ample time for various voices to be heard, for minority opinions to be considered, and for bills to be amended, which is part of the fine-tuning process. At any moment during the process a bill can die, which means only the bills with the greatest support ultimately make it to the floor for a vote.

Legislative action may begin in one of four different forms. They may be a bill, a Joint Resolution, Concurrent Resolution, or a Simple Resolution. There is not much difference between a bill and a Joint Resolution, and a Joint Resolution (H.J. Res. or S.J. Res.) does not mean that it has to jointly begin in both houses. However, if a Joint Resolution is used to amend the Constitution of the United States, and it is approved by two-thirds vote of both chambers, then the Joint Resolution does not seek approval from the President. Rather, it is sent directly to the States for approval. If three-fourths of the states approve it within a prescribed period of time, then it becomes a part of the Constitution without ever requiring the President's signature.

© bernie_moto_photo/Shutterstock.com

Neither a concurrent resolution, nor a simple resolution, has been found by the Supreme Court to actually constitute legislative character, since neither requires approval from the President. A concurrent resolution, contrary to how it sounds, does not have to concurrently start in both chambers. It may originate in either the House (H. Con. Res.) or the Senate (S. Con. Res.), and once it passes both houses it is signed not by the President, but by the Clerk of the House and the Secretary of the Senate. It is then published so the public may read the resolution. A concurrent resolution usually revolves around some situation that impacts both chambers, and is more or less simply a statement of agreed upon fact or opinion of both chambers.

A simple resolution is a statement of opinion or fact concerning an issue that only impacts one particular chamber. Therefore, if the issue affects the Senate only, then it would originate in the Senate (S. Res.), and if it passes, would be signed by the Secretary of the Senate. Conversely, if the issue affects the House only, then it would originate in the house (H. Res.), and if it passes, would be signed by the Clerk of the House.

House Chamber © Drop of Light/Shutterstock.com

The procedure for how a bill becomes a law is a long, detailed process. A single Congressman (Primary Sponsor) or several Congressmen (Cosponsors) may introduce a bill. Once a bill is introduced it is then referred to the appropriate committee or committees. The committee process is the process that most thoroughly vets the bill. This is also the time during which Congress allows the public to be heard. Additionally, one of the first actions of the committee is to send the bill to the relevant Governmental Agency for a formal report. The committees are not bound to follow these reports. However, it is easy to see how it would be challenging for a bill that significantly cuts the role or responsibility of a Governmental Agency to make it out of committee.

If the Committee determines the bill to be sufficiently important, then a public hearing may be set. The date, time and place of the hearing are to be provided to the public at least one week prior to the hearing. However, there is a process whereby this date may be scheduled earlier if there is deemed to be good cause to do so.

The committee then will vote whether to report the bill favorably for consideration by the respective chamber. It may report it favorably, unfavorably, without recommendation, or favorably with amendments. If the amendments are extensive, it essentially reports a substitute bill for consideration.

Senate Chamber © Marzolino/Shutterstock.com

The bill is then presented to the chamber for an established amount of time for general debate. Once this time lapses, the bill is then presented for "second reading." This is when the bill is read through section by section. This is also the time when amendments may be made to each respective section. It is required that any amendment presented for consideration must be **germane**—relevant—to the subject matter of the bill.

Debate on the bill may be stopped by majority vote of the chamber, when a **quorum** of the voting members is present. Then the Speaker of the

House, if the bill is in the House of Representatives, asks whether the bill should be **engrossed**, which means the bill will be read a third and final time. However, the third time it is simply read by title, not content, and then placed before the chamber for a vote.

The engrossed bill is then sent to the other chamber for consideration. If that chamber is the Senate, then the President of the Senate, or Vice President of the United States, sends the bill to the appropriate committee(s) for consideration. The bill then goes through the exact same process that it had already undergone in the other chamber, with the noted distinction between the rules of procedure governing the Senate and those governing the House. A bill may not become law unless the identical bill has passed through both chambers. Therefore, if the Senate amends the engrossed House version, then it is no longer the same bill that passed the House. Consequently, the Senate would send its version of the bill back to the House for approval. If the House votes to pass this amended version, then the bill is sent to the President for his approval and signature.

If the President approves and signs the bill, then it becomes law. If the President fails to return the

© docstockmedia/Shutterstock.com

bill with his objections to the chamber from which it originated within ten days, excluding Sundays, then the bill becomes a law. If, however, the President is prohibited from returning it to Congress during the prescribed ten days, due to Congress' **adjournment**, this constitutes a pocket veto. Any bill that has been vetoed must then pass through both chambers with a two-thirds majority vote in order to override the President's veto. If both chambers vote with a two-thirds vote or greater to pass the bill, then the President's veto is overridden and the bill still becomes a law.

Amendment XX

Section. 1

The terms of the President and Vice President shall end at noon on the 20th day of January, and the terms of Senators and Representatives at noon on the 3d day of January, of the years in which such terms would have ended if this article had not been ratified; and the terms of their successors shall then begin.

Section. 2

The Congress shall assemble at least once in every year, and such meeting shall begin at noon on the 3d day of January, unless they shall by law appoint a different day.

Section. 3

If, at the time fixed for the beginning of the term of the President, the President elect shall have died, the Vice President elect shall become President. If a President shall not have been chosen before the time fixed for the beginning of his term, or if the President elect shall have failed to qualify, then the Vice President elect shall act as President until a President shall have qualified; and the Congress may by law provide for the case wherein neither a President elect nor a Vice President elect shall have qualified, declaring who shall then act as President, or the manner in which one who is to act shall be selected, and such person shall act accordingly until a President or Vice President shall have qualified.

Section. 4

The Congress may by law provide for the case of the death of any of the persons from whom the House of Representatives may choose a President whenever the right of choice shall have devolved upon them, and for the case of the death of any of the persons from whom the Senate may choose a Vice President whenever the right of choice shall have devolved upon them.

Section. 5

Sections 1 and 2 shall take effect on the 15th day of October following the ratification of this article.

Section. 6

This article shall be inoperative unless it shall have been ratified as an amendment to the Constitution by the legislatures of three-fourths of the several states within seven years from the date of its submission.

QUESTIONS

1. What are the four basic forms of legislation?

2. What is required for an amendment to the Constitution?

3. What is the legislative process that most thoroughly vets a Bill?

4. What is the process to override a Presidential Veto to a Bill?

Chapter 4
WAYS CITIZENS SHAPE AND INFLUENCE THE GOVERNMENT

Original Sources:
1. Two Treatises of Government, Book II, Chapter VII
2. 9th and 10th Amendments
3. Madison's Memorial and Remonstrance

We will review more thoroughly what it means to be a Republic in Chapter 9. In this chapter, we will discuss the citizen's role within our government. This role is uniquely balanced between being a government of laws, not of men, and at the same time being a government of the people, by the people and for the people. In short, how do we shape and influence government, without resorting to majority or mob rule?

First it is important to note that our society, or civil body politic, was made by the coming together of thirteen colonies to voluntarily form one nation. When man decides to come together in community, he is voluntarily setting down some of his individual rights or autonomy for the united protection of society. Tension arises from the need to form a government that adequately governs the people, and at the same time form a government that is accountable to the people such that it cannot oppress them.

We as Americans possess exactly the type of governance that we choose. We can make our voices heard in many different ways. First, most of us possess the privilege of being able to vote for our elected representatives. Unfortunately, while many are not happy with how we are represented, they do not avail themselves of the opportunity to vote. Or more importantly, to become informed voters who research the candidates and their positions. In 2012, a Presidential Election year, only 58% of eligible voters voted. In 2014, a mid-term election year, only 36.4% of eligible voters cast ballots.

© Carolyn Franks/Shutterstock.com

We have the ability to tremendously influence and shape our government by selecting the men and women who represent us. This is our most basic and fundamental means of controlling our government. When we don't vote, and when we don't stay informed on how our elected officials are governing, then we waive much of our right to govern through the selection of our representatives.

"When you become entitled to exercise the right of voting for public officers, let it be impressed on your mind that God commands you to choose for rulers just men who will rule in the fear of God. The preservation of a republican government depends on the faithful discharge of this duty; if the citizens neglect their duty and place unprincipled men in office, the government will soon be corrupted; laws will be made not for the public good so much as for selfish or local purposes; corrupt or incompetent men will be appointed to execute the laws; the public revenues will be squandered on unworthy men; and the rights of the citizens will be violated or disregarded. If a republican government fails to secure

public prosperity and happiness, it must be because the citizens neglect the Divine commands and elect bad men to make and administer the laws."

Noah Webster,
Letters to a Young Gentlemen

We also have the right of Petition. The government doesn't give this right to us. Rather it's a right we inherently possess from which Congress is prohibited in any way from infringing. This right is preserved to us in the 1st Amendment of the Bill of Rights. More specifically it says that Congress shall make no law respecting the "right of the people . . . to petition the Government for a redress of grievances."

This right to petition the government for relief was a right found within the British **common law** as detailed by Sir William Blackstone in his Commentaries on the Laws of England. The common law and all of its intrinsic rights were embraced by the thirteen colonies, and viewed as their birthright. This unlegislated form of the law of nature presented the right to petition the King for redress of grievances as a right given by God and possessed by all individuals. As such, it was viewed as an **unalienable** right, and could not, therefore, be taken away by the government.

© Zerbor/Shutterstock.com

Congress threatened our right to petition when they began receiving unwanted petitions for the abolition of slavery. Congress passed the Gag Rule in 1836, prohibiting the reading of anti-slavery petitions from the House floor. Two notable Congressmen on opposite sides of this debate were John Quincy Adams, a former President of the United States, and James K. Polk, a future President of the United States. Polk threatened John Quincy Adams with censure for reading petitions regarding slavery. Quincy Adams used this threat and the resultant proceedings as a platform to discuss the evils of slavery. The Gag Rule was not repealed until December 1844.

While the Right of Petition may not be well understood or frequently used, it is an important means of preserving our rights and liberty. The ability to confront the government about areas of oppression is a right we possess and one we should use.

The federal government was vested with eighteen enumerated powers over which it was authorized to enact legislation. All other powers and authorities were preserved to the states and to the people. This was expressly done through the 10th Amendment. This reservation of all other powers in the hands of the states and the people justify the constitutional **Doctrine of Nullification**. This doctrine was based upon the belief that the states were their own sovereigns in all areas outside of those expressly granted to the **General Government**, a name given to the Federal Government by Thomas Jefferson. Therefore, the Doctrine of Nullification allowed states to ignore the General Government in any of its attempts to exert authority over those areas outside of those expressly enumerated to the General Government.

Thomas Jefferson © Everett Historical/Shutterstock.com

This means that where the government oversteps its bounds, the authority resorts back to the states and, ultimately, the people. It is at this point that the voices of the people should be the loudest, whether in the form of voting elected officials out of office, or lobbying or petitioning for change. The Founders viewed usurped or wrongful authority as tyranny, and viewed the people who submitted to such authority as slaves. James Madison, our 4th President, also known as the Father of our Constitution, warned,

James Madison © Everett Historical/Shutterstock.com

"The preservation of a free Government requires not merely, that the metes and bounds which separate each department of power be invariably maintained; but more especially that neither of them be suffered to overleap the great Barrier which defends the rights of the people. The Rulers who are guilty of such an encroachment, exceed the commission from which they derive their authority, and are Tyrants. The People who submit to it are governed by laws made neither by themselves nor by an authority derived from them, and are slaves. Because it is proper to take alarm at the first experiment on our liberties. We hold this prudent jealousy to be the first duty of Citizens, and one of the noblest characteristics of the late Revolution. The free men of America did not wait till usurped power had strengthened itself by exercise, and entangled the question in precedents. They saw all the consequences in the principle, and they avoided the consequences by denying the principle. We revere this lesson too much soon to forget it."

Madison's Memorial and Remonstrance, Articles 2 & 3

This meant that if the government, through any of its branches—Legislative, Executive or Judicial—were to attempt to impose control that the Founders viewed tyrannical, or unjust, they believed that it ultimately fell to the people to take action to eliminate such tyranny.

"Tyranny is the exercise of some power over a man, which is not warranted by law, or necessary for the public safety. A people can never be deprived of their liberties, while they retain in their own hands, a power sufficient to any other power in the state."

—Noah Webster

The 9th and 10th Amendments to the U.S. Constitution underscore this acceptance that government is to be at all times for the people, and not imposed upon them with tyrannical oppression. These Amendments stem from an acceptance that there are rights and authority inherently possessed by the people, and they are not to be diminished by the exercise of government beyond its established jurisdiction. These two amendments, along with the prior eight of the Bill of Rights, should teach us that the delegation of rights and authority actually are unalienable rights possessed by the people and protected from the government, rather than rights created by the government and granted to the people.

Amendment IX

The enumeration in the Constitution, of certain rights, shall not be construed to deny or disparage others retained by the people.

Amendment X

The powers not delegated to the United States by the Constitution, nor prohibited by it to the States, are reserved to the States respectively, or to the people.

If this flow of authority is forgotten, it can cause both the people and the government to begin to believe that the government has created and granted to the people their Rights. This view is historically and constitutionally inaccurate. The Bill of Rights is a statement of Rights that the people inherently possess, and over which, the government is forbidden to invade.

While Congress is the branch specifically prohibited from legislating within these areas, this does not mean that the Executive and Judicial Branches are free to intrude. Rather, since there could be no laws enacted within these areas, there would likewise be no laws for the Executive Branch to execute, nor any laws for the Judicial Branch to **adjudicate**. Consequently, the Bill of Rights ensured that none of the three branches of government could tread upon rights inherently possessed by the people.

Two Treatises of Civil Government
John Locke

Chap. VII.

Of Political or Civil Society. §. 77. GOD having made man such a creature, that in his own judgment, it was not good for him to be alone, put him under strong obligations of necessity, convenience, and inclination to drive him into society, as well as fitted him with understanding and language to continue and enjoy it. The first society was between man and wife, which gave beginning to that between parents and children; to which, in time, that between master and servant came to be added: and though all these might, and commonly did meet together, and make up but one family, wherein the master or mistress of it had some sort of rule proper to a family; each of these, or all together, came short of political society, as we shall see, if we consider the different ends, ties, and bounds of each of these.

§. 87. Man being born, as has been proved, with a title to perfect freedom, and an uncontrouled enjoyment of all the rights and privileges of the law of nature, equally with any other man, or number of men in the world, hath by nature a power, not only to preserve his property, that is, his life, liberty and estate, against the injuries and attempts of other men; but to judge of, and punish the breaches of that law in others, as he is persuaded the offence deserves, even with death itself, in crimes where the heinousness of the fact, in his opinion, requires it. But because no political society can be, nor subsist, without having in itself the power to preserve the property, and in order thereunto, punish the offences of all those of that society; there, and there only is political society, where every one of the members hath quitted this natural power, resigned it up into the hands of the community in all cases that exclude him not from appealing for protection to the law established by it. And thus all private judgment of every particular member being excluded, the community comes to be umpire, by settled standing rules, indifferent, and the same to all parties; and by men having authority from the community, for the execution of those rules, decides all the differences that may happen between any members of that society concerning any matter of right; and punishes those offences which any member hath committed against the society, with such penalties as the law has established: whereby it is easy to discern, who are, and who are not, in political society together.

Those who are united into one body, and have a common established law and judicature to appeal to, with authority to decide controversies between them, and punish offenders, are in civil society one with another: but those who have no such common people, I mean on earth, are still in the state of nature, each being, where there is no other, judge for himself, and executioner; which is, as I have before shewed it, the perfect state of nature. §. 88. And thus the common-wealth comes by a power to set down what punishment shall belong to the several transgressions which they think worthy of it, committed amongst the members of that society, (which is the power of making laws) as well as it has the power to punish any injury done unto any of its members, by any one that is not of it, (which is the power of war and peace;) and all this for the preservation of the property of all the members of that society, as far as is possible. But though every man who hasentered into civil society, and is become a member of any common-wealth, has thereby quitted his power to punish offences, against the law of nature, in prosecution of his own private judgment, yet with the judgment of offences, which he has given up to the legislative in all cases, where he can appeal to the magistrate, he has given a right to the common-wealth to employ his force, for the execution of the judgments of the common-wealth, whenever he shall be called to it; which indeed are his own judgments, they being made by himself, or his representative. And herein we have the original of the legislative and executive power of civil society, which is to judge by standing laws, how far offences are to be punished, when committed within the common-wealth; and also to determine, by occasional judgments founded on the present circumstances of the fact, how far injuries from without are to be vindicated; and in both these to employ all the force of all the members, when there shall be need. §. 89. Where-ever therefore any number of men are so united into one society, as to quit every one his executive power of the law of nature, and to resign it to the public, there and there only is a political, or civil society. And this is done, where-ever any number of men, in the state of nature, enter into society to make one people, one body politic, under one supreme government; or else when any one joins himself to, and incorporates with any government already made: for hereby he authorizes the society, or which is all one, the legislative thereof, to make laws for him, as the public good of the society shall require; to the execution whereof, his own assistance (as to his own decrees) is due. And this puts men out of a state of nature into that of a common-wealth, by setting up a judge on earth, with authority to determine all the controversies, and redress the injuries that may happen to any member of the common-wealth; which judge is the legislative, or magistrates appointed by it. And where-ever there are any number of men, however associated, that have no such decisive power to appeal to, there they are still in the state of nature.

Memorial and Remonstrance against Religious Assessments

James Madison

20 June 1785 Papers 8:298—304
To the Honorable the General Assembly of the Commonwealth of Virginia
A Memorial and Remonstrance

We the subscribers, citizens of the said Commonwealth, having taken into serious consideration, a Bill printed by order of the last Session of General Assembly, entitled "A Bill establishing a provision for Teachers of the Christian Religion," and conceiving that the same if finally armed with the sanctions of a law, will be a dangerous abuse of power, are bound as faithful members of a free State to remonstrate against it, and to declare the reasons by which we are determined. We remonstrate against the said Bill,

1. Because we hold it for a fundamental and undeniable truth, "that Religion or the duty which we owe to our Creator and the manner of discharging it, can be directed only by reason and conviction, not by force or violence." [Virginia Declaration of Rights, art. 16] The Religion then of every man must be left to the conviction and conscience of every man; and it is the right of every man to exercise it as these may dictate. This right is in its nature an unalienable right. It is unalienable, because the opinions of men, depending only on the evidence contemplated by their own minds cannot follow the dictates of other men: It is unalienable also, because what is here a right towards men, is a duty towards the Creator. It is the duty of every man to render to the Creator such homage and such only as he believes to be acceptable to him. This duty is precedent, both in order of time and in degree of obligation, to the claims of Civil Society. Before any man can be considered as a member of Civil Society, he must be considered as a subject of the Governour of the Universe: And if a member of Civil Society, who enters into any subordinate Association, must always do it with a reservation of his duty to the General Authority; much more must every man who becomes a member of any particular Civil Society, do it with a saving of his allegiance to the Universal Sovereign. We maintain therefore that in matters of Religion, no mans right is abridged by the institution of Civil Society and that Religion is wholly exempt from its cognizance. True it is, that no other rule exists, by which any question which may divide a Society, can be ultimately determined, but the will of the majority; but it is also true that the majority may trespass on the rights of the minority.

2. Because if Religion be exempt from the authority of the Society at large, still less can it be subject to that of the Legislative Body. The latter are but the creatures and vicegerents of the former. Their jurisdiction is both derivative and limited: it is limited with regard to the co-ordinate departments, more necessarily is it limited with regard to the constituents. The preservation of a free Government requires not merely, that the metes and bounds which separate each department of power be invariably maintained; but more especially that neither of them be suffered to overleap the great Barrier which defends the rights of the people. The Rulers who are guilty of such an encroachment, exceed the commission from which they derive their authority, and are Tyrants. The People who submit to it are governed by laws made neither by themselves nor by an authority derived from them, and are slaves.

3. Because it is proper to take alarm at the first experiment on our liberties. We hold this prudent jealousy to be the first duty of Citizens, and one of the noblest characteristics of the late Revolution. The free men of America did not wait till usurped power had strengthened itself by exercise, and entangled the question in precedents. They saw all the consequences in the principle, and they avoided the consequences by denying the principle. We revere this lesson too much soon to forget it. Who does not see that the same authority which can establish Christianity, in exclusion of all other Religions, may establish with the same ease any particular sect of Christians, in exclusion of all other Sects? that the same authority which can force a citizen to contribute three pence only of his property for the support of any one establishment, may force him to conform to any other establishment in all cases whatsoever?

4. Because the Bill violates that equality which ought to be the basis of every law, and which is more indispensible, in proportion as the validity or expediency of any law is more liable to be impeached. If "all men are by nature equally free and independent," [Virginia Declaration of Rights, art. 1] all men are to be considered as entering into Society on equal conditions; as relinquishing no more, and therefore retaining no less, one than another, of their natural rights. Above all are they to be considered as retaining an "equal title to the free exercise of Religion according to the dictates of Conscience." [Virginia Declaration of Rights, art. 16] Whilst we assert for ourselves a freedom to embrace, to profess and to observe the Religion which we believe to

be of divine origin, we cannot deny an equal freedom to those whose minds have not yet yielded to the evidence which has convinced us. If this freedom be abused, it is an offence against God, not against man: To God, therefore, not to man, must an account of it be rendered. As the Bill violates equality by subjecting some to peculiar burdens, so it violates the same principle, by granting to others peculiar exemptions. Are the Quakers and Menonists the only sects who think a compulsive support of their Religions unnecessary and unwarrantable? Can their piety alone be entrusted with the care of public worship? Ought their Religions to be endowed above all others with extraordinary privileges by which proselytes may be enticed from all others? We think too favorably of the justice and good sense of these denominations to believe that they either covet pre-eminences over their fellow citizens or that they will be seduced by them from the common opposition to the measure.

5. Because the Bill implies either that the Civil Magistrate is a competent Judge of Religious Truth; or that he may employ Religion as an engine of Civil policy. The first is an arrogant pretension falsified by the contradictory opinions of Rulers in all ages, and throughout the world: the second an unhallowed perversion of the means of salvation.

6. Because the establishment proposed by the Bill is not requisite for the support of the Christian Religion. To say that it is, is a contradiction to the Christian Religion itself, for every page of it disavows a dependence on the powers of this world: it is a contradiction to fact; for it is known that this Religion both existed and flourished, not only without the support of human laws, but in spite of every opposition from them, and not only during the period of miraculous aid, but long after it had been left to its own evidence and the ordinary care of Providence. Nay, it is a contradiction in terms; for a Religion not invented by human policy, must have pre-existed and been supported, before it was established by human policy. It is moreover to weaken in those who profess this Religion a pious confidence in its innate excellence and the patronage of its Author; and to foster in those who still reject it, a suspicion that its friends are too conscious of its fallacies to trust it to its own merits.

7. Because experience witnesseth that ecclesiastical establishments, instead of maintaining the purity and efficacy of Religion, have had a contrary operation. During almost fifteen centuries has the legal establishment of Christianity been on trial. What have been its fruits? More or less in all places, pride and indolence in the Clergy, ignorance and servility in the laity, in both, superstition, bigotry and persecution. Enquire of the Teachers of Christianity for the ages in which it appeared in its greatest lustre; those of every sect, point to the ages prior to its incorporation with Civil policy. Propose a restoration of this primitive State in which its Teachers depended on the voluntary rewards of their flocks, many of them predict its downfall. On which Side ought their testimony to have greatest weight, when for or when against their interest?

8. Because the establishment in question is not necessary for the support of Civil Government. If it be urged as necessary for the support of Civil Government only as it is a means of supporting Religion, and it be not necessary for the latter purpose, it cannot be necessary for the former. If Religion be not within the cognizance of Civil Government how can its legal establishment be necessary to Civil Government? What influence in fact have ecclesiastical establishments had on Civil Society? In some instances they have been seen to erect a spiritual tyranny on the ruins of the Civil authority; in many instances they have been seen upholding the thrones of political tyranny: in no instance have they been seen the guardians of the liberties of the people. Rulers who wished to subvert the public liberty, may have found an established Clergy convenient auxiliaries. A just Government instituted to secure & perpetuate it needs them not. Such a Government will be best supported by protecting every Citizen in the enjoyment of his Religion with the same equal hand which protects his person and his property; by neither invading the equal rights of any Sect, nor suffering any Sect to invade those of another.

9. Because the proposed establishment is a departure from that generous policy, which, offering an Asylum to the persecuted and oppressed of every Nation and Religion, promised a lustre to our country, and an accession to the number of its citizens. What a melancholy mark is the Bill of sudden degeneracy? Instead of holding forth an Asylum to the persecuted, it is itself a signal of persecution. It degrades from the equal rank of Citizens all those whose opinions in Religion do not bend to those of the Legislative authority. Distant as it may be in its present form from the Inquisition, it differs from it only in degree. The one is the first step, the other the last in the career of intolerance. The magnanimous sufferer under this cruel scourge in foreign Regions, must view the Bill as a Beacon on our Coast, warning him to seek some other haven, where liberty and philanthrophy in their due extent, may offer a more certain repose from his Troubles.

10. Because it will have a like tendency to banish our Citizens. The allurements presented by other situations are every day thinning their number. To superadd a fresh motive to emigration by revoking the liberty which they

now enjoy, would be the same species of folly which has dishonoured and depopulated flourishing kingdoms.

11. Because it will destroy that moderation and harmony which the forbearance of our laws to intermeddle with Religion has produced among its several sects. Torrents of blood have been spilt in the old world, by vain attempts of the secular arm, to extinguish Religious discord, by proscribing all difference in Religious opinion. Time has at length revealed the true remedy. Every relaxation of narrow and rigorous policy, wherever it has been tried, has been found to assuage the disease. The American Theatre has exhibited proofs that equal and compleat liberty, if it does not wholly eradicate it, sufficiently destroys its malignant influence on the health and prosperity of the State. If with the salutary effects of this system under our own eyes, we begin to contract the bounds of Religious freedom, we know no name that will too severely reproach our folly. At least let warning be taken at the first fruits of the threatened innovation. The very appearance of the Bill has transformed "that Christian forbearance, love and charity," [Virginia Declaration of Rights, art. 16] which of late mutually prevailed, into animosities and jealousies, which may not soon be appeased. What mischiefs may not be dreaded, should this enemy to the public quiet be armed with the force of a law?

12. Because the policy of the Bill is adverse to the diffusion of the light of Christianity. The first wish of those who enjoy this precious gift ought to be that it may be imparted to the whole race of mankind. Compare the number of those who have as yet received it with the number still remaining under the dominion of false Religions; and how small is the former! Does the policy of the Bill tend to lessen the disproportion? No; it at once discourages those who are strangers to the light of revelation from coming into the Region of it; and countenances by example the nations who continue in darkness, in shutting out those who might convey it to them. Instead of Levelling as far as possible, every obstacle to the victorious progress of Truth, the Bill with an ignoble and unchristian timidity would circumscribe it with a wall of defence against the encroachments of error.

13. Because attempts to enforce by legal sanctions, acts obnoxious to so great a proportion of Citizens, tend to enervate the laws in general, and to slacken the bands of Society. If it be difficult to execute any law which is not generally deemed necessary or salutary, what must be the case, where it is deemed invalid and dangerous? And what may be the effect of so striking an example of impotency in the Government, on its general authority?

14. Because a measure of such singular magnitude and delicacy ought not to be imposed, without the clearest evidence that it is called for by a majority of citizens, and no satisfactory method is yet proposed by which the voice of the majority in this case may be determined, or its influence secured. "The people of the respective counties are indeed requested to signify their opinion respecting the adoption of the Bill to the next Session of Assembly." But the representation must be made equal, before the voice either of the Representatives or of the Counties will be that of the people. Our hope is that neither of the former will, after due consideration, espouse the dangerous principle of the Bill. Should the event disappoint us, it will still leave us in full confidence, that a fair appeal to the latter will reverse the sentence against our liberties.

15. Because finally, "the equal right of every citizen to the free exercise of his Religion according to the dictates of conscience" is held by the same tenure with all our other rights. If we recur to its origin, it is equally the gift of nature; if we weigh its importance, it cannot be less dear to us; if we consult the "Declaration of those rights which pertain to the good people of Virginia, as the basis and foundation of Government," it is enumerated with equal solemnity, or rather studied emphasis. Either then, we must say, that the Will of the Legislature is the only measure of their authority; and that in the plenitude of this authority, they may sweep away all our fundamental rights; or, that they are bound to leave this particular right untouched and sacred: Either we must say, that they may controul the freedom of the press, may abolish the Trial by Jury, may swallow up the Executive and Judiciary Powers of the State; nay that they may despoil us of our very right of suffrage, and erect themselves into an independent and hereditary Assembly or, we must say, that they have no authority to enact into law the Bill under consideration. We the Subscribers say, that the General Assembly of this Commonwealth have no such authority: And that no effort may be omitted on our part against so dangerous an usurpation, we oppose to it, this remonstrance; earnestly praying, as we are in duty bound, that the Supreme Lawgiver of the Universe, by illuminating those to whom it is addressed, may on the one hand, turn their Councils from every act which would affront his holy prerogative, or violate the trust committed to them: and on the other, guide them into every measure which may be worthy of his blessing, may redound to their own praise, and may establish more firmly the liberties, the prosperity and the happiness of the Commonwealth.

QUESTIONS

1. According to Webster what is the reason for the failure of a Republican government to secure public prosperity and happiness?

2. According to Locke from where does man receive his right to freedom and his enjoyment of rights and privileges of the law of nature?

3. Who did Madison feel was responsible for taking alarm at usurped power and preventing its authority from becoming steeped in precedent?

4. According to the Bill of Rights, to whom are all the rights for those beyond the eighteen specifically enumerated in the Constitution reserved?

Chapter 5

AMERICAN EXCEPTIONALISM

American Exceptionalism is the belief that America, through all its charter principles and character, was exceptional. It is this belief that perceived America's very existence against seemingly insurmountable odds was nothing short of **providential**, and that the prosperity and blessings that were hers as a nation were in every way atypical and exemplary. This lofty perception appeared to be validated through numerous societal goals and accomplishments, a few of which are listed within this chapter.

Science

The Founding Fathers were concerned with anything that could serve to promote and advance the progress of the nation through science and the useful arts. It was for this reason that the protection of intellectual property rights was listed as one of the eighteen powers granted to the General Government to oversee.

© Bimbim/Shutterstock.com

"To promote the Progress of Science and useful Arts, by securing for limited Times to Authors and Inventors the exclusive Right to their respective Writings and Discoveries;

Constitution, Article I, Section 8

Agriculture

The majority of our Founding Fathers were farmers or some type of cultivators of the land. This provided them with a strong support for an **agrarian** society. They found an agricultural economy to not only provide stability and safety in being our own suppliers of food, but actually saw that the type of character found within a more rural, agrarian society, to be preferable for numerous reasons.

"Cultivators of the earth are the most valuable citizens. They are the most vigorous, the most independent, the most virtuous, and they are tied to their country and wedded to its liberty and interests by the most lasting bands."

—Thomas Jefferson

Agriculture . . . is our wisest pursuit, because it will in the end contribute most to real wealth, good morals and happiness."

—Thomas Jefferson

"I know of no pursuit in which more real and important services can be rendered to any country than by improving its agriculture, its breed of useful animals, and other branches of a husbandman's cares."

—George Washington

© Everett Historical/Shutterstock.com

"There seem to be but three ways for a nation to acquire wealth. The first is by war, as the Romans did, in plundering their conquered neighbors. This is robbery. The second by commerce, which is generally cheating. The third by agriculture, the only honest way, wherein man receives a real increase of the seed thrown into the ground, in a kind of continual miracle, wrought by the hand of God in his favor, as a reward for his innocent life and his virtuous industry."

—Benjamin Franklin

Query XIX Manufactures: Those who labor in the earth are the chosen people of God, if ever he had a chosen people, whose breasts he has made his peculiar deposit for substantial and genuine virtue. It is the focus in which he keeps alive that sacred fire, which other might escape from the face of the earth. Corruption of morals in the mass of cultivators is a phenomenon of which no age nor nation has furnished an example. It is the mark set on those, who not looking up to heaven, to their own soil and industry, as does the husbandman, for their subsistence, depend for it on the casualties and caprice of customers. Dependence begets subservience and venality, suffocates the germ of virtue, and prepares fit tools for the designs of ambition. This, the natural progress and consequence of the arts, has sometimes been retarded by accidental circumstances: but, generally speaking, the proportion which the aggregate of the other classes of citizens bears in any state to that of its husbandmen, is the proportion of its unsound to its healthy parts, and is a good-enough barometer whereby to measure its degree of corruption. While we have land to labor then, let us never wish to see our citizens occupied at a work-bench, or twirling a distaff. Carpenters, masons, smiths, are wanting in husbandry: but, for the general operations of manufacture, let our workshops remain in Europe.

Notes on the State of Virginia,
Thomas Jefferson (1784–85)

Economics

Our Founding Fathers believed in the benefit of individual industry as being the best source of productivity and wealth, just as they preferred self-governance to dictatorial control. To this end they desired to see the people free in their economic pursuits. This required a government that would honor and preserve property rights, including real, personal and intellectual, and keep regulation and control of commerce to a minimum, allowing the market instead to drive the economy.

Department of Treasury © Joseph Sohm/Shutterstock.com

"Government is instituted to protect property of every sort; as well that which lies in the various rights of individuals, as that which the term particularly expresses. This being the end of government, that alone is a just government which impartially secures to every man whatever is his own."

—James Madison,
Essay on Property, 1792

"A people . . . who are possessed of the spirit of commerce, who see and who will pursue their advantages may achieve almost anything."

—George Washington

Education

The goal of promoting, or encouraging, education was fervently embraced as essential by our Founding Fathers. Having well-educated citizens was seen as crucial to preserving our liberties, and keeping the society, as a whole, from being led astray through its inability to think through ideals and principles. While the promotion of education was deemed essential, the financial provision of education in the form of socialized education was not perceived as a legitimate role of the government. This is underscored by the fact that education was not even included by the Founders within the eighteen enumerated powers of the Constitution.

> "Religion, morality, and knowledge, being necessary to good government and the happiness of mankind, schools shall forever be **encouraged.**
>
> Article 3 of the Northwest Ordinance;
> July 13, 1787

© Joseph Sohm/Shutterstock.com

> "If Congress . . . may establish teachers in every state, county, and parish, and pay them out of the public Treasury; they may take into their own hands the education of children establishing in like manner schools throughout the Union. . . . I would venture to declare it as my opinion . . . it would subvert the very foundation and transmute the very nature of the **limited Government** established by the people of America. . . ."
>
> James Madison,
> "Father of the Constitution"
> Remarks on the House Floor,
> debates on Cod Fishery Bill (February 1792)

> "The education of youth should be watched with the most scrupulous attention. It is much easier to introduce and establish an effectual system . . . than to correct by penal statutes the ill effects of a bad system. The education of youth . . . lays the foundations on which both law and gospel rest for success."
>
> Noah Webster,
> A Collection of Papers on Political,
> Literary, and Moral Subjects, 1843.

Justice

The Founding Fathers implemented many means of ensuring justice for all. The rights to a trial by jury, a speedy trial, and due process were some of the means of preserving for the people the beautiful character of a system of justice. A jury, it was understood, allowed people the ability to be tried by twelve of their peers, to avoid concerns of bias. Originally, jurors assessed both the law as well as fact, having a final say in a given case or controversy as to the fairness and equity of an application of the law. Today, the jury is only allowed the ability to examine the facts, not the law.

Due Process can be reduced to two things, both of which are essential to preserving your rights and freedoms. They are the requirement that prior to a person having either their freedom or their property impacted by a court of law they must be given notice and an opportunity to be heard. Unlike other countries, American courts are not allowed to pass judgment until such time as the person whose freedom or property are being threatened has been made sufficiently aware of the charges, and has been provided a sufficient opportunity to defend himself or his position.

Additionally, while the legislative body is not generally seen as the branch responsible for justice, it is in fact inextricably involved. The legislature, being the sole branch vested with legislative authority, has a process whereby laws are publicly enacted and cannot be made **retroactive**. The courts are prohibited from making laws. These checks and balances are vital to the preservation of justice because they place the American people on notice concerning the law. There can be no laws imposed upon U.S. citizens that are made through the impulse of the judiciary. It is this firmness, uniformity, and prior notice that act as additional protectors of justice. Should this check upon the judiciary ever be removed, justice would also be removed.

Without justice being freely, fully, and impartially administered, neither our persons, nor our rights, nor our property, can be protected. And if these, or either of them, are regulated by no certain laws, and are subject to no certain principles, and are held by no certain tenure, and are redressed, when violated, by no certain remedies, society fails of all its value; and men may as well return to a state of savage and barbarous independence.

Justice Joseph Story
Commentaries on the Constitution, 1833

Human Rights

One of the most blatant proofs against the doctrine of American Exceptionalism is the inhumane treatment of certain individuals on the basis of race and gender. This treatment, though allowed to continue for far too long, and even into today's society, is more a proof of the embarrassing frailty of humanity, than the broad sweeping opinions of our nation's Founders. It is undeniable that our Declaration of Independence boldly proclaimed the belief that all are created equal. It affirmed that all are invested with certain rights given to them by their Creator from which they cannot be deprived, not even voluntarily. Despite this declaration of inherent human worth, many continued to blindly act as though this were mere lip service. However, the lack of conviction of some, if not many, did not change the truth of the Declaration. Nor did it confirm there were no Founding Fathers who devoutly adopted these beliefs and encouraged their universal implementation. The legitimacy of these underlying principles coupled with the existence of those who would defend them passionately, both attest to American Exceptionalism.

© igo.stevanovic/Shutterstock.com

"Justice and humanity require it—Christianity commands it. Let every benevolent... pray for the glorious period when the last slave who fights for freedom shall be restored to the possession of that inestimable right."

Noah Webster,
In writings, Effect of Slavery
on Morals and Industry

The utmost good faith shall always be observed towards the Indians; their lands and property shall never be taken from them without their consent; and, in their property, rights, and liberty, they shall never be invaded or disturbed, unless in just and lawful wars authorized by Congress; but laws founded in justice and humanity, shall from time to time be made for preventing wrongs being done to them, and for preserving peace and friendship with them.

Northwest Ordinance, Article 3
July 13, 1787

If we mean to have Heroes, Statesmen and Philosophers, we should have learned women. The world perhaps would laugh at me, and accuse me of vanity, but you know I have a mind too enlarged and liberal to disregard the Sentiment. If much depends as is allowed upon the early Education of youth and the first principals which are instill'd take the deepest root, great benefit must arise from literary accomplishments in women.

Abigail Adams
Letter to her husband,
John Adams, 2nd President

Standard of Living

The Founding Fathers believed in individual responsibility for provision, and opposed redistribution of wealth on the basis of lack. They saw socialistic involvement by the government that punished prosperity through uneven taxation as an unacceptable governmental intrusion. They perceived such involvement would chill industry, hard work and ingenuity.

"To take from one, because it is thought his own industry and that of his fathers has acquired too much, in order to spare to others, who, or whose

fathers, have not exercised equal industry and skill, is to violate arbitrarily the first principle of association, the guarantee to everyone the free exercise of his industry and the fruits acquired by it."

—Thomas Jefferson,
letter to Joseph Milligan, April 6, 1816

"A wise and frugal government . . . shall restrain men from injuring one another, shall leave them otherwise free to regulate their own pursuits of industry and improvement, and shall not take from the mouth of labor the bread it has earned. This is the sum of good government."

Thomas Jefferson,
First Inaugural Address, March 4, 1801

Liberty

© Edwin Verin/Shutterstock.com

The Founding Fathers believed in a type of liberty that brought with it true happiness. When the Declaration of Independence spoke of the unalienable right to liberty and the pursuit of happiness, these rights were deemed inseparable. The significance of tying these two principles together was that there were only certain actions that they believed would tend to man's ultimate happiness. Those were the actions that aligned with the laws of nature and of nature's god. This liberty tied to an objective standard found within the preexisting law of nature was clear and identifiable.

America's founders did not perceive of a liberty that would bring with it sorrow or bondage. They believed any freedom to act in such a way that was ultimately harmful to the actor himself was not in fact liberty, but rather licentiousness. Consequently, it was this definition of liberty tied to the pursuit of happiness that was believed to be a right inherent within man. Governments were to be instituted for the purpose of preserving this specific definition of liberty and the pursuit of happiness. The pursuit of happiness had a very specific understanding, and it was never meant to be unclear words, subjectively interpreted. Consequently, a definition of liberty that granted to man the ability to do whatever subjectively made him happy was never deemed an unalienable right, and was never intended to be preserved.

Without liberty, law loses its nature and its name, and becomes oppression. Without law, liberty also loses its nature and its name, and becomes licentiousness.

James Wilson,
Of the Study of the Law
in the United States, Circa

[W]here there is no law, there is no liberty; and nothing deserves the name of law but that which is certain and universal in its operation upon all the members of the community.

Benjamin Rush,
letter to David Ramsay,
Circa April, 1788

© Marcio Jose Bastos Silva/Shutterstock.com

QUESTIONS

1. How did the founding fathers perceive the importance of agriculture?

2. What were some of the views present during the ratification of the Constitution that stood in opposition to the denial of human rights?

3. What was the rationale behind encouraging education according to the Northwest Ordinance?

4. How did Jefferson perceive the redistribution of wealth?

DECLARATION OF INDEPENDENCE

Original Sources:
1. The Olive Branch Petition
2. The Dominion of Providence over the Passions of Man
3. Blackstone's Commentaries, Section Second (see page 36)

A. CIVIL DISOBEDIENCE

[Why we were willing to war against our own king?]

B. LAWS OF NATURE AND NATURE'S GOD

[What were our values?]

C. JUST AND UNJUST LAWS

[How had tyranny to taken away those values?]

A. CIVIL DISOBEDIENCE

One of the initial questions that had to be addressed by our Founders was whether it was lawful for us to separate from England. While this may not seem like a question that would even require any contemplation, you must remember that our Founding Fathers believed in the preexistence of law, so men couldn't simply make up whatever laws they wanted.

Drafting of Declaration © Everett Historical/Shutterstock.com

The Founder's believed in the Doctrine of Civil Disobedience. This Doctrine of Civil Disobedience held that when those who were ruling over you were operating in ways beyond their legitimate authority, such overreaching of authority was tyrannical and was, therefore, the basis for the people to "lawfully" disobey them. When such abuses became commonplace or numerous, to the point that the people were routinely oppressed by the ruling powers, then Civil Disobedience could be exhibited in the form of separating from all connection.

America fighting "John Bull" aka England © Everett Historical/Shutterstock.com

It was this belief in the legitimacy of the Doctrine of Civil Disobedience that impressed upon the Founders the legal right of the Colonists to separate from England. Because they did not believe in the random whims of the people to justify this separation, they felt a responsibility to list and detail to the world the grievances the Colonists had suffered at the hands of King George to justify their separation. They further felt the need to state the legal basis upon which their Civil Disobedience was merited, and the legal foundation upon which the new nation, its government, and all its laws were to be based. All of this information along with a detailed list of grievances was included in the Declaration of Independence.

"Prudence, indeed, will dictate that Governments long established should not be changed for light and transient causes; and accordingly all experience hath shewn, that mankind are more disposed to suffer, while evils are sufferable, than to right themselves by abolishing the forms to which they are accustomed. But when a long train of abuses and usurpations, pursuing invariably the same Object evinces a design to reduce them under absolute Despotism, it is their right, it is their duty, to throw off such Government, and to provide new Guards for their future security.—Such has been the patient sufferance of these Colonies; and such is now the necessity which constrains them to alter their former Systems of Government. The history of the present King of Great Britain is a history of repeated injuries and usurpations, all having in direct object the establishment of an absolute Tyranny over these States. To prove this, let Facts be submitted to a candid world.

He has refused his Assent to Laws, the most wholesome and necessary for the public good.

He has forbidden his Governors to pass Laws of immediate and pressing importance, unless suspended in their operation till his Assent should be obtained; and when so suspended, he has utterly neglected to attend to them.

He has refused to pass other Laws for the accommodation of large districts of people, unless those people would relinquish the right of Representation in the Legislature, a right inestimable to them and formidable to tyrants only.

He has called together legislative bodies at places unusual, uncomfortable, and distant from the depository of their public Records, for the sole purpose of fatiguing them into compliance with his measures.

He has dissolved Representative Houses repeatedly, for opposing with manly firmness his invasions on the rights of the people.

He has refused for a long time, after such dissolutions, to cause others to be elected; whereby the Legislative powers, incapable of Annihilation, have returned to the People at large for their exercise; the State remaining in the mean time exposed to all the dangers of invasion from without, and convulsions within.

He has endeavoured to prevent the population of these States; for that purpose obstructing the Laws for Naturalization of Foreigners; refusing to pass others to encourage their migrations hither, and raising the conditions of new Appropriations of Lands. He has obstructed the Administration of Justice, by refusing his Assent to Laws for establishing Judiciary powers.

He has made Judges dependent on his Will alone, for the tenure of their offices, and the amount and payment of their salaries.

He has erected a multitude of New Offices, and sent hither swarms of Officers to harrass our people, and eat out their substance.

He has kept among us, in times of peace, Standing Armies without the Consent of our legislatures.

He has affected to render the Military independent of and superior to the Civil power.

He has combined with others to subject us to a jurisdiction foreign to our constitution, and unacknowledged by our laws; giving his Assent to their Acts of pretended Legislation:

For Quartering large bodies of armed troops among us:

For protecting them, by a mock Trial, from punishment for any Murders which they should commit on the Inhabitants of these States:

For cutting off our Trade with all parts of the world:

For imposing Taxes on us without our Consent:

For depriving us in many cases, of the benefits of Trial by Jury:

For transporting us beyond Seas to be tried for pretended offences

For abolishing the free System of English Laws in a neighbouring Province, establishing therein an Arbitrary government, and enlarging its Boundaries so as to render it at once an example and fit instrument for introducing the same absolute rule into these Colonies:

For taking away our Charters, abolishing our most valuable Laws, and altering fundamentally the Forms of our Governments:

For suspending our own Legislatures, and declaring themselves invested with power to legislate for us in all cases whatsoever.

He has abdicated Government here, by declaring us out of his Protection and waging War against us.

He has plundered our seas, ravaged our Coasts, burnt our towns, and destroyed the lives of our people.

He is at this time transporting large Armies of foreign Mercenaries to compleat the works of death, desolation and tyranny, already begun with circumstances of Cruelty & perfidy scarcely paralleled in the most barbarous ages, and totally unworthy the Head of a civilized nation.

He has constrained our fellow Citizens taken Captive on the high Seas to bear Arms against their Country, to become the executioners of their friends and Brethren, or to fall themselves by their Hands.

He has excited domestic insurrections amongst us, and has endeavoured to bring on the inhabitants of our frontiers, the merciless Indian Savages, whose known rule of warfare, is an undistinguished destruction of all ages, sexes and conditions.

In every stage of these Oppressions We have Petitioned for Redress in the most humble terms: Our repeated Petitions have been answered only by repeated injury. A Prince whose character is thus marked by every act which may define a Tyrant, is unfit to be the ruler of a free people."

Declaration of Independence [excerpt]

B. LAWS OF NATURE AND NATURE'S GOD

Our Declaration, in its thesis statement, identified the source of authority to which we looked to establish a new government and system of laws. *". . . to acquire from among the powers of the earth that separate but equal station to which the laws of nature and nature's God entitle us. . . ."*[1] This most specific form of natural law, the laws of nature and nature's god, was defined by Sir William Blackstone as the Will of our Maker as revealed through His holy scriptures.[2] It was based upon a belief in a preexisting law established by our Creator that was supreme over all the globe and binding upon all nations, a system of law that was superior to all others.[3]

This preexisting law legitimized one unified people declaring to the world the basis for severing ties from its prior sovereign. Thomas Jefferson's words,

"[w]hen in the Course of human events it becomes necessary for one people to dissolve the political bands which have connected them with another.., a decent respect to the opinions of mankind requires that they should declare the causes which impel them to the separation"[4]

provided support for the principle of civil disobedience, as it was founded within the laws of nature's god. It was of utmost importance that this clear declaration to the world was that of "one people." If this charter document did not function to formally establish solidarity as a nation, then the remainder of its declaration would serve no meaningful purpose (see Chapter 8). Not only did this document declare one people, it served to formally solidify their union through the corporate opposition of a common enemy. The legitimacy of this opposition was found in the principle of justified, lawful resistance, in contrast to mere tyrannical mutiny.

The concern this fledgling nation had for universally providing justification for its Declaration of Independence evidences its abiding respect for conformity to the preexisting laws of nature and nature's god. It was understood that in order for any law to be deemed valid, it in no way could fail to align with the laws of nature and nature's god.[5] Were America's course of action to be deemed just and defensible, it would, of necessity, need to be lawful. For its action to be lawful, it would need to align with the laws of nature and nature's god. For its action to align with the laws of nature and nature's god, it would need to conform to the will of the Maker as revealed through the Holy Scriptures. Therefore, the grievances charged against its prior sovereign were justifications for the utilization of the biblical principle of civil disobedience, which was to be found within the source of all laws, the laws of nature and nature's god.

---

1 Declaration of Independence.
2 Blackstone's Commentaries on the Laws of England, Section the Second. Of the Nature of Laws in General.
3 Id.
4 Declaration of Independence.
5 Blackstone's Commentaries on the Laws of England, Section the Second. Of the Nature of Laws in General.

By identifying the source of law and the basis upon which this new government was to be founded, the United States was not only establishing legal authority, but also simultaneously legitimizing its rightful authority to resist tyranny, even to the point of open declaration of formal resistance. Such right to resist would cast any impending military skirmish as a just war, rather than an unjustified display of anarchy.

C. JUST AND UNJUST LAWS

Just as civil disobedience found its support within the laws of nature and nature's god, so too did the laws of nature and nature's god underscore the belief in just and unjust laws. Our Founders believed that laws that did not comply with the preexisting laws of nature were inherently unjust, and governments that upheld such laws contrary to the laws of nature were themselves illegitimate. *"Government, in my humble opinion, should be formed to secure and to enlarge the exercise of the natural rights of its members; and every government, which has not this in view, as its principal object, is not a government of the legitimate kind."* [6]

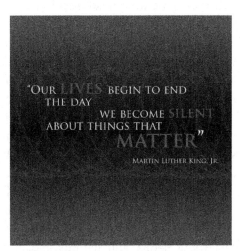

© Tom Tom/Shutterstock.com

Our Founders embraced the belief that just laws preexisted the societies of men and were to be discovered, rather than impulsively made by the ever-changing mind and will of man. This belief in inherently just and unjust laws was espoused for centuries prior to our nation's founding. It would be relied upon in later years during our nation's battle for the establishment of civil rights for all. The belief was simply that the preexisting laws of nature and nature's god established eternal and never-changing laws of right and wrong, and for man and society to operate outside of these prescribed laws would do disservice and harm to both themselves, as well as others. The Founding Fathers did not create the belief in just and unjust law. This belief had been clearly detailed by St. Augustine and later affirmed by St. Thomas Aquinas centuries before our nation's founding.

> *"As Augustine says . . . 'that which is not just seems to be no law at all': wherefore the force of a law depends on the extent of its justice. Now in human affairs a thing is said to be just, from being right, according to the rule of reason. But the first rule of reason is the law of nature. . . . Consequently every human law has just so much of the nature of law, as it is derived from the law of nature. But if in any point it deflects from the law of nature, it is no longer a law but a perversion of law."*
>
> St. Thomas Aquinas,
> Summa Theologica, Treatise on Law, Question 95—Of Human Law, Article (2) Its Origin

It was this same belief in just and unjust laws that Martin Luther King, Jr. would later use as the very foundation to legitimize the entire civil rights movement.

St. Augustine © Renata Sedmakova/Shutterstock.com

---

6 James Wilson, Lectures on Law, 1791.

One may well ask: "How can you advocate breaking some laws and obeying others?" The answer lies in the fact that there are two types of laws: just and unjust. I would be the first to advocate obeying just laws. One has not only a legal but a moral responsibility to obey just laws. Conversely, one has a moral responsibility to disobey unjust laws. I would agree with St. Augustine that "an unjust law is no law at all.

Now, what is the difference between the two? How does one determine whether a law is just or unjust? A just law is a man made code that squares with the moral law or the law of God. An unjust law is a code that is out of harmony with the moral law. To put it in the terms of St. Thomas Aquinas: "An unjust law is a human law that is not rooted in eternal law and natural law."

Martin Luther King, Jr.
Letter from the Birmingham Jail, 1963

All three of these principles espoused within our Declaration of Independence: **civil disobedience, laws of nature and nature's god, and just and unjust laws,** are all interdependent upon the central principle, the legitimacy of all laws arising from the laws of nature and nature's god. It is the acceptance of the authority of the laws of nature and nature's god that validates the existence of just and unjust laws and, consequently, the practice of civil disobedience, which vindicates the actions of those who disobey unjust laws. The Founder's obvious acceptance of the laws of nature and nature's god provided justification for their disobedience against the laws of England, and their ability to declare the American Revolution a "Just War."

John Knox Witherspoon was the only college president to sign the Declaration of Independence. While President of the College of New Jersey, now Princeton University, he preached a fiery sermon in support of the Declaration in May of 1776. His words were highly influential; the College of New Jersey with Witherspoon at its helm educated nine members of the Constitutional Convention, one President, James Madison, one Vice President, Aaron Burr, along with three Supreme Court Justices and numerous congressmen and governors. His views perceiving religious freedom as inextricably linked to liberty in general provided the foundation for the establishment of the first amendment. He explained the danger of usurped authority leading to unjust decisions, and that the colonies' responses to such were birthed out of conviction, justifying the need for a Revolutionary War. Peaceful petition had been made; the necessity for arms was at hand.

© 360b/Shutterstock.com

Valley Forge © Everett Historical/Shutterstock.com

The Olive Branch Petition

July 5, 1775

John Dickinson

Approved by the Second Continental Congress on July 5, 1775
Submitted to King George on July 8, 1775
King George declared the colonists to be in "open and avowed rebellion" on August 23, 1775

To the King's Most Excellent Majesty. Most Gracious Sovereign,

We your Majesty's faithful subjects of the colonies of New-hampshire, Massachusetts-bay, Rhode island and Providence plantations, Connecticut, New-York, New-Jersey, Pennsylvania, the counties of New Castle, Kent, and Sussex on Delaware, Maryland, Virginia, North Carolina and South Carolina, in behalf of ourselves and the inhabitants of these colonies, who have deputed us to represent them in general Congress, entreat your Majesty's gracious attention to this our humble petition.

The union between our Mother Country and these colonies, and the energy of mild and just government, produced benefits so remarkably important, and afforded such an assurance of their permanency and increase, that the wonder and envy of other Nations were excited, while they beheld Great Britain riseing to a power the most extraordinary the world had ever known.

Her rivals observing, that there was no probability of this happy connection being broken by civil dissentions, and apprehending its future effects, if left any longer undisturbed, resolved to prevent her receiving such continual and formidable accessions of wealth and strength, by checking the growth of these settlements from which they were to be derived.

In the prosecution of this attempt events so unfavourable to the design took place, that every friend to the interests of Great Britain and these colonies entertained pleasing and reasonable expectations of seeing an additional force and extention immediately given to the operations of the union hitherto experienced, by an enlargement of the dominions of the Crown, and the removal of ancient and warlike enemies to a greater distance.

At the conclusion therefore of the late war, the most glorious and advantagious that ever had been carried on by British arms, your loyal colonists having contributed to its success, by such repeated and strenuous exertions, as frequently procured them the distinguished approbation of your Majesty, of the late king, and of Parliament, doubted not but that they should be permitted with the rest of the empire, to share in the blessings of peace and the emoluments of victory and conquest. While these recent and honorable acknowledgments of their merits remained on record in the journals and acts of the august legislature the Parliament, undefaced by the imputation or even the suspicion of any offence, they were alarmed by a new system of Statutes and regulations adopted for the administration of the colonies, that filled their minds with the most painful fears and jealousies; and to their inexpressible astonishment perceived the dangers of a foreign quarrel quickly succeeded by domestic dangers, in their judgment of a more dreadful kind.

Nor were their anxieties alleviated by any tendancy in this system to promote the welfare of the Mother Country. For 'tho its effects were more immediately felt by them, yet its influence appeared to be injurious to the commerce and prosperity of Great Britain.

We shall decline the ungrateful task of describing the irksome variety of artifices practised by many of your Majestys ministers, the delusive pretences, fruitless terrors, and unavailing severities, that have from time to time been dealt out by them, in their attempts to execute this impolitic plan, or of traceing thro' a series of years past the progress of the unhappy differences between Great Britain and these colonies which have flowed from this fatal source.

Your Majestys ministers persevering in their measures and proceeding to open hostilities for enforcing them, have compelled us to arm in our own defence, and have engaged us in a controversy so peculiarly abhorrent to the affection of your still faithful colonists, that when we consider whom we must oppose in this contest, and if it continues, what may be the consequences, our own particular misfortunes are accounted by us, only as parts of our distress.

Knowing, to what violent resentments and incurable animosities, civil discords are apt to exasperate and inflame the contending parties, we think ourselves required by indispensable obligations to Almighty God, to your Majesty, to our fellow subjects, and to ourselves, immediately to use all the means in our power not incompatible with our safety, for stopping the further effusion of blood, and for averting the impending calamities that threaten the British Empire.

Thus called upon to address your Majesty on affairs of such moment to America, and probably to all your dominions, we are earnestly desirous of performing this office with the utmost deference for your Majesty; and we therefore pray, that your royal magnanimity and benevolence may make the most favourable construction of our expressions on so uncommon an occasion. Could we represent in their full force the sentiments that agitate the minds of us your dutiful subjects, we are persuaded, your Majesty would ascribe any seeming deviation from reverence, and our language, and even in our conduct, not to any reprehensible intention but to the impossibility or reconciling the usual appearances of respect with a just attention to our own preservation against those artful and cruel enemies, who abuse your royal confidence and authority for the purpose of effecting our destruction.

Attached to your Majestys person, family and government with all the devotion that principle and affection can inspire, connected with Great Britain by the strongest ties that can unite societies, and deploring every event that tends in any degree to weaken them, we solemnly assure your Majesty, that we not only most ardently desire the former harmony between her and these colonies may be restored but that a concord may be established between them upon so firm a basis, as to perpetuate its blessings uninterrupted by any future dissentions to succeeding generations in both countries, and to transmit your Majestys name to posterity adorned with that signal and lasting glory that has attended the memory of those illustrious personages, whose virtues and abilities have extricated states from dangerous convulsions, and by securing happiness to others, have erected the most noble and durable monuments to their own fame.

We beg leave further to assure your Majesty that notwithstanding the sufferings of your loyal colonists during the course of the present controversy, our breasts retain too tender a regard for the kingdom from which we derive our origin to request such a reconciliation as might in any manner be inconsistent with her dignity or her welfare. These, related as we are to her, honor and duty, as well as inclination induce us to support and advance; and the apprehensions that now oppress our hearts with unspeakable grief, being once removed, your Majesty will find your faithful subjects on this continent ready and willing at all times, as they ever have been with their lives and fortunes to assert and maintain the rights and interests of your Majesty and of our Mother Country.

We therefore beseech your Majesty, that your royal authority and influence may be graciously interposed to procure us releif [sic] from our afflicting fears and jealousies occasioned by the system before mentioned, and to settle peace through every part of your dominions, with all humility submitting to your Majesty's wise consideration, whether it may not be expedient for facilitating those important purposes, that your Majesty be pleased to direct some mode by which the united applications of your faithful colonists to the throne, in pursuance of their common councils, may be improved into a happy and permanent reconciliation; and that in the meantime measures be taken for preventing the further destruction of the lives of your Majesty's subjects; and that such statutes as more immediately distress any of your Majestys colonies be repealed: For by such arrangements as your Majesty's wisdom can form for collecting the united sense of your American people, we are convinced, your Majesty would receive such satisfactory proofs of the disposition of the colonists towards their sovereign and the parent state, that the wished for opportunity would soon be restored to them, of evincing the sincerity of their professions by every testimony of devotion becoming the most dutiful subjects and the most affectionate colonists.

That your Majesty may enjoy a long and prosperous reign, and that your descendants may govern your dominions with honor to themselves and happiness to their subjects is our sincere and fervent prayer.

The Dominion of Providence Over The Passions of Men

By John Witherspoon

May, 1776

In the first place, I would take the opportunity on this occasion, and from this subject, to press every hearer to a sincere concern for his own soul's salvation. There are times when the mind may be expected to be more awake to divine truth, and the conscience more open to the arrows of conviction than at others. A season of public judgment is of this kind. Can you have a clearer view of the sinfulness of your nature, than when the rod of the oppressor is lifted up, and when you see men putting on the habit of the warrior, and collecting on every hand the weapons of hostility and instruments of death? I do not blame your ardour in preparing for the resolute defense of your temporal rights; but consider, I beseech you, the truly infinite importance of the salvation of your souls. Is it of much moment whether you and your children shall be rich or poor, at liberty or in bonds? Is it of much moment whether this beautiful country shall increase in fruitfulness from year to year, being cultivated by active industry, and possessed by independent freemen, or the scanty produce of the neglected fields shall be eaten up by hungry publicans, while the timid owner trembles at the tax-gatherer's approach? And is it of less moment, my brethren, whether you shall be the heirs of glory of the heirs of hell? Is your state on earth for a few fleeting years of so much moment? And is it of less moment what shall be your state through endless ages! Have you assembled together willingly to hear what shall be said on public affairs, and to join in imploring the blessing of God on the counsels and arms of the United Colonies, and can you be unconcerned what shall become of you for ever, when all the monuments of human greatness shall be laid in ashes, for "the earth itself, and all the works that are therein shall be burnt up."

Wherefore, my beloved hearers, as the ministry of reconciliation is committed to me, I beseech you in the most earnest manner, to attend to "the things that belong to your peace, before they are hid from your eyes". How soon, and in what manner a seal shall be set upon the character and state of every person here present, it is impossible to know. But you may rest assured, that there is no time more suitable, and there is none so safe as that which is present, since it is wholy uncertain whether any other shall be yours. Those who shall first fall in battle, have not many more warnings to receive.

There are some few daring and hardened sinners, who despise eternity itself, and set their Maker at defiance; but the far greater number, by staving off their convictions to a more convenient season, have been taken unprepared, and thus eternally lost. I would therefore earnestly press the apostle's exhortation, 2 Cor 6: 1–2 . . . "Behold, now is the accepted time; behold, now is the day of salvation."

Suffer me to beseech you, or rather to give you warning, not to rest satisfied with a form of godliness, denying the power thereof. There can be no true religion, till there be a discovery of your lost state by nature and practice, and an unfeigned acceptance of Christ Jesus, as he is offered in the gospel. Unhappy are they who either despise his mercy, or are ashamed of his cross. Believe it, "There is no salvation in any other." "There is no other name under heaven given amongst men by which we must be saved." Unless you are united to him by a lively faith, not the resentment of a haughty monarch, the sword of divine justice hangs over you, and the fulness of divine vengeance shall speedily overtake you. I do not speak this only to the heaven-daring profligate or grovelling sensualist, but to every insensible, secure sinner; to all those, however decent and orderly in their civildeportment, who live to themselves, and have their part and portion in this life; in fine, to all who are yet in a state of nature, for "except a man be born again, he cannot see the kingdom of God". The fear of man may make you hide your profanity; prudence and experience may make you abhor intemperance and riot; as you advance in life one vice may supplant another and hold its place; but nothing less than the sovereign grace of God can produce a saving change of heart and temper, or fit you for his immediate presence.

While we give praise to God, the supreme Disposer of all events, for his interposition in our behalf, let us guard against the dangerous error of trusting in, or boasting of an arm of flesh. I could earnestly wish, that while our arms are crowned with success, we might content ourselves with a modest ascription of it to the power of the Highest. It has given me great uneasiness to read some ostentatious, vaunting expressions in our newspapers, though happily, I think, much restrained of late. Let us not return to them again. If I am not mistaken, not only the Holy Scriptures in general, and the truths of the glorious gospel in particular, but the whole course of providence, seem intended to abase the pride of man, and lay the vain-glorious in the dust.

From what has been said you may learn what encouragement you have to put your trust in God, and hope for his assistance in the present important conflict. He is the Lord of hosts, great in might, and strong in battle. Whoever hath his countenance and approbation, shall have the best at last. I do not mean to speak prophetically, but agreeably to the analogy of faith, and the principles of God's moral government. I leave this as a matter rather of conjecture than certainty, but observe, that if your conduct is prudent, you need not fear the multitude of opposing hosts.

If your cause is just, you may look with confidence to the Lord, and intreat him to plead it as his own. You are all my witnesses, that this is the first time of my introducing any political subject into the pulpit. **At this season, however, it is not only lawful but necessary, and I willingly embrace the opportunity of declaring my opinion without any hesitation, that the cause in which America is now in arms, is the cause of justice, of liberty, and of human nature. So far as we have hitherto proceeded, I am satisfied that the confederacy of the colonies has not been the effect of pride, resentment, or sedition, but of a deep and general conviction that our civil and religious liberties, and consequently in a great measure the temporal and eternal happiness of us and our posterity, depended on the issue. The knowledge of God and his truths have from the beginning of the world been chiefly, if not entirely confined to those parts of the earth where some degree of liberty and political justice were to be seen, and great were the difficulties with which they had to struggle, from the imperfection of human society, and the unjust decisions of unsurped authority. There is not a single instance in history, in which civil liberty was lost, and religious liberty preserved entire. If therefore we yield up our temporal property, we at the same time deliver the conscience into bondage.**

QUESTIONS

1. What did Martin Luther King define as, "a man-made code that squares with the moral law or the law of God?"

2. How did John Witherspoon perceive the connection between civil liberty and religious liberty?

3. How would Blackstone define the laws of nature?

4. "But when a long train of abuses and usurpations, pursuing invariably the same Object evinces a design to reduce them under absolute Despotism, it is their right, it is their duty, to throw off such Government," is an example of which doctrine?

Chapter 7
THE CONSTITUTION

Original Sources:
1. Madison's Federalist Paper No. 41
2. Jefferson's Draft of the Kentucky Resolution of 1798
3. Justice Story's Commentaries on the Constitution, 2 §§904–925, 1833

Our Constitution serves as the Rule of Law for our general government. Every elected official, whether Federal, State, or Local, takes an oath swearing to uphold the Constitution. It would seem only fitting, then, that all U.S. citizens should have a clear understanding of the Constitution, its scope and authority. As you shall read in Chapter 8, while the Declaration of Independence created us as a nation, it is the Constitution that governs us as a nation. The Constitution of the United States did not, nor could it, serve to replace the Declaration of Independence. Rather, it replaced the Articles of Confederation.

© Janece Flippo/Shutterstock.com

Our charter document, the Declaration of Independence, declared us to the world to be one unified and new nation. The Articles of Confederation were drafted to govern these unified confederacies, or states. However, the Articles proved to be rather weak or insufficient in their ability to govern our new nation. The Constitutional Convention was convened for this reason.

While the general government needed greater strength and authority in order to function properly, the citizenry as a whole were still fearful of a strong centralized government. It is for this reason that during the time leading up to the ratification of the Constitution there were arguments made by **Federalists** and **Anti-Federalists**, but there were no arguments to be found by Nationalists. Federalists argued for the ratification of the Constitution because they believed that it adequately preserved the rights and liberties to the co-sovereigns of the states, as well as ultimately to the people. Anti-federalists argued against ratification of the Constitution because they feared that it did not adequately preserve the rights of the co-sovereigns of the states, and, thereby ultimately placed the rights of the people at risk. However, nobody was making the argument that the general government should be stronger than its co-sovereigns, the states. Such an argument would have shown strong **Nationalist** sentiment, and such sentiments did not exist at the time of the ratification of our Constitution; they first appeared in the 1820s with Martin Van Buren.

> *"Those who have wrought great changes in the world never succeeded by gaining over chiefs; but always by exciting the multitude. The first is the resource of intrigue and produces only secondary results, the second is the resort of genius and transforms the face of the universe."*
>
> Martin Van Buren citing Emperor Napolean
> Memoirs of the Life, Exile, and Conversations
> of the Emperor Napoleon, Volume 2, By
> Emmanuel-Auguste-Dieudonnécomte de Las Cases

Such a Nationalist view of majority opinion controlling did not become widely accepted within the United States until the Progressive Era. The Founders, both Federalist and Anti-federalist alike, all held strong opposition to the idea of a ruling majority. The principle of **Federalism**, or division of power among sovereigns, was seen as the great barrier to tyrannical control by any one governing authority. It was this principle of federalism that was the basis for a **bicameral legislature**, with one chamber representing the will of the individual states, and another chamber representing the corporate will of the people. It was likewise the principle of federalism that was the foundation for the **Electoral College**, with individual votes being granted to the people but with such votes to be collectively cast by the states. This unique balance was a means of preserving Federalism over Nationalism; by preventing popular vote from always being determinative, Nationalism was likewise frustrated from being implemented. The Founding Fathers saw this as a positive protective tool that would preserve the vertical balance of power between the States and the general government.

Therefore, states' rights were viewed in a positive light and were the principles behind the 10th Amendment. In order to not create a vehicle by which the general government could potentially usurp more and more power from the states, the Constitution was drafted as a document of **Enumerated Powers.** Article I of the Constitution gave Congress authority to create laws over eighteen specifically enumerated areas. Article II gave the Executive Branch the authority to execute—enforce—only those laws constitutionally enacted by Congress, and Article III provided the Judicial Branch the authority to **adjudicate** cases or controversies involving those laws constitutionally enacted. This kept all three branches tethered to the eighteen enumerated powers. There were no parts of the Constitution intended to extend authority to the general government beyond those eighteen enumerated powers; for to do so through other Constitutional terms or phrases would have served to negate the very character of the Constitution as a document of enumerated powers.

This includes the more ambiguously constructed terms of **necessary and proper** and **general welfare**. Both necessary and proper and general welfare are clauses in Article I, Section 8 and they were intended as limiting language. The eighteen enumerated powers were only to be legislated to the extent they were necessary and proper. Additionally, Congress only had the power to lay taxes that served the welfare of the general public through the preservation of the union, rather than the welfare of special interests. If these clauses were not interpreted in such a limiting fashion, then, according to **Justice Joseph Story** in his Commentaries on the Constitution, the enumeration of powers would be rendered meaningless.

> *The constitution was, from its very origin, contemplated to be the frame of a national government, of special and enumerated powers, and not of general and unlimited powers. This is apparent, as will be presently seen, from the history of the proceedings of the convention, which framed it; and it has formed the admitted basis of all legislative and judicial reasoning upon it, ever since it was put into operation, by all, who have been its open friends and advocates, as well as by all, who have been its enemies and opponents. If the clause, "to pay the debts and provide for the common defence and general welfare of the United States," is construed to be an independent and substantive grant of power, it not only renders wholly unimportant and unnecessary the subsequent enumeration of specific powers; but it plainly extends far beyond them, and creates a general authority in congress to pass all laws, which they may deem for the common defence or general welfare. Under such circumstances, the constitution would practically create an unlimited national government. The enumerated powers would tend to embarrassment and confusion; since they would only give rise to doubts, as to the true extent of the general power, or of the enumerated powers.*

Perhaps, no greater misunderstanding and misapplication of Constitutional principles has served to deconstruct the principles of Federalism and limited governance than has the use of these two clauses. Some interpret these clauses to expand the authority of the general government beyond its enumerated powers by reading these clauses as providing to Congress the ability to do anything they believe is necessary and proper or for the general welfare. This interpretation expands the power of Congress, rather than contain it soundly within the specifically enumerated powers. This expansion of power in the general government has been used to substantially shrink the rights reserved to the States' without directly assaulting the 10th Amendment. It is this latter interpretation of both the general welfare clause and the necessary and proper clause that is ultimately responsible for Federal Government's regulation of numerous areas beyond those listed within the eighteen enumerated powers.

The enumerated powers are not the only safeguards against federal government expansion to have been ignored. The historic doctrines of **Nullification** and **Non-Acquiescence** were intended as means of correcting unconstitutional government expansion, either by the general government over the states, or by one of the three branches over the others, respectively. The argument has been made that the Civil War ended the validity of the doctrine of Nullification because it defeated the assertion of States' rights. However, while the Civil War did end the debate among the states for succession of the Confederacy, it could not have removed the doctrine of Nullification as to the residual rights of the states beyond the eighteen enumerated powers, without amending or removing the 10th Amendment.

Likewise, non-acquiescence has been diminished through the more recent acceptance of Supreme Court decisions as the Supreme Law of the land, rather than the Constitution itself. However, while non-acquiescence in its pure form is diminished by the tendency to view Article III (Judicial) power as supreme, it is still frequently used. Even if particular branches no longer expressly defend their actions as a means of non-acquiescence, we still witness the refusal of one branch to honor the actions of another.

One particularly notable time in history when both a state government and the Executive Branch were in vehement opposition to the position taken by the United States Supreme Court was during the handing down of the opinion in the case of ***Georgia v Worcester***. In this case the SCOTUS struck down the opinions of the Georgia Courts regarding the Cherokee Reservations. The Supreme Court did this by declaring the Tribes as independent nations with whom only the Federal government, not the states, could negotiate.

During this time President Andrew Jackson was ordering the Cherokee Indians to be forcibly relocated to western reservations. It is estimated that this evacuation of 20,000 Indians, monitored by the U.S. Military, occasioned the deaths of one-fourth of those removed from their ancestral lands. This became known as the Cherokee Trail of Tears. Justice Joseph Story, one of the Justices deciding this case, anticipated the Supreme Court's opinion would elicit a particular response from both President Jackson, as well as the state of Georgia. While he and the Supreme Court had made their position clear, he was well aware of the fact that they did not possess the power to override opposing positions from either the states or other branches of the government.

> *"We have just decided the Cherokee case, and reversed the decisions of the State Court of Georgia, and declared her laws unconstitutional. The decision produced a very strong sensation in both houses; Georgia is full of anger and violence. . . . Probably she will resist the execution of our judgment, and if she does I do not believe the President will interefere. . . . The Court has done its duty. Let the Nation do theirs.*
>
> Justice Joseph Story,
> Letter to Professor Ticknor, March 8, 1832

> *Yesterday morning the Chief Justice delivered the opinion of the court in the Cherokee case, in favor of the missionaries. It was a very able opinion in his best manner. Thanks be to God the Court can wash their hands clean of the iniquity of oppressing the Indians and disregarding their rights. . . .*
>
> Justice Joseph Story,
> Letter to his Wife, March 4, 1832

From these letters we can see that Justice Story was persuaded that the Supreme Court had made the right decision. However, we can also see that he understood that the Court's decision did not prohibit either the President, through non-acquiescence, or the state of Georgia, through nullification, from taking a position opposing the court's opinion. Story, the author of the Commentaries of the Constitution of the United States, was fully aware of both the vertical and horizontal checks and balances between the federal government and the states, and the three branches of government. It was his understanding that the Constitution did not grant to the Supreme Court of the United States supreme control to prevent all opposition.

Federalist Papers No. 41
General View of the Powers Conferred by the Constitution
For the Independent Journal.
Author: James Madison

To the People of the State of New York:

THE Constitution proposed by the convention may be considered under two general points of view. The FIRST relates to the sum or quantity of power which it vests in the government, including the restraints imposed on the States. The SECOND, to the particular structure of the government, and the distribution of this power among its several branches. Under the FIRST view of the subject, two important questions arise: 1. Whether any part of the powers transferred to the general government be unnecessary or improper? 2. Whether the entire mass of them be dangerous to the portion of jurisdiction left in the several States? Is the aggregate power of the general government greater than ought to have been vested in it? This is the FIRST question. It cannot have escaped those who have attended with candor to the arguments employed against the extensive powers of the government, that the authors of them have very little considered how far these powers were necessary means of attaining a necessary end. They have chosen rather to dwell on the inconveniences which must be unavoidably blended with all political advantages; and on the possible abuses which must be incident to every power or trust, of which a beneficial use can be made. This method of handling the subject cannot impose on the good sense of the people of America. It may display the subtlety of the writer; it may open a boundless field for rhetoric and declamation; it may inflame the passions of the unthinking, and may confirm the prejudices of the misthinking: but cool and candid people will at once reflect, that the purest of human blessings must have a portion of alloy in them; that the choice must always be made, if not of the lesser evil, at least of the GREATER, not the PERFECT, good; and that in every political institution, a power to advance the public happiness involves a discretion which may be misapplied and abused. They will see, therefore, that in all cases where power is to be conferred, the point first to be decided is, whether such a power be necessary to the public good; as the next will be, in case of an affirmative decision, to guard as effectually as possible against a perversion of the power to the public detriment. That we may form a correct judgment on this subject, it will be proper to review the several powers conferred on the government of the Union; and that this may be the more conveniently done they may be reduced into different classes as they relate to the following different objects: 1. Security against foreign danger; 2. Regulation of the intercourse with foreign nations; 3. Maintenance of harmony and proper intercourse among the States; 4. Certain miscellaneous objects of general utility; 5. Restraint of the States from certain injurious acts; 6. Provisions for giving due efficacy to all these powers. The powers falling within the FIRST class are those of declaring war and granting letters of marque; of providing armies and fleets; of regulating and calling forth the militia; of levying and borrowing money. Security against foreign danger is one of the primitive objects of civil society. It is an avowed and essential object of the American Union. The powers requisite for attaining it must be effectually confided to the federal councils. Is the power of declaring war necessary? No man will answer this question in the negative. It would be superfluous, therefore, to enter into a proof of the affirmative. The existing Confederation establishes this power in the most ample form. Is the power of raising armies and equipping fleets necessary? This is involved in the foregoing power. It is involved in the power of self-defense. But was it necessary to give an INDEFINITE POWER of raising TROOPS, as well as providing fleets; and of maintaining both in PEACE, as well as in war? The answer to these questions has been too far anticipated in another place to admit an extensive discussion of them in this place. The answer indeed seems to be so obvious and conclusive as scarcely to justify such a discussion in any place. With what color of propriety could the force necessary for defense be limited by those who cannot limit the force of offense? If a federal Constitution could chain the ambition or set bounds to the exertions of all other nations, then indeed might it prudently chain the discretion of its own government, and set bounds to the exertions for its own safety.

How could a readiness for war in time of peace be safely prohibited, unless we could prohibit, in like manner, the preparations and establishments of every hostile nation? The means of security can only be regulated by the means and the danger of attack. They will, in fact, be ever determined by these rules, and by no others. It is in vain to oppose constitutional barriers to the impulse of self-preservation. It is worse than in vain; because it plants in the Constitution itself necessary usurpations of power, every precedent of which is a germ of unnecessary and multiplied repetitions. If one nation maintains constantly a disciplined army, ready for the service of ambition or revenge, it obliges the most pacific nations who may be within the reach of its enterprises to take corresponding precautions.

The fifteenth century was the unhappy epoch of military establishments in the time of peace. They were introduced by Charles VII. of France. All Europe has followed, or been forced into, the example. Had the example not been followed by other nations, all Europe must long ago have worn the chains of a universal monarch. Were every nation except France now to disband its peace establishments, the same event might follow. The veteran legions of Rome were an overmatch for the undisciplined valor of all other nations and rendered her the mistress of the world. Not the less true is it, that the liberties of Rome proved the final victim to her military triumphs; and that the liberties of Europe, as far as they ever existed, have, with few exceptions, been the price of her military establishments. A standing force, therefore, is a dangerous, at the same time that it may be a necessary, provision. On the smallest scale it has its inconveniences. On an extensive scale its consequences may be fatal. On any scale it is an object of laudable circumspection and precaution. A wise nation will combine all these considerations; and, whilst it does not rashly preclude itself from any resource which may become essential to its safety, will exert all its prudence in diminishing both the necessity and the danger of resorting to one which may be inauspicious to its liberties. The clearest marks of this prudence are stamped on the proposed Constitution. The Union itself, which it cements and secures, destroys every pretext for a military establishment which could be dangerous. America united, with a handful of troops, or without a single soldier, exhibits a more forbidding posture to foreign ambition than America disunited, with a hundred thousand veterans ready for combat. It was remarked, on a former occasion, that the want of this pretext had saved the liberties of one nation in Europe. Being rendered by her insular situation and her maritime resources impregnable to the armies of her neighbors, the rulers of Great Britain have never been able, by real or artificial dangers, to cheat the public into an extensive peace establishment. The distance of the United States from the powerful nations of the world gives them the same happy security. A dangerous establishment can never be necessary or plausible, so long as they continue a united people. But let it never, for a moment, be forgotten that they are indebted for this advantage to the Union alone. The moment of its dissolution will be the date of a new order of things. The fears of the weaker, or the ambition of the stronger States, or Confederacies, will set the same example in the New, as Charles VII. did in the Old World. The example will be followed here from the same motives which produced universal imitation there. Instead of deriving from our situation the precious advantage which Great Britain has derived from hers, the face of America will be but a copy of that of the continent of Europe. It will present liberty everywhere crushed between standing armies and perpetual taxes. The fortunes of disunited America will be even more disastrous than those of Europe. The sources of evil in the latter are confined to her own limits. No superior powers of another quarter of the globe intrigue among her rival nations, inflame their mutual animosities, and render them the instruments of foreign ambition, jealousy, and revenge. In America the miseries springing from her internal jealousies, contentions, and wars, would form a part only of her lot. A plentiful addition of evils would have their source in that relation in which Europe stands to this quarter of the earth, and which no other quarter of the earth bears to Europe. This picture of the consequences of disunion cannot be too highly colored, or too often exhibited. Every man who loves peace, every man who loves his country, every man who loves liberty, ought to have it ever before his eyes, that he may cherish in his heart a due attachment to the Union of America, and be able to set a due value on the means of preserving it.

Next to the effectual establishment of the Union, the best possible precaution against danger from standing armies is a limitation of the term for which revenue may be appropriated to their support. This precaution the Constitution has prudently added. I will not repeat here the observations which I flatter myself have placed this subject in a just and satisfactory light. But it may not be improper to take notice of an argument against this part of the Constitution, which has been drawn from the policy and practice of Great Britain. It is said that the continuance of an army in that kingdom requires an annual vote of the legislature; whereas the American Constitution has lengthened this critical period to two years. This is the form in which the comparison is usually stated to the public: but is it a just form? Is it a fair comparison? Does the British Constitution restrain the parliamentary discretion to one year? Does the American impose on the Congress appropriations for two years? On the contrary, it cannot be unknown to the authors of the fallacy themselves, that the British Constitution fixes no limit whatever to the discretion of the legislature, and that the American ties down the legislature to two years, as the longest admissible term. Had the argument from the British example been truly stated, it would have stood thus: The term for which supplies may be appropriated to the army establishment, though unlimited by the British

Constitution, has nevertheless, in practice, been limited by parliamentary discretion to a single year. Now, if in Great Britain, where the House of Commons is elected for seven years; where so great a proportion of the members are elected by so small a proportion of the people; where the electors are so corrupted by the representatives, and the representatives so corrupted by the Crown, the representative body can possess a power to make appropriations to the army for an indefinite term, without desiring, or without daring, to extend the term beyond a single year, ought not suspicion herself to blush, in pretending that the representatives of the United States, elected FREELY by the WHOLE BODY of the people, every SECOND YEAR, cannot be safely intrusted with the discretion over such appropriations, expressly limited to the short period of TWO YEARS? A bad cause seldom fails to betray itself. Of this truth, the management of the opposition to the federal government is an unvaried exemplification. But among all the blunders which have been committed, none is more striking than the attempt to enlist on that side the prudent jealousy entertained by the people, of standing armies. The attempt has awakened fully the public attention to that important subject; and has led to investigations which must terminate in a thorough and universal conviction, not only that the constitution has provided the most effectual guards against danger from that quarter, but that nothing short of a Constitution fully adequate to the national defense and the preservation of the Union, can save America from as many standing armies as it may be split into States or Confederacies, and from such a progressive augmentation, of these establishments in each, as will render them as burdensome to the properties and ominous to the liberties of the people, as any establishment that can become necessary, under a united and efficient government, must be tolerable to the former and safe to the latter. The palpable necessity of the power to provide and maintain a navy has protected that part of the Constitution against a spirit of censure, which has spared few other parts. It must, indeed, be numbered among the greatest blessings of America, that as her Union will be the only source of her maritime strength, so this will be a principal source of her security against danger from abroad. In this respect our situation bears another likeness to the insular advantage of Great Britain. The batteries most capable of repelling foreign enterprises on our safety, are happily such as can never be turned by a perfidious government against our liberties. The inhabitants of the Atlantic frontier are all of them deeply interested in this provision for naval protection, and if they have hitherto been suffered to sleep quietly in their beds; if their property has remained safe against the predatory spirit of licentious adventurers; if their maritime towns have not yet been compelled to ransom themselves from the terrors of a conflagration, by yielding to the exactions of daring and sudden invaders, these instances of good fortune are not to be ascribed to the capacity of the existing government for the protection of those from whom it claims allegiance, but to causes that are fugitive and fallacious. If we except perhaps Virginia and Maryland, which are peculiarly vulnerable on their eastern frontiers, no part of the Union ought to feel more anxiety on this subject than New York. Her seacoast is extensive. A very important district of the State is an island. The State itself is penetrated by a large navigable river for more than fifty leagues. The great emporium of its commerce, the great reservoir of its wealth, lies every moment at the mercy of events, and may almost be regarded as a hostage for ignominious compliances with the dictates of a foreign enemy, or even with the rapacious demands of pirates and barbarians. Should a war be the result of the precarious situation of European affairs, and all the unruly passions attending it be let loose on the ocean, our escape from insults and depredations, not only on that element, but every part of the other bordering on it, will be truly miraculous. In the present condition of America, the States more immediately exposed to these calamities have nothing to hope from the phantom of a general government which now exists; and if their single resources were equal to the task of fortifying themselves against the danger, the object to be protected would be almost consumed by the means of protecting them. The power of regulating and calling forth the militia has been already sufficiently vindicated and explained. The power of levying and borrowing money, being the sinew of that which is to be exerted in the national defense, is properly thrown into the same class with it. This power, also, has been examined already with much attention, and has, I trust, been clearly shown to be necessary, both in the extent and form given to it by the Constitution. I will address one additional reflection only to those who contend that the power ought to have been restrained to external taxation by which they mean, taxes on articles imported from other countries. It cannot be doubted that this will always be a valuable source of revenue; that for a considerable time it must be a principal source; that at this moment it is an essential one. But we may form very mistaken ideas on this subject, if we do not call to mind in our calculations, that the extent of revenue drawn from foreign commerce must vary with the variations, both in the extent and the kind of imports; and that these variations do not correspond with the progress of population, which must be the general measure of the public wants. As long as agriculture continues the sole field of labor, the importation of manufactures must increase as the consumers multiply. As soon as domestic manufactures are begun by the hands not called for by agriculture, the imported manufactures will decrease as the numbers of people increase. In a more remote stage, the imports may consist in a considerable part of raw materials, which will be wrought into articles for exportation, and will, therefore, require rather the encouragement of bounties, than to be loaded with discouraging duties. A system of government, meant for duration, ought to contemplate these revolutions, and be able to accommodate itself to them. Some, who have not denied the necessity of the power of taxation, have grounded a very fierce attack against the Constitution, on the language in which it is defined. **It has been urged and echoed, that the power "to lay and collect taxes, duties, imposts, and excises, to pay the debts, and provide for the common defense and general welfare of the United States," amounts to an unlimited commission to exercise every power which may be alleged to be necessary for the common defense or general welfare. No stronger proof could be given of the distress under which these writers labor for objections, than their stooping to such a misconstruction. Had no other enumeration or definition of the powers of the Congress been found in the Constitution, than the general expressions just cited, the authors of the objection might have had some color for it; though it would have been difficult to find a reason for so awkward a form of describing an authority to legislate in all possible cases. A power to destroy the freedom of the press, the trial by jury, or even to regulate the course of descents, or the forms of conveyances, must be very singularly expressed by the terms "to raise money for the general welfare." But what color can the objection have, when a specification of the objects alluded to by these general terms immediately follows, and is not even separated by a longer pause than a semicolon? If the different parts of the same instrument ought to be so expounded, as to give meaning to every part which will bear it, shall one part of the same sentence be excluded altogether from a share in the meaning; and shall the more doubtful and indefinite terms be retained in their full extent, and the clear and precise expressions be denied any signification whatsoever? For what purpose could the enumeration of particular powers be inserted, if these and all others were meant to be included in the preceding general power? Nothing is more natural nor common than first to use a general phrase, and then to explain and qualify it by a recital of particulars. But the idea of an enumeration of particulars which neither explain nor qualify the general meaning, and can have no other effect than to confound and mislead, is an absurdity, which, as we are reduced to the dilemma of charging either on the authors of the objection or on the authors of the Constitution, we must take the liberty of supposing, had not its origin with the latter.** The objection here is the more extraordinary, as it appears that the language used by the convention is a copy from the articles of Confederation. The objects of the Union among the States, as described in article third, are "their common defense, security of their liberties, and mutual and general welfare. "The terms of article eighth are still more identical: "All charges of war and all other expenses that shall be incurred for the common defense or general welfare, and allowed by the United States in Congress, shall be defrayed out of a common treasury," etc. A similar language again occurs in article ninth. Construe either of these articles by the rules which would justify the construction put on the new Constitution, and they vest in the existing Congress a power to legislate in all cases whatsoever.

But what would have been thought of that assembly, if, attaching themselves to these general expressions, and disregarding the specifications which ascertain and limit their import, they had exercised an unlimited power of providing for the common defense and general welfare? I appeal to the objectors themselves, whether they would in that case have employed the same reasoning in justification of Congress as they now make use of against the convention. How difficult it is for error to escape its own condemnation!

PUBLIUS.

Draft of the Kentucky Resolutions

Thomas Jefferson

October 1798

1. _Resolved_, **That the several States composing the United States of America, are not united on the principle of unlimited submission to their General Government; but that, by a compact under the style and title of a Constitution for the United States, and of amendments thereto, they constituted a General Government for special purposes,—delegated to that government certain definite powers, reserving, each State to itself, the residuary mass of right to their own self-government; and that whensoever the General Government assumes undelegated powers, its acts are unauthoritative, void, and of no force; that to this compact each State acceded as a State, and is an integral party, its co-States forming, as to itself, the other party: that the government created by this compact was not made the exclusive or final judge of the extent of the powers delegated to itself; since that would have made its discretion, and not the Constitution, the measure of its powers; but that, as in all other cases of compact among powers having no common judge, each party has an equal right to judge for itself, as well of infractions as of the mode and measure of redress.**

2. _Resolved_, That the Constitution of the United States, having delegated to Congress a power to punish treason, counterfeiting the securities and current coin of the United States, piracies, and felonies committed on the high seas, and offences against the law of nations, and no other crimes whatsoever; and it being true as a general principle, and one of the amendments to the Constitution having also declared, that "the powers not delegated to the United States by the Constitution, nor prohibited by it to the States, are reserved to the States respectively, or to the people," therefore the act of Congress, passed on the 14th day of July, 1798, and intituled "An Act in addition to the act intituled An Act for the punishment of certain crimes against the United States," as also the act passed by them on the—day of June, 1798, intituled "An Act to punish frauds committed on the bank of the United States," (and all their other acts which assume to create, define, or punish crimes, other than those so enumerated in the Constitution,) are altogether void, and of no force; and that the power to create, define, and punish such other crimes is reserved, and, of right, appertains solely and exclusively to the respective States, each within its own territory.

3. _Resolved_, That it is true as a general principle, and is also expressly declared by one of the amendments to the Constitution, that "the powers not delegated to the United States by the Constitution, nor prohibited by it to the States, are reserved to the States respectively, or to the people;" and that no power over the freedom of religion, freedom of speech, or freedom of the press being delegated to the United States by the Constitution, nor prohibited by it to the States, all lawful powers respecting the same did of right remain, and were reserved to the States or the people: that thus was manifested their determination to retain to themselves the right of judging how far the licentiousness of speech and of the press may be abridged without lessening their useful freedom, and how far those abuses which cannot be separated from their use should be tolerated, rather than the use be destroyed. And thus also they guarded against all abridgment by the United States of the freedom of religious opinions and exercises, and retained to themselves the right of protecting the same, as this State, by a law passed on the general demand of its citizens, had already protected them from all human restraint or interference. And that in addition to this general principle and express declaration, another and more special provision has been made by one of the amendments to the Constitution, which expressly declares, that "Congress shall make no law respecting an establishment of religion, or prohibiting the free exercise thereof, or abridging the freedom of speech or of the press:" thereby guarding in the same sentence, and under the same words, the freedom of religion, of speech, and of the press: insomuch, that whatever violated either, throws down the sanctuary which covers the others, and that libels, falsehood, and defamation, equally with heresy and false religion, are withheld from the cognizance of federal tribunals. That, therefore, the act of Congress of the United States, passed on the 14th day of July, 1798, intituled "An Act in addition to the act intituled An Act for the punishment of certain crimes against the United States," which does abridge the freedom of the press, is not law, but is altogether void, and of no force.

4. _Resolved_, That alien friends are under the jurisdiction and protection of the laws of the State wherein they are: that no power over them has been

delegated to the United States, nor prohibited to the individual States, distinct from their power over citizens. And it being true as a general principle, and one of the amendments to the Constitution having also declared, that "the powers not delegated to the United States by the Constitution, nor prohibited by it to the States, are reserved to the States respectively, or to the people," the act of the Congress of the United States, passed on the—day of July, 1798, intituled "An Act concerning aliens," which assumes powers over alien friends, not delegated by the Constitution, is not law, but is altogether void, and of no force.

5. _Resolved_, That in addition to the general principle, as well as the express declaration, that powers not delegated are reserved, another and more special provision, inserted in the Constitution from abundant caution, has declared that "the migration or importation of such persons as any of the States now existing shall think proper to admit, shall not be prohibited by the Congress prior to the year 1808;" that this commonwealth does admit the migration of alien friends, described as the subject of the said act concerning aliens: that a provision against prohibiting their migration, is a provision against all acts equivalent thereto, or it would be nugatory: that to remove them when migrated, is equivalent to a prohibition of their migration, and is, therefore, contrary to the said provision of the Constitution, and void.

6. _Resolved_, That the imprisonment of a person under the protection of the laws of this commonwealth, on his failure to obey the simple _order_ of the President to depart out of the United States, as is undertaken by said act intituled "An Act concerning aliens," is contrary to the Constitution, one amendment to which has provided that "no person shall be deprived of liberty without due process of law;" and that another having provided that "in all criminal prosecutions the accused shall enjoy the right to public trial by an impartial jury, to be informed of the nature and cause of the accusation, to be confronted with the witnesses against him, to have compulsory process for obtaining witnesses in his favor, and to have the assistance of counsel for his defence," the same act, undertaking to authorize the President to remove a person out of the United States, who is under the protection of the law, on his own suspicion, without accusation, without jury, without public trial, without confrontation of the witnesses against him, without hearing witnesses in his favor, without defence, without counsel, is contrary to the provision also of the Constitution, is therefore not law, but utterly void, and of no force: that transferring the power of judging any person, who is under the protection of the laws, from the courts to the President of the United States, as is undertaken by the same act concerning aliens, is against the article of the Constitution which provides that "the judicial power of the United States shall be vested in courts, the judges of which shall hold their offices during good behavior;" and that the said act is void for that reason also. And it is further to be noted, that this transfer of judiciary power is to that magistrate of the General Government who already possesses all the Executive, and a negative on all legislative powers.

7. _Resolved_, **That the construction applied by the General Government (as is evidenced by sundry of their proceedings) to those parts of the Constitution of the United States which delegate to Congress a power "to lay and collect taxes, duties, imports, and excises, to pay the debts, and provide for the common defence and general welfare of the United States," and "to make all laws which shall be necessary and proper for carrying into execution the powers vested by the Constitution in the government of the United States, or in any department or officer thereof," goes to the destruction of all limits prescribed to their power by the Constitution: that words meant by the instrument to be subsidiary only to the execution of limited powers, ought not to be so construed as themselves to give unlimited powers, nor a part to be so taken as to destroy the whole residue of that instrument: that the proceedings of the General Government under color of these articles, will be a fit and necessary subject of revisal and correction, at a time of greater tranquillity, while those specified in the preceding resolutions call for immediate redress.**

8th. _Resolved_, That a committee of conference and correspondence be appointed, who shall have in charge to communicate the preceding resolutions to the legislatures of the several States; to assure them that this commonwealth continues in the same esteem of their friendship and union which it has manifested from that moment at which a common danger first suggested a common union: that it considers union, for specified national purposes, and particularly to those specified in their late federal compact, to be friendly to the peace, happiness and prosperity of all the States: that faithful to that compact, according to the plain intent and meaning in which it was understood and acceded to by the several parties, it is sincerely anxious for its preservation: that it does also believe, that to take from the States all the powers of self-government and transfer them to a general and consolidated government, without regard to the special delegations and reservations solemnly agreed to in that compact, is not for the peace, happiness or prosperity of these States; and that therefore this commonwealth is determined, as it doubts not its co-States are, to submit to undelegated, and consequently unlimited powers in no man, or body of men on earth: that in cases of an abuse of the delegated powers, the members of the General Government, being chosen by the people, a change by the people would be the constitutional remedy; but, where powers are assumed which have not been delegated, a nullification of the act is the rightful remedy: that every State has a natural right in cases not within the compact, (casus non foederis,) to nullify of their own authority all assumptions of power by others within their limits: that without this right, they would be under the dominion, absolute and unlimited, of whosoever might exercise this right of judgment for them: that nevertheless, this commonwealth, from motives of regard and respect for its co-States, has wished to communicate with them on the subject: that with them alone it is proper to communicate, they alone being parties to the compact, and solely authorized to judge in the last resort of the powers exercised under it, Congress being not a party, but merely the creature of the compact, and subject as to its assumptions of power to the final judgment of those by whom, and for whose use itself and its powers were all created and modified: that if the acts before specified should stand, these conclusions would flow from them; that the General Government may place any act they think proper on the list of crimes, and punish it themselves whether enumerated or not enumerated by the Constitution as cognizable by them: that they may transfer its cognizance to the President, or any other person, who may himself be the accuser, counsel, judge and jury, whose _suspicions_ may be the evidence, his _order_ the sentence, his _officer_ the executioner, and his breast the sole record of the transaction: that a very numerous and valuable description of the inhabitants of these States being, by this precedent, reduced, as outlaws, to the absolute dominion of one man, and the barrier of the Constitution thus swept away from us all, no rampart now remains against the passions and the powers of a majority in Congress to protect from a like exportation, or other more grievous punishment, the minority of the same body, the legislatures, judges, governors, and counsellors of the States, nor their other peaceable inhabitants, who may venture to reclaim the constitutional rights and liberties of the States and people, or who for other causes, good or bad, may be obnoxious to the views, or marked by the suspicions of the President, or be thought dangerous to his or their election, or other interests, public or personal: that the friendless alien has indeed been selected as the safest subject of a first experiment; but the citizen will soon follow, or rather, has already followed, for already has a sedition act marked him as its prey: that these and successive acts of the same character, unless arrested at the threshold, necessarily drive these States into revolution and blood, and will furnish new calumnies against republican government, and new pretexts for those who wish it to be believed that man cannot be governed but by a rod of iron: that it would be a dangerous delusion were a confidence in the men of our choice to silence our fears for the safety of our rights: that confidence is everywhere the parent of despotism—free government is founded in jealousy, and not in confidence; it is jealousy and not confidence which prescribes limited constitutions, to bind down those whom we are obliged to trust with power: that our Constitution has accordingly fixed the limits to which, and no further, our confidence may go; and let the honest advocate of confidence read the alien and sedition acts, and say if the Constitution has not been wise in fixing limits to the government it created, and whether we should be wise in destroying those limits. Let him say what the government is, if it be not a tyranny, which the men of our choice have conferred on our President, and the President of our choice has assented to, and accepted over the friendly strangers to whom the mild spirit of our country and its laws have pledged hospitality and protection: that the men of our choice have more respected the bare _suspicions_ of the President, than the solid right of innocence, the claims of justification, the sacred force of truth, and the forms and substance of law and justice. In questions of power, then, let no more be heard of confidence in man, but bind him down from mischief by the chains of the Constitution. That this commonwealth does therefore call on its co-States for an expression of their sentiments on the acts concerning aliens, and for the punishment of certain crimes herein before specified, plainly declaring whether these acts are or are not authorized by the federal compact. And it doubts not that their sense will be so announced as to prove their attachment unaltered to limited government, whether general or particular. And that the rights and liberties of their co-States will be exposed to no dangers by remaining embarked in a common bottom with their own. That they will concur with this commonwealth in considering the said acts as so palpably against the Constitution as to amount to an undisguised declaration that that compact is not meant to be the measure of the powers of the General Government, but that it will proceed in the exercise over these States, of all powers whatsoever: that they will view this as seizing the rights of the States, and consolidating them in the hands of the General Government, with a power assumed to bind the States, not merely as the cases made federal, (casus foederis,) but in all cases whatsoever, by laws made, not with their consent, but by others against their consent: that this would be to surrender the form of government we have chosen, and live under one deriving its powers from its own will, and not from our authority; and that the co-States, recurring to their natural right in cases not made federal, will concur in declaring these acts void, and of no force, and will each take measures of its own for providing that neither these acts, nor any others of the General Government not plainly and intentionally authorized by the Constitution, shall be exercised within their respective territories.

9th. _Resolved_, That the said committee be authorized to communicate by writing or personal conferences, at any times or places whatever, with any person or person who may be appointed by any one or more co-States to correspond or confer with them; and that they lay their proceedings before the next session of Assembly.

Commentaries on the Constitution

2 : §§ 904—25

Joseph Story

1833

§ 904. Before proceeding to consider the nature and extent of the power conferred by this clause, and the reasons, on which it is founded, it seems necessary to settle the grammatical construction of the clause, and to ascertain its true reading. Do the words, "to lay and collect taxes, duties, imposts, and excises," constitute a distinct, substantial power; and the words, "to pay debts and provide for the common defence, and general welfare of the United States," constitute another distinct and substantial power? Or are the latter words connected with the former, so as to constitute a qualification upon them? This has been a topic of political controversy; and has furnished abundant materials for popular declamation and alarm. If the former be the true interpretation, then it is obvious, that under colour of the generality of the words to "provide for the common defence and general welfare," the government of the United States is, in reality, a government of general and unlimited powers, notwithstanding the subsequent enumeration of specific powers; if the latter be the true construction, then the power of taxation only is given by the clause, and it is limited to objects of a national character, "for the common defence and the general welfare."

§ 905. The former opinion has been maintained by some minds of great ingenuity, and liberality of views. The latter has been the generally received sense of the nation, and seems supported by reasoning at once solid and impregnable. The reading, therefore, which will be maintained in these commentaries, is that, which makes the latter words a qualification of the former; and this will be best illustrated by supplying the words, which are necessarily to be understood in this interpretation. They will then stand thus: "The congress shall have power to lay and collect taxes, duties, imposts, and excises, in order to pay the debts, and to provide for the common defence and general welfare of the United States;" that is, for the purpose of paying the public debts, and providing for the common defence and general welfare of the United States. In this sense, congress has not an unlimited power of taxation; but it is limited to specific objects,—the payment of the public debts, and providing for the common defence and general welfare. A tax, therefore, laid by congress for neither of these objects, would be unconstitutional, as an excess of its legislative authority. In what manner this is to be ascertained, or decided, will be considered hereafter.

At present, the interpretation of the words only is before us; and the reasoning, by which that already suggested has been vindicated, will now be reviewed.

§ 906. The constitution was, from its very origin, contemplated to be the frame of a national government, of special and enumerated powers, and not of general and unlimited powers. This is apparent, as will be presently seen, from the history of the proceedings of the convention, which framed it; and it has formed the admitted basis of all legislative and judicial reasoning upon it, ever since it was put into operation, by all, who have been its open friends and advocates, as well as by all, who have been its enemies and opponents. If the clause, "to pay the debts and provide for the common defence and general welfare of the United States," is construed to be an independent and substantive grant of power, it not only renders wholly unimportant and unnecessary the subsequent enumeration of specific powers; but it plainly extends far beyond them, and creates a general authority in congress to pass all laws, which they may deem for the common defence or general welfare. Under such circumstances, the constitution would practically create an unlimited national government. The enumerated powers would tend to embarrassment and confusion; since they would only give rise to doubts, as to the true extent of the general power, or of the enumerated powers.

§ 907. One of the most common maxims of interpretation is, (as has been already stated,) that, as an exception strengthens the force of a law in cases not excepted, so enumeration weakens it in cases not enumerated. But, how could it be applied with success to the interpretation of the constitution of the United States, if the enumerated powers were neither exceptions from, nor additions to, the general power to provide for the common defence and general welfare? To give the enumeration of the specific powers any sensible place or operation in the constitution, it is indispensable to construe them, as not wholly and necessarily embraced in the general power. The common principles of interpretation would seem to instruct us, that the different parts of the same instrument ought to be so expounded, as to give meaning to every part, which will bear it. Shall one part of the same sentence be excluded altogether from a share in the meaning; and shall the more doubtful and indefinite terms be retained in their full extent, and the clear and precise expressions be denied any signification? For what purpose could the enumeration of particular powers be inserted, if these and all others were meant to be included in the preceding general power? Nothing is more natural or common, than first to use a general phrase, and then to qualify it by a recital of particulars. But the idea of an enumeration of particulars, which neither explain, nor qualify the general meaning, and can have no other effect, than to confound and mislead, is an absurdity, which no one ought to charge on the enlightened authors of the constitution. It would be to charge them either with premeditated folly, or premeditated fraud.

§ 908. On the other hand, construing this clause in connexion with, and as a part of the preceding clause, giving the power to lay taxes, it becomes sensible and operative. It becomes a qualification of that clause, and limits the taxing power to objects for the common defence or general welfare. It then contains no grant of any power whatsoever; but it is a mere expression of the ends and purposes to be effected by the preceding power of taxation.

§ 909. An attempt has been sometimes made to treat this clause, as distinct and independent, and yet as having no real significancy per se, but (if it may be so said) as a mere prelude to the succeeding enumerated powers. It is not improbable, that this mode of explanation has been suggested by the fact, that in the revised draft of the constitution in the convention the clause was separated from the preceding exactly in the same manner, as every succeeding clause was, viz. by a semicolon, and a break in the paragraph; and that it now stands, in some copies, and it is said, that it stands in the official copy, with a semicolon interposed. But this circumstance will be found of very little weight, when the origin of the clause, and its progress to its present state are traced in the proceedings of the convention. It will then appear, that it was first introduced as an appendage to the power to lay taxes. But there is a fundamental objection to the interpretation thus attempted to be maintained, which is, that it robs the clause of all efficacy and meaning. No person has a right to assume, that any part of the constitution is useless, or is without a meaning; and a fortiori no person has a right to rob any part of a meaning, natural and appropriate to the language in the connexion, in which it stands. Now, the words have such a natural and appropriate meaning, as a qualification of the preceding clause to lay taxes. Why, then, should such a meaning be rejected?

§ 910. It is no sufficient answer to say, that the clause ought to be regarded, merely as containing "general terms, explained and limited, by the subjoined specifications, and therefore requiring no critical attention, or studied precaution;" because it is assuming the very point in controversy, to assert, that the clause is connected with any subsequent specifications. It is not said, to "provide for the common defence, and general welfare, in manner following, viz.," which would be the natural expression, to indicate such an intention. But it stands entirely disconnected from every subsequent clause, both in sense and punctuation; and is no more a part of them, than they are of the power to lay taxes. Besides; what suitable application, in such a sense, would there be of the last clause in the enumeration, viz., the clause to make all laws, necessary and proper for carrying into execution the foregoing powers, & Surely, this clause is as applicable to the power to lay taxes, as to any other; and no one would dream of its being a mere specification, under the power to provide for the common defence, and general welfare.

§ 911. It has been said [in James Madison's 1800 Report on the Virginia Resolutions] in support of this construction, that in the articles of confederation (art. 8) it is provided, that "all charges of war, and all other expenses, that shall be incurred for the common defence, or general welfare, and allowed by the United States in congress assembled, shall be defrayed out of a common treasury, &c.;" and that "the similarity in the use of these same phrases in these two great federal charters may well be considered, as rendering their meaning less liable to misconstruction; because it will scarcely be said, that in the former they were ever understood to be either a general grant or power, or to authorize the requisition or application of money by the old congress to the common defence and [or] general welfare, except in the cases afterwards enumerated, which explained and limited their meaning; and if such was the limited meaning attached to these phrases in the very instrument revised and remodelled by the present constitution, it can never be supposed, that when copied into this constitution, a different meaning ought to be attached to them." Without stopping to consider, whether the constitution can in any just and critical sense be deemed a revision and remodelling of the confederation, if the argument here stated be of any value, it plainly establishes, that the words ought to be construed, as a qualification or limitation of the power to lay taxes. By the confederation, all expenses incurred for the common defence, or general welfare, are to be defrayed out of a common treasury, to be supplied by requisitions upon the states. Instead of requisitions, the constitution gives the right to the national government directly to lay taxes. So, that the only difference in this view between the two clauses is, as to the mode of obtaining the money, not as to the objects or purposes, to which it is to be applied. If then the constitution were to be construed according to the true bearing of this argument, it would read thus: congress shall have power to lay taxes for "all charges of war, and all other expenses, that shall be incurred for the common defence or general welfare." This plainly makes it a qualification of the taxing power; and not an independent provision, or a general index to the succeeding specifications of power. There is not, however, any solid ground, upon which it can be for a moment maintained, that the language of the constitution is to be enlarged, or restricted by the language of the confederation. That would be to make it speak, what its words do not import, and its objects do not justify. It would be to append it, as a codicil, to an instrument, which it was designed wholly to supercede and vacate.

§ 912. But the argument in its other branch rests on an assumed basis, which is not admitted. It supposes, that in the confederation no expenses, not strictly incurred under some of the subsequent specified powers given to the continental congress, could be properly payable out of the common treasury. Now, that is a proposition to be proved; and is not to be taken for granted. The confederation was not finally ratified, so as to become a binding instrument on any of the states, until March, 1781. Until that period there could be no practice or construction under it; and it is not shown, that subsequently there was any exposition to the effect now insisted on. Indeed, after the peace of 1783, if there had been any such exposition, and it had been unfavourable to the broad exercise of the power, it would have been entitled to less weight, than usually belongs to the proceedings of public bodies in the administration of their powers; since the decline and fall of the confederation was so obvious, that it was of little use to exert them. The states notoriously disregarded the rights and prerogatives admitted to belong to the confederacy; and even the requisitions of congress, for objects most unquestionably within their constitutional authority, were openly denied, or silently evaded. Under such circumstances, congress would have little inclination to look closely to their powers; since, whether great or small, large or narrow, they were of little practical value, and of no practical cogency.

§ 913. But it does so happen, that in point of fact, no such unfavourable or restrictive interpretation or practice was ever adopted by the continental congress. On the contrary, they construed their power on the subject of requisitions and taxation, exactly as it is now contended for, as a power to make requisitions on the states for all expenses, which they might deem proper to incur for the common defence and general welfare; and to appropriate all monies in the treasury to the like purposes. This is admitted to be of such notoriety, as to require no proof. Surely, the practice of that body in questions of this nature must be of far higher value, than the mere private interpretation of any persons in the present times, however respectable. But the practice was conformable to the constitutional authority of congress under the confederation. The ninth article expressly delegates to congress the power "to ascertain the necessary sums to be raised for the service of the United States, and to appropriate and apply the same for defraying the public expenses;" and then provides, that congress shall not "ascertain the sums and expenses necessary for the defence and welfare of the United States, or any of them, &c. unless nine states assent to the same." So that here we have, in the eighth article, a declaration, that "all charges of war and all other expenses, that shall be incurred for the common defence or general welfare, &c. shall be defrayed out of a common treasury;" and in the ninth article, an express power to ascertain the necessary sums of money to be raised for the public service; and then, that the necessary sums for the defence and welfare of the United States, (and not of the United States alone, for the words are added,) or of any of them, shall be ascertained by the assent of nine states. Clearly therefore, upon the plain language of the articles, the words "common defence and general welfare," in one, and "defence and welfare," in another, and "public service," in another, were not idle words, but were descriptive of the very intent and objects of the power; and not confined even to the defence and welfare of all the states, but extending to the welfare and defence of any of them. The power then is, in this view, even larger, than that conferred by the constitution.

§ 914. But there is no ground whatsoever, which authorizes any resort to the confederation, to interpret the power of taxation, which is conferred on congress by the constitution. The clause has no reference whatsoever to the confederation; nor indeed to any other clause of the constitution. It is, on its face, a distinct, substantive, and independent power. Who, then, is at liberty to say, that it is to be limited by other clauses, rather than they to be enlarged by it; since there is no avowed connexion, or reference from the one to the others? Interpretation would here desert its proper office, that, which requires, that "every part of the expression ought, if possible, to be allowed some meaning, and be made to conspire to some common end."

§ 915. It has been farther said [in Madison's 1800 Report], in support of the construction now under consideration, that "whether the phrases in question are construed to authorize every measure relating to the common defence and general welfare, as contended by some; or every measure only, in which there might be an application of money, as suggested by the caution of others; the effect must substantially be the same, in destroying the import and force of the particular enumeration of powers, which follow these general phrases in the constitution. For it is evident, that there is not a single power whatsoever, which may not have some reference to the common defence, or the general welfare; nor a power of any magnitude, which, in its exercise, does not involve, or admit an application of money. The government, therefore, which possesses power in either one, or the other of these extents, is a government without limitations, formed by a particular enumeration of powers; and consequently the meaning and effect of this particular enumeration is destroyed by the exposition given to these general phrases." The conclusion deduced from these premises is, that under the confederation, and the constitution, "congress is authorized to provide money for the common defence and general welfare. In both is subjoined to this authority an enumeration of the cases, to which their powers shall extend. Money cannot be applied to the general welfare otherwise, than by an application of it to some particular measure, conducive to the general welfare. Whenever, therefore, money has been raised by the general authority, and is to be applied to a particular measure, a question arises, whether the particular measure be within the enumerated authorities vested in the congress. If it be, the money requisite for it may be applied to it; if it be not, no such application can be made. This fair and obvious interpretation coincides with, and is enforced by the clause in the constitution, which declares, that no money shall be drawn from the treasury but in consequence of appropriations by law. An appropriation of money to the general welfare would be deemed rather a mockery, than an observance of this constitutional injunction."

§ 916. Stripped of the ingenious texture, by which this argument is disguised, it is neither more nor less, than an attempt to obliterate from the constitution the whole clause, "to pay the debts, and provide for the common defence and general welfare of the United States," as entirely senseless, or inexpressive of any intention whatsoever. Strike them out, and the constitution is exactly what the argument contends for. It is, therefore, an argument, that the words ought not to be in the constitution; because if they are, and have any meaning, they enlarge it beyond the scope of certain other enumerated powers, and this is both mischievous and dangerous. Being in the constitution, they are to be deemed, voxetpreterea nihil, an empty sound and vain phraseology, a finger-board pointing to other powers, but having no use whatsoever, since these powers are sufficiently apparent without. Now, it is not too much to say, that in a constitution of government, framed and adopted by the people, it is a most unjustifiable latitude of interpretation to deny effect to any clause, if it is sensible in the language, in which it is expressed, and in the place, in which it stands. If words are inserted, we are bound to presume, that they have some definite object, and intent; and to reason them out of the constitution upon arguments ab inconvenienti, (which to one mind may appear wholly unfounded, and to another wholly satisfactory,) is to make a new constitution, not to construe the old one. It is to do the very thing, which is so often complained of, to make a constitution to suit our own notions and wishes, and not to administer, or construe that, which the people have given to the country.

§ 917. But what is the argument, when it is thoroughly sifted? It reasons upon a supposed dilemma, upon which it suspends the advocates of the two contrasted opinions. If the power to provide for the common defence and general welfare is an independent power, then it is said, that the government is unlimited, and the subsequent enumeration of powers is unnecessary and useless. If it is a mere appendage or qualification of the power to lay taxes, still it involves a power of general appropriation of the monies so raised, which indirectly produces the same result. Now, the former position may be safely admitted to be true by those, who do not deem it an independent power; but the latter position is not a just conclusion from the premises, which it states, that it is a qualified power. It is not a logical, or a practical sequence from the premises; it is a non sequitur.

§ 918. A dilemma, of a very different sort, might be fairly put to those, who contend for the doctrine, that the words are not a qualification of the power to lay taxes, and, indeed, have no meaning, or use per se. The words are found in the clause respecting taxation, and as a part of that clause. If the power to tax extends simply to the payment of the debts of the United States, then congress has no power to lay any taxes for any other purpose. If so, then congress could not appropriate the money raised to any other purposes; since the restriction is to taxes for payment of the debts of the United States, that is, of the debts then existing. This would be almost absurd. If, on the other hand, congress have a right to lay taxes, and appropriate the money to any other objects, it must be, because the words, "to provide for the common defence and general welfare," authorize it, by enlarging the power to those objects; for there are no other words, which belong to the clause. All the other powers are in distinct clauses, and do not touch taxation. No advocate for the doctrine of a restrictive power will contend, that the power to lay taxes to pay debts, authorizes the payment of all debts, which the United States may choose to incur, whether for national or constitutional objects, or not. The words, "to pay debts," are therefore, either antecedent debts, or debts to be incurred "for the common defence and general welfare," which will justify congress in incurring any debts for such purposes. But the language is not confined to the payment of debts for the common defence and general welfare. It is not "to pay the debts" merely; but "to provide for the common defence and general welfare." That is, congress may lay taxes to provide means for the common defence and general welfare. So that there is a difficulty in rejecting one part of the qualifying clause, without rejecting the whole, or enlarging the words for some purposes, and restricting them for others.

§ 919. A power to lay taxes for any purposes whatsoever is a general power; a power to lay taxes for certain specified purposes is a limited power. A power to lay taxes for the common defence and general welfare of the United States is not in common sense a general power. It is limited to those objects. It cannot constitutionally transcend them. If the defence proposed by a tax be not the common defence of the United States, if the welfare be not general, but special, or local, as contradistinguished from national, it is not within the scope of the constitution. If the tax be not proposed for the common defence, or general welfare, but for other objects, wholly extraneous, (as for instance, for propagating Mahometanism among the Turks, or giving aids and subsidies to a foreign nation, to build palaces for its kings, or erect monuments to its heroes,) it would be wholly indefensible upon constitutional principles. The power, then, is, under such circumstances, necessarily a qualified power. If it is so, how then does it affect, or in the slightest degree trench upon the other enumerated powers? No one will pretend, that the power to lay taxes would, in general, have superseded, or rendered unnecessary all the other enumerated powers. It would neither enlarge, nor qualify them. A power to tax does not include them. Nor would they, (as unhappily the confederation too clearly demonstrated,) necessarily include a power to tax. Each has its appropriate office and objects; each may exist without necessarily interfering with, or annihilating the other. No one will pretend, that the power to lay a tax necessarily includes the power to declare war, to pass naturalization and bankrupt laws, to coin money, to establish post-offices, or to define piracies and felonies on the high seas. Nor would either of these be deemed necessarily to include the power to tax. It might be convenient; but it would not be absolutely indispensable.

§ 920. The whole of the elaborate reasoning upon the propriety of granting the power of taxation, pressed with so much ability and earnestness, both in and out of the convention, as vital to the operations of the national government, would have been useless, and almost absurd, if the power was included in the subsequently enumerated powers. If the power of taxing was to be granted, why should it not be qualified according to the intention of the framers of the constitution? But then, it is said, if congress may lay taxes for the common defence and general welfare, the money may be appropriated for those purposes, although not within the scope of the other enumerated powers. Certainly it may be so appropriated; for if congress is authorized to lay taxes for such purposes, it would be strange, if, when raised, the money could not be applied to them. That would be to give a power for a certain end, and then deny the end intended by the power. It is added, "that there is not a single power whatsoever, which may not have some reference to the common defence or general welfare; nor a power of any magnitude, which, in its exercise, does not involve, or admit an application of money." If by the former language is meant, that there is not any power belonging, or incident to any government, which has not some reference to the common defence or general welfare, the proposition may be peremptorily denied. Many governments possess powers, which have no application to either of these objects in a just sense; and some possess powers repugnant to both. If it is meant, that there is no power belonging, or incident to a good government, and especially to a republican government, which may not have some reference to those objects, that proposition may, or may not be true; but it has nothing to do with the present inquiry. The only question is, whether a mere power to lay taxes, and appropriate money for the common defence and general welfare, does include all the other powers of government; or even does include the other enumerated powers (limited as they are) of the national government. No person can answer in the affirmative to either part of the inquiry, who has fully considered the subject. The power of taxation is but one of a multitude of powers belonging to governments; to the state governments, as well as the national government. Would a power to tax authorize a state government to regulate the descent and distribution of estates; to prescribe the form of conveyances; to establish courts of justice for general purposes; to legislate respecting personal rights, or the general dominion of property; or to punish all offences against society? Would it confide to congress the power to grant patent rights for intervention; to provide for counterfeiting the public securities and coin; to constitute judicial tribunals with the powers confided by the third article of the constitution; to declare war, and raise armies and navies, and make regulations for their government; to exercise exclusive legislation in the territories of the United States, or in other ceded places; or to make all laws necessary and proper to carry into effect all the powers given by the constitution? The constitution itself upon its face refutes any such notion. It gives the power to tax, as a substantive power; and gives others, as equally substantive and independent.

§ 921. That the same means may sometimes, or often, be resorted to, to carry into effect the different powers, furnishes no objection; for that is common to all governments. That an appropriation of money may be the usual, or best mode of carrying into effect some of these powers, furnishes no objection; for it is one of the purposes, for which, the argument itself admits, that the power of taxation is given. That it is indispensable for the due exercise of all the powers, may admit of some doubt. The only real question is, whether even admitting the power to lay taxes is appropriate for some of the purposes of other enumerated powers, (for no one will contend, that it will, of itself, reach, or provide for them all,) it is limited to such appropriations, as grow out of the exercise of those powers. In other words, whether it is an incident to those powers, or a substantive power in other cases, which may concern the common defence and the general welfare. If there are no other cases, which concern the common defence and general welfare, except those within the scope of the other enumerated powers, the discussion is merely nominal and frivolous. If there are such cases, who is at liberty to say, that, being for the common defence and general welfare, the constitution did not intend to embrace them? The preamble of the constitution declares one of the objects to be, to provide for the common defence, and to promote the general welfare; and if the power to lay taxes is in express terms given to provide for the common defence and general welfare, what ground can there be to construe the power, short of the object? To say, that it shall be merely auxiliary to other enumerated powers, and not coextensive with its own terms, and its avowed objects? One of the best established rules of interpretation, one, which common sense and reason forbid us to overlook, is, that when the object of a power is clearly defined by its terms, or avowed in the context, it ought to be construed, so as to obtain the object, and not to defeat it. The circumstance, that so construed the power may be abused, is no answer. All powers may be abused; but are they then to be abridged by those, who are to administer them, or denied to have any operation? If the people frame a constitution, the rulers are to obey it. Neither rulers, nor any other functionaries, much less any private persons, have a right to cripple it, because it is according to their own views inconvenient, or dangerous, unwise or impolitic, of narrow limits, or of wide influence.

§ 922. Besides; the argument itself admits, that "congress is authorized to provide money for the common defence and general welfare." It is not pretended, that, when the tax is laid, the specific objects, for which it is laid, are to be specified, or that it is to be solely applied to those objects. That would be to insert a limitation, no where stated in the text. But it is said, that it must be applied to the general welfare; and that can only be by an application of it to some particular measure, conducive to the general welfare. This is admitted. But then, it is added, that this particular measure must be within the enumerated authorities vested in congress, (that is, within some of the powers not embraced in the first clause,) otherwise the application is not authorized. Why not, since it is for the general welfare? No reason is assigned, except, that not being within the scope of those enumerated powers, it is not given by the constitution. Now, the premises may be true; but the conclusion does not follow, unless the words common defence and general welfare are limited to the specifications included in those powers. So, that after all, we are led back to the same reasoning, which construes the words, as having no meaning per se, but as dependent upon, and an exponent of, the enumerated powers. Now, this conclusion is not justified by the natural connexion or collocation of the words; and it strips them of all reasonable force and efficacy. And yet we are told, that "this fair and obvious interpretation coincides with, and is enforced by, the clause of the constitution, which provides, that no money shall be drawn from the treasury, but in consequence of appropriations by law;" as if the clause did not equally apply, as a restraint upon drawing money, whichever construction is adopted. Suppose congress to possess the most unlimited power to appropriate money for the general welfare; would it not be still true, that it could not be drawn from the treasury, until an appropriation was made by some law passed by congress? This last clause is a limitation, not upon the powers of congress, but upon the acts of the executive, and other public officers, in regard to the public monies in the treasury.

§ 923. The argument in favour of the construction, which treats the clause, as a qualification of the power to lay taxes, has, perhaps, never been presented in a more concise or forcible shape, than in an official opinion, deliberately given by one of our most distinguished statesmen [Jefferson]. "To lay taxes to provide for the general welfare of the United States, is," says he, "to lay taxes for the purpose, of providing for the general welfare. For the laying of taxes is the power, and the general welfare the purpose, for which the power is to be exercised. Congress are not to lay taxes ad libitum, for any purpose they please; but only to pay the debts, or provide for the welfare of the Union. In like manner they are not to do any thing they please, to provide for the general welfare; but only to lay taxes for that purpose. To consider the latter phrase, not as describing the purpose of the first, but as giving a distinct and independent power to do any act they please, which might be for the good of the Union, would render all the preceding and subsequent enumerations of power completely useless. It would reduce the whole instrument to a single phrase, that of instituting a congress with power to do whatever would be for the good of the United States; and, as they would be the sole judges of the good or evil, it would also be a power to do whatever evil they pleased. It is an established rule of construction, where a phrase will bear either of two meanings, to give that, which will allow some meaning to the other parts of the instrument, and not that, which will render all the others useless. Certainly, no such universal power was meant to be given them. It was intended to lace them up strictly within the enumerated powers, and those, without which, as means, those powers could not be carried into effect."

§ 924. The same opinion has been maintained at different and distant times by many eminent statesmen. It was avowed, and apparently acquiesed in, in the state conventions, called to ratify the constitution: and it has been, on various occasions, adopted by congress, and may fairly be deemed, that which the deliberate sense of a majority of the nation has at all times supported. This, too, seems to be the construction maintained by the Supreme Court of the United States. In the case of Gibbons v. Ogden, Mr. Chief Justice Marshall, in delivering the opinion of the court, said, "Congress is authorized to lay and collect taxes, &c. to pay the debts, and provide for the common defence and general welfare of the United States. This does not interefere with the power of the states to tax for the support of their own governments; nor is the exercise of that power by the states an exercise of any portion of the power, that is granted to the United States. In imposing taxes for state purposes, they are not doing, what congress is empowered to do. Congress is not empowered to tax for those purposes, which are within the exclusive province of the states. When, then, each government is exercising the power of taxation, neither is exercising the power of the other." Under such circumstances, it is not, perhaps, too much to contend, that it is the truest, the safest, and the most authoritative construction of the constitution.

§ 925. The view thus taken of this clause of the constitution will receive some confirmation, (if it should be thought by any person necessary,) by an historical examination of the proceedings of the convention.

QUESTIONS

1. According to James Madison, Thomas Jefferson, and Justice Story how should the necessary and proper clause and the general welfare clause be construed?

2. In Justice Story's letter to his wife, what does the attitude he anticipates from the state of Georgia in response to the Supreme Court's decision of Worcester v Georgia evidence? What does is the attitude he anticipates from President Andrew Jackson evidence?

3. Which doctrine is evidenced by the Obama Administration's refusal to enforce the DOMA laws passed by Congress?

4. According to Madison's, Jefferson's, and/or Story's view of our Constitution, which, if any, of the eighteen enumerated powers within the Constitution would provide grounds for the DOE's development of Common Core State Standards for schools to teach English Language Arts and Math?

Chapter 8
THE DECLARATION, CONSTITUTION, AND BILL OF RIGHTS

Original Sources:
1. Federalist Paper No. 2
2. Madison's Memorial and Remonstrance (see page 62)
3. Rehnquist's Dissent in Wallace v Jaffree

Our Declaration of Independence and the U.S. Constitution with its Bill of Rights all work together. The Declaration of Independence is the document that created us as one nation. The U.S. Constitution was enacted as the **bylaws** by which our nation, created by the Declaration, was to be governed. The Bill of Rights were provided as an affirmation to the American people that their ratification of the Constitution would not deprive them of certain rights that were to be beyond the reach of the general government. All three of these documents must operate fully at the same time. The Constitution should never be read in such a way that would do violence to the Declaration of Independence, neither should it ever be read in such a way as to tread upon the rights of the people preserved within its Bill of Rights.

© Todd Taulman/Shutterstock.com

One may think there is no need to defend our Declaration of Independence. Most assume that the significance of this document is beyond question. While its significance should indeed be beyond question, there is a very real and active effort to make the Declaration nothing more than a historic, yet old-fashioned and outdated, piece of paper.

The Declaration both formed one nation, as well as established the foundation for our laws and government. Historical documentation of this fact exposes the incorrect arguments that the Declaration did nothing substantively and that we were not founded as one nation until 1787 with the ratification of the Constitution. The truth that we were indeed founded as one nation and one people by and through our Declaration of Independence is not only factually defensible, it is necessary knowledge to the preservation of our Republic as our Founders intended.

At the time of the Declaration's drafting, the significance of this document was known to be profound. Its effectiveness in establishing one nation and one people had not been forgotten by the time of the Constitutional convention. The very basis for calling a Constitutional convention was to discern and implement the most effective means of preserving the union that had already been established. This historical reality lies in stark contrast to the modern-day argument that the Constitution served to create us as a nation for the first time.

Founders at Independence Hall © JohnKwan/Shutterstock.com

The authors of the Federalist papers diligently undertook the task of deliberating upon the impact of, and justifying the need for, a new constitution. It was clear to them that the preservation of the union, not the creation of one, was the forceful impetus behind such an effort. "The utility of the UNION . . . [and] the insufficiency of the present confederation to preserve that union . . ."[1] were the subject matter of Alexander Hamilton's intended writings. It is irrational to speak of preserving a union if in fact such a union had not already been established. His fear of the "dismemberment of the union"[2] and the dangers that would result to the states "from its dissolution"[3] is the very basis for his asserting the need for a stronger federal form of governance through the ratification of the Constitution.

John Jay criticized the argument of moving forward by dividing the nation into separate states as opposed to the wisdom of remaining one people:

> "It has until lately been a received and uncontradicted opinion that the prosperity of the people of America depended on their continuing firmly united, and the wishes, prayers, and efforts of our best and wisest citizens have been constantly directed to that object. But politicians now appear, who insist that this opinion is erroneous, and that instead of looking for safety and happiness in union, we ought to seek it in a division of the States into distinct confederacies or sovereignties. However extraordinary this new doctrine may appear, it nevertheless has its advocates; and certain characters who were much opposed to it formerly, are at present of the number. Whatever may be the arguments or inducements which have wrought this change in the sentiments and declarations of these gentlemen, it certainly would not be wise in the people at large to adopt these new political tenets. . . ."[4]

His unwavering support was for "continuing firmly united."[5] Again it would be entirely illogical for him to speak of the continuation of a nation had one not yet been formed. Unquestionably, both Hamilton and Jay were of the opinion that at the time of the Constitutional Convention we had already been firmly established as one union. In fact, the very thought of dissolving our union into separate confederacies was criticized by Jay as an "extraordinary new doctrine;"[6] such a new doctrine could in no way be a clear presentation of the current state of affairs.

Jay further documented evidence of the reality that we already existed as a Nation prior to the time of our Constitutional convention:

> "To all general purposes we have uniformly been one people each individual citizen everywhere enjoying the same national rights, privileges, and protection. As a nation we have made peace and war; as a nation we have vanquished our common enemies; as a nation we have formed alliances, and made treaties, and entered into various compacts and conventions with foreign states."[7]

He continued to paint a picture with descriptive clarity of the timing relevant to our formal founding as one Nation:

> "A strong sense of the value and blessings of union induced the people, at a very early period, to institute a federal government to preserve and perpetuate it. They were in flames, when many of their citizens were bleeding. . . ."[8]

The remainder of his discussion rationalized why, at such a time of intense hostility, the question of how to form the most effective means of governing one unified people must be the focus. That after some time for reflection and experiment, the defects of the Articles of Confederation had exposed the need for a stronger government capable of preserving the union that the people had grown to appreciate. The goal, therefore, of the Constitutional Convention of 1787 was to preserve the union already established which the people embraced to the same degree as liberty and were persuaded that the latter would be endangered by the dissolution of the former.[9]

In short, to embrace the belief that the Declaration was of no effect, that it was replaced and made

---

1 Hamilton, Alexander; Jay, John; Madison, James (2011-03-24). The Federalist Papers, No. 1 By Alexander Hamilton (p. 10). Kindle Edition.
2 Id.
3 Id.
4 Hamilton, Alexander; Jay, John; Madison, James (2011-03-24). The Federalist Papers, No. 2 By John Jay (p. 11). Kindle Edition.
5 Id.
6 Id.
7 Id., at 12.
8 Hamilton, Alexander; Jay, John; Madison, James (2011-03-24). The Federalist Papers, No. 2 By John Jay (p. 12). Kindle Edition.
9 Id.

obsolete by the Constitution, that the Constitution was instead the document that first created us as a nation, is to completely rewrite American history. The entire purpose of the Constitutional Convention was finding the best way for the continuation of the Union. It was widely recognized, as asserted by Jay, "... that the prosperity of America depended on its Union. To preserve and perpetuate it was the great object of the people in forming that convention...."[10]

The Declaration had already effectively established us as one unified nation and declared our formal identity to the world as the United States of America. The convention was held in 1787, inclusively the twelfth year of our existence as a nation as created by the Declaration. With this in mind, it makes complete sense that when the members of the convention set their signatures to the proposed Constitution they did so with the following punctuation, "Done in Convention by the Unanimous Consent of the States present the Seventeenth Day of September in the Year of our Lord one thousand seven hundred and eighty seven and of the Independence of the United States of America the Twelfth."[11] By this simple act of referencing our Declaration of Independence, the signers of our Constitution not only acknowledged its importance, they assured its unending existence through the four corners of this new document.

The ratification of the Bill of Rights was a way of satisfying the uneasiness of the American people that this new form of Constitutional governance would not violate their most precious rights and liberties. These rights were inherently possessed by the American people, granted to them by their Creator, and they desired to guarantee that this general government would not intrude upon those rights by taking them into its jurisdiction and control. This belief that all people were possessed with certain rights and duties that preexisted the creation of any civil government was clearly expressed by the founding fathers. The right to worship God according to the dictates of one's conscience, for example, was viewed as being completely outside of the government's grasp.

> *The Religion then of every man must be left to the conviction and conscience of every man; and it is the right of every man to exercise it as these may dictate.... It is the duty of every man to render to the Creator such homage and such only as he believes to be acceptable to him. This duty is precedent, both in order of time and in degree of obligation, to the claims of Civil Society. We maintain therefore that in matters of Religion, no mans right is abridged by the institution of Civil Society and that Religion is wholly exempt from its cognizance.*[12]

There were those, such as Hamilton, who argued that such a Bill of Rights was unnecessary, since the government was only a government of eighteen specifically enumerated powers and had absolutely no authority to abridge such rights. However, in the end, although arguably unnecessary, the Bill of Rights was added as an express statement of protection. The government was not seen as granting these rights, but merely as acknowledging them and expressing the continual protection of such rights. The Bill of Rights is a statement of rights that the people possess; rights over which the government is not to intrude. This should be kept in mind when reading the Bill of Rights. Such a view is helpful in understanding what the main concerns were of the Founding Fathers in drafting the first 10 Amendments. For example, the religious liberty preserved in the First Amendment is the Free Exercise Clause, which maintains the unalienable right of conscience. The No Establishment Clause would make no sense as an unalienable right itself; therefore, one can clearly see that the function of the No Establishment Clause is to further underscore and protect the Free Exercise Clause.

These unalienable rights were so clearly understood by the Founding Fathers as to require little to no clarification. One of the clearest and most thorough discussions of the history and congressional debates surrounding the Bill of Rights would not be penned until almost 200 years later in a dissenting opinion in the Supreme Court case of Wallace v Jaffree.

© Cheryl Casey/Shutterstock.

---

10 Id., at 13.
11 Article VII of the U.S. Constitution.
12 Madison's Memorial and Remonstrance.

Federalist Papers: No. 2

Concerning Dangers from Foreign Force and Influence

John Jay

To the People of the State of New York:

WHEN the people of America reflect that they are now called upon to decide a question, which, in its consequences, must prove one of the most important that ever engaged their attention, the propriety of their taking a very comprehensive, as well as a very serious, view of it, will be evident.

Nothing is more certain than the indispensable necessity of government, and it is equally undeniable, that whenever and however it is instituted, the people must cede to it some of their natural rights in order to vest it with requisite powers. It is well worthy of consideration therefore, whether it would conduce more to the interest of the people of America that they should, to all general purposes, be one nation, under one federal government, or that they should divide themselves into separate confederacies, and give to the head of each the same kind of powers which they are advised to place in one national government.

It has until lately been a received and uncontradicted opinion that the prosperity of the people of America depended on their continuing firmly united, and the wishes, prayers, and efforts of our best and wisest citizens have been constantly directed to that object. But politicians now appear, who insist that this opinion is erroneous, and that instead of looking for safety and happiness in union, we ought to seek it in a division of the States into distinct confederacies or sovereignties. However extraordinary this new doctrine may appear, it nevertheless has its advocates; and certain characters who were much opposed to it formerly, are at present of the number. Whatever may be the arguments or inducements which have wrought this change in the sentiments and declarations of these gentlemen, it certainly would not be wise in the people at large to adopt these new political tenets without being fully convinced that they are founded in truth and sound policy.

It has often given me pleasure to observe that independent America was not composed of detached and distant territories, but that one connected, fertile, widespreading country was the portion of our western sons of liberty. Providence has in a particular manner blessed it with a variety of soils and productions, and watered it with innumerable streams, for the delight and accommodation of its inhabitants. A succession of navigable waters forms a kind of chain round its borders, as if to bind it together; while the most noble rivers in the world, running at convenient distances, present them with highways for the easy communication of friendly aids, and the mutual transportation and exchange of their various commodities.

With equal pleasure I have as often taken notice that Providence has been pleased to give this one connected country to one united people—a people descended from the same ancestors, speaking the same language, professing the same religion, attached to the same principles of government, very similar in their manners and customs, and who, by their joint counsels, arms, and efforts, fighting side by side throughout a long and bloody war, have nobly established general liberty and independence.

This country and this people seem to have been made for each other, and it appears as if it was the design of Providence, that an inheritance so proper and convenient for a band of brethren, united to each other by the strongest ties, should never be split into a number of unsocial, jealous, and alien sovereignties.

Similar sentiments have hitherto prevailed among all orders and denominations of men among us. To all general purposes we have uniformly been one people each individual citizen everywhere enjoying the same national rights, privileges, and protection. As a nation we have made peace and war; as a nation we have vanquished our common enemies; as a nation we have formed alliances, and made treaties, and entered into various compacts and conventions with foreign states.

A strong sense of the value and blessings of union induced the people, at a very early period, to institute a federal government to preserve and perpetuate it. They formed it almost as soon as they had a political existence; nay, at a time when their habitations were in flames, when many of their citizens were bleeding, and when the progress of hostility and desolation left little room for those calm and mature inquiries and reflections which must ever precede the formation of a wise and wellbalanced government for a free people. It is not to be wondered at, that a government instituted in times so inauspicious, should on experiment be found greatly deficient and inadequate to the purpose it was intended to answer.

This intelligent people perceived and regretted these defects. Still continuing no less attached to union than enamored of liberty, they observed the danger which immediately threatened the former and more remotely the latter; and being pursuaded that ample security for both could only be found in a national government more wisely framed, they as with one voice, convened the late convention at Philadelphia, to take that important subject under consideration.

This convention composed of men who possessed the confidence of the people, and many of whom had become highly distinguished by their patriotism, virtue and wisdom, in times which tried the minds and hearts of men, undertook the arduous task. In the mild season of peace, with minds unoccupied by other subjects, they passed many months in cool, uninterrupted, and daily consultation; and finally, without having been awed by power, or influenced by any passions except love for their country, they presented and recommended to the people the plan produced by their joint and very unanimous councils.

Admit, for so is the fact, that this plan is only RECOMMENDED, not imposed, yet let it be remembered that it is neither recommended to BLIND approbation, nor to BLIND reprobation; but to that sedate and candid consideration which the magnitude and importance of the subject demand, and which it certainly ought to receive. But this (as was remarked in the foregoing number of this paper) is more to be wished than expected, that it may be so considered and examined. Experience on a former occasion teaches us not to be too sanguine in such hopes. It is not yet forgotten that well-grounded apprehensions of imminent danger induced the people of America to form the memorable Congress of 1774. That body recommended certain measures to their constituents, and the event proved their wisdom; yet it is fresh in our memories how soon the press began to teem with pamphlets and weekly papers against those very measures. Not only many of the officers of government, who obeyed the dictates of personal interest, but others, from a mistaken estimate of consequences, or the undue influence of former attachments, or whose ambition aimed at objects which did not correspond with the public good, were indefatigable in their efforts to pursuade the people to reject the advice of that patriotic Congress. Many, indeed, were deceived and deluded, but the great majority of the people reasoned and decided judiciously; and happy they are in reflecting that they did so.

They considered that the Congress was composed of many wise and experienced men. That, being convened from different parts of the country, they brought with them and communicated to each other a variety of useful information. That, in the course of the time they passed together in inquiring into and discussing the true interests of their country, they must have acquired very accurate knowledge on that head. That they were individually interested in the public liberty and prosperity, and therefore that it was not less their inclination than their duty to recommend only such measures as, after the most mature deliberation, they really thought prudent and advisable.

These and similar considerations then induced the people to rely greatly on the judgment and integrity of the Congress; and they took their advice, notwithstanding the various arts and endeavors used to deter them from it. But if the people at large had reason to confide in the men of that Congress, few of whom had been fully tried or generally known, still greater reason have they now to respect the judgment and advice of the convention, for it is well known that some of the most distinguished members of that Congress, who have been since tried and justly approved for patriotism and abilities, and who have grown old in acquiring political information, were also members of this convention, and carried into it their accumulated knowledge and experience.

It is worthy of remark that not only the first, but every succeeding Congress, as well as the late convention, have invariably joined with the people in thinking that the prosperity of America depended on its Union. To preserve and perpetuate it was the great object of the people in forming that convention, and it is also the great object of the plan which the convention has advised them to adopt. With what propriety, therefore, or for what good purposes, are attempts at this particular period made by some men to depreciate the importance of the Union? Or why is it suggested that three or four confederacies would be better than one? I am persuaded in my own mind that the people have always thought right on this subject, and that their universal and uniform attachment to the cause of the Union rests on great and weighty reasons, which I shall endeavor to develop and explain in some ensuing papers. They who promote the idea of substituting a number of distinct confederacies in the room of the plan of the convention, seem clearly to foresee that the rejection of it would put the continuance of the Union in the utmost jeopardy. That certainly would be the case, and I sincerely wish that it may be as clearly foreseen by every good citizen, that whenever the dissolution of the Union arrives, America will have reason to exclaim, in the words of the poet: "FAREWELL! A LONG FAREWELL TO ALL MY GREATNESS."

PUBLIUS.

Wallace V. Jaffree
United States Supreme Court
Justice Rehnquist's Dissent
472 U.S. 38, 105 S.Ct. 2479
Argued Dec. 4, 1984.
Decided June 4, 1985

Thirty-eight years ago this Court, in Everson v. Board of Education, 330 U.S. 1, 16, 67 S.Ct. 504, 512, 91 L.Ed. 711 (1947), summarized its exegesis of Establishment Clause doctrine thus:

"In the words of Jefferson, the clause against establishment of religion by law was intended to erect 'a wall of separation between church and State.' Reynolds v. United States, [98 U.S. 145, 164, 25 L.Ed. 244 (1879)]."

This language from Reynolds, a case involving the Free Exercise Clause of the First Amendment rather than the Establishment Clause, quoted from Thomas Jefferson's letter to the Danbury Baptist Association the phrase "I contemplate with sovereign reverence that act of the whole American people which declared that their legislature should 'make no law respecting an establishment of religion, or prohibiting the free exercise thereof,' thus building a wall of separation between church and State." 8 Writings of Thomas Jefferson 113 (H. Washington ed. 1861).(1)

It is impossible to build sound constitutional doctrine upon a mistaken understanding of constitutional history, but unfortunately the Establishment Clause has been expressly freighted with Jefferson's misleading metaphor for nearly 40 years. Thomas Jefferson was of course in France at the time the constitutional Amendments known as the Bill of Rights were passed by Congress and ratified by the States. His letter to the Danbury Baptist Association was a short note of courtesy, written 14 years after the Amendments were passed by Congress. He would seem to any detached observer as a less than ideal source of contemporary history as to the meaning of the Religion Clauses of the First Amendment.

Jefferson's fellow Virginian, James Madison, with whom he was joined in the battle for the enactment of the Virginia Statute of Religious Liberty of 1786, did play as large a part as anyone in the drafting of the Bill of Rights. He had two advantages over Jefferson in this regard: he was present in the United States, and he was a leading Member of the First Congress. But when we turn to the record of the proceedings in the First Congress leading up to the adoption of the Establishment Clause of the Constitution, including Madison's significant contributions thereto, we see a far different picture of its purpose than the highly simplified "wall of separation between church and State."

During the debates in the Thirteen Colonies over ratification of the Constitution, one of the arguments frequently used by opponents of ratification was that without a Bill of Rights guaranteeing individual liberty the new general Government carried with it a potential for tyranny. The typical response to this argument on the part of those who favored ratification was that the general Government established by the Constitution had only delegated powers, and that these delegated powers were so limited that the Government would have no occasion to violate individual liberties. This response satisfied some, but not others, and of the 11 Colonies which ratified the Constitution by early 1789, 5 proposed one or another amendments guaranteeing individual liberty. Three—New Hampshire, New York, and Virginia—included in one form or another a declaration of religious freedom. See 3 J. Elliot, Debates on the Federal Constitution 659 (1891); 1 id., at 328. Rhode Island and North Carolina flatly refused to ratify the Constitution in the absence of amendments in the nature of a Bill of Rights. 1 id., at 334; 4 id., at 244. Virginia and North Carolina proposed identical guarantees of religious freedom:

"[A]ll men have an equal, natural and unalienable right to the free exercise of religion, according to the dictates of conscience, and . . . no particular religious sect or society ought to be favored or established, by law, in preference to others." 3 id., at 659; 4 id., at 244.(2)

On June 8, 1789, James Madison rose in the House of Representatives and "reminded the House that this was the day that he had heretofore named for bringing forward amendments to the Constitution." 1 Annals of Cong. 424. Madison's subsequent remarks in urging the House to adopt his drafts of the proposed amendments were less those of a dedicated advocate of the wisdom of such measures than those of a prudent statesman seeking the enactment of measures sought by a number of his fellow citizens which could surely do no harm and might do a great deal of good. He said, inter alia:

"It appears to me that this House is bound by every motive of prudence, not to let the first session pass over without proposing to the State Legislatures, some things to be incorporated into the Constitution, that will render it as acceptable to the whole people of the United States, as it has been found acceptable to a majority of them. I wish, among other reasons why something should be done, that those who had been friendly to the adoption of this Constitution may have the opportunity of proving to those who were opposed to it that they were as sincerely devoted to liberty and a Republican Government, as those who charged them with wishing the adoption of this Constitution in order to lay the foundation of an aristocracy or despotism. It will be a desirable thing to extinguish from the bosom of every member of the community, any apprehensions that there are those among his countrymen who wish to deprive them of the liberty for which they valiantly fought and honorably bled. And if there are amendments desired of such a nature as will not injure the Constitution, and they can be ingrafted so as to give satisfaction to the doubting part of our fellow-citizens, the friends of the Federal Government will evince that spirit of deference and concession for which they have hitherto been distinguished." Id., at 431–432.

The language Madison proposed for what ultimately became the Religion Clauses of the First Amendment was this:

"The civil rights of none shall be abridged on account of religious belief or worship, nor shall any national religion be established, nor shall the full and equal rights of conscience be in any manner, or on any pretext, infringed." Id., at 434.

On the same day that Madison proposed them, the amendments which formed the basis for the Bill of Rights were referred by the House to a Committee of the Whole, and after several weeks' delay were then referred to a Select Committee consisting of Madison and 10 others. The Committee revised Madison's proposal regarding the establishment of religion to read:

"[N]o religion shall be established by law, nor shall the equal rights of conscience be infringed." Id., at 729.

The Committee's proposed revisions were debated in the House on August 15, 1789. The entire debate on the Religion Clauses is contained in two full columns of the "Annals," and does not seem particularly illuminating. See id., at 729–731. Representative Peter Sylvester of New York expressed his dislike for the revised version, because it might have a tendency "to abolish religion altogether." Representative John Vining suggested that the two parts of the sentence be transposed; Representative Elbridge Gerry thought the language should be changed to read "that no religious doctrine shall be established by law." Id., at 729. Roger Sherman of Connecticut had the traditional reason for opposing provisions of a Bill of Rights—that Congress had no delegated authority to "make religious establishments"—and therefore he opposed the adoption of the amendment. Representative Daniel Carroll of Maryland thought it desirable to adopt the words proposed, saying "[h]e would not contend with gentlemen about the phraseology, his object was to secure the substance in such a manner as to satisfy the wishes of the honest part of the community."

Madison then spoke, and said that "he apprehended the meaning of the words to be, that Congress should not establish a religion, and enforce the legal observation of it by law, nor compel men to worship God in any manner contrary to their conscience." Id., at 730. He said that some of the state conventions had thought that Congress might rely on the Necessary and Proper Clause to infringe the rights of conscience or to establish a national religion, and "to prevent these effects he presumed the amendment was intended, and he thought it as well expressed as the nature of the language would admit." Ibid.

Representative Benjamin Huntington then expressed the view that the Committee's language might "be taken in such latitude as to be extremely hurtful to the cause of religion. He understood the amendment to mean what had been expressed by the gentleman from Virginia; but others might find it convenient to put another construction upon it." Huntington, from Connecticut, was concerned that in the New England States, where state-established religions were the rule rather than the exception, the federal courts might not be able to entertain claims based upon an obligation under the bylaws of a religious organization to contribute to the support of a minister or the building of a place of worship. He hoped that "the amendment would be made in such a way as to secure the rights of conscience, and a free exercise of the rights of religion, but not to patronize those who professed no religion at all." Id., at 730–731.

Madison responded that the insertion of the word "national" before the word "religion" in the Committee version should satisfy the minds of those who had criticized the language. "He believed that the people feared one sect might obtain a pre-eminence, or two combine together, and establish a religion to which they would compel others to conform. He thought that if the word 'national' was introduced, it would point the amendment directly to the object it was intended to prevent." Id., at 731. Representative Samuel Livermore expressed himself as dissatisfied with Madison's proposed amendment, and thought it would be better if the Committee language were altered to read that "Congress shall make no laws touching religion, or infringing the rights of conscience." Ibid.

Representative Gerry spoke in opposition to the use of the word "national" because of strong feelings expressed during the ratification debates that a federal government, not a national government, was created by the Constitution. Madison thereby withdrew his proposal but insisted that his reference to a "national religion" only referred to a national establishment and did not mean that the Government was a national one. The question was taken on Representative Livermore's motion, which passed by a vote of 31 for and 20 against. Ibid.

The following week, without any apparent debate, the House voted to alter the language of the Religion Clauses to read "Congress shall make no law establishing religion, or to prevent the free exercise thereof, or to infringe the rights of conscience." Id., at 766. The floor debates in the Senate were secret, and therefore not reported in the Annals. The Senate on September 3, 1789, considered several different forms of the Religion Amendment, and reported this language back to the House:

"Congress shall make no law establishing articles of faith or a mode of worship, or prohibiting the free exercise of religion." C. Antieau, A. Downey, & E. Roberts, Freedom From Federal Establishment 130 (1964).

The House refused to accept the Senate's changes in the Bill of Rights and asked for a conference; the version which emerged from the conference was that which ultimately found its way into the Constitution as a part of the First Amendment.

"Congress shall make no law respecting an establishment of religion, or prohibiting the free exercise thereof."

The House and the Senate both accepted this language on successive days, and the Amendment was proposed in this form.

On the basis of the record of these proceedings in the House of Representatives, James Madison was undoubtedly the most important architect among the Members of the House of the Amendments which became the Bill of Rights, but it was James Madison speaking as an advocate of sensible legislative compromise, not as an advocate of incorporating the Virginia Statute of Religious Liberty into the United States Constitution. During the ratification debate in the Virginia Convention, Madison had actually opposed the idea of any Bill of Rights. His sponsorship of the Amendments in the House was obviously not that of a zealous believer in the necessity of the Religion Clauses, but of one who felt it might do some good, could do no harm, and would satisfy those who had ratified the Constitution on the condition that Congress propose a Bill of Rights.(3) His original language "nor shall any national religion be established" obviously does not conform to the "wall of separation" between church and State idea which latter-day commentators have ascribed to him. His explanation on the floor of the meaning of his language—"that Congress should not establish a religion, and enforce the legal observation of it by law" is of the same ilk. When he replied to Huntington in the debate over the proposal which came from the Select Committee of the House, he urged that the language "no religion shall be established by law" should be amended by inserting the word "national" in front of the word "religion."

It seems indisputable from these glimpses of Madison's thinking, as reflected by actions on the floor of the House in 1789, that he saw the Amendment as designed to prohibit the establishment of a national religion, and perhaps to prevent discrimination among sects. He did not see it as requiring neutrality on the part of government between religion and irreligion. Thus the Court's opinion in Everson—while correct in bracketing Madison and Jefferson together in their exertions in their home State leading to the enactment of the Virginia Statute of Religious Liberty—is totally incorrect in suggesting that Madison carried these views onto the floor of the United States House of Representatives when he proposed the language which would ultimately become the Bill of Rights.

The repetition of this error in the Court's opinion in Illinois ex rel. McCollum v. Board of Education, 333 U.S. 203, 68 S.Ct. 461, 92 L.Ed. 649 (1948), and, inter alia, Engel v. Vitale, 370 U.S. 421, 82 S.Ct. 1261, 8 L.Ed.2d 601 (1962), does not make it any sounder historically. Finally, in Abington School District v. Schempp, 374 U.S. 203, 214, 83 S.Ct. 1560, 1567, 10 L.Ed.2d 844 (1963), the Court made the truly remarkable statement that "the views of Madison and Jefferson, preceded by Roger Williams, came to be incorporated not only in the Federal Constitution but likewise in those of most of our States" (footnote omitted). On the basis of what evidence we have, this statement is demonstrably incorrect as a matter of history. (4) And its repetition in varying forms in succeeding opinions of the Court can give it no more authority than it possesses as a matter of fact; stare decisis may bind courts as to matters of law, but it cannot bind them as to matters of history.

None of the other Members of Congress who spoke during the August 15th debate expressed the slightest indication that they thought the language before them from the Select Committee, or the evil to be aimed at, would require that the Government be absolutely neutral as between religion and irreligion. The evil to be aimed at, so far as those who spoke who concerned, appears to have been the establishment of a national church, and perhaps the preference of one religious sect over another; but it was definitely not concerned about whether the Government might aid all religions evenhandedly. If one were to follow the advice of Justice BRENNAN, concurring in Abington School District v. Schempp, supra, at 236, 83 S.Ct., at 1578, 10 L.Ed.2d 844, and construe the Amendment in the light of what particular "practices . . . challenged threaten those consequences which the Framers deeply feared; whether, in short, they tend to promote that type of interdependence between religion and state which the First Amendment was designed to prevent," one would have to say that the First Amendment Establishment Clause should be read no more broadly than to prevent the establishment of a national religion or the governmental preference of one religious sect over another.

The actions of the First Congress, which reenacted the Northwest Ordinance for the governance of the Northwest Territory in 1789, confirm the view that Congress did not mean that the Government should be neutral between religion and irreligion. The House of Representatives took up the Northwest Ordinance on the same day as Madison introduced his proposed amendments which became the Bill of Rights; while at that time the Federal Government was of course not bound by draft amendments to the Constitution which had not yet been proposed by Congress, say nothing of ratified by the States, it seems highly unlikely that the House of Representatives would simultaneously consider proposed amendments to the Constitution and enact an important piece of territorial legislation which conflicted with the intent of those proposals. The Northwest Ordinance, 1 Stat. 50, reenacted the Northwest Ordinance of 1787 and provided that "[r]eligion, morality, and knowledge, being necessary to good government and the happiness of mankind, schools and the means of education shall forever be encouraged." Id., at 52, n. (a). Land grants for schools in the Northwest Territory were not limited to public schools. It was not until 1845 that Congress limited land grants in the new States and Territories to nonsectarian schools. 5 Stat. 788; C. Antieau, A. Downey, & E. Roberts, Freedom From Federal Establishment 163 (1964).

On the day after the House of Representatives voted to adopt the form of the First Amendment Religion Clauses which was ultimately proposed and ratified, Representative Elias Boudinot proposed a resolution asking President George Washington to issue a Thanksgiving Day Proclamation. Boudinot said he "could not think of letting the session pass over without offering an opportunity to all the citizens of the United States of joining with one voice, in returning to Almighty God their sincere thanks for the many blessings he had poured down upon them." 1 Annals of Cong. 914 (1789). Representative Aedanas Burke objected to the resolution because he did not like "this mimicking of European customs"; Representative Thomas Tucker objected that whether or not the people had reason to be satisfied with the Constitution was something that the States knew better than the Congress, and in any event "it is a religious matter, and, as such, is proscribed to us." Id., at 915. Representative Sherman supported the resolution "not only as a laudable one in itself, but as warranted by a number of precedents in Holy Writ: for instance, the solemn thanksgivings and rejoicings which took place in the time of Solomon, after the building of the temple, was a case in point. This example, he thought, worthy of Christian imitation on the present occasion. . . ." Ibid.

Boudinot's resolution was carried in the affirmative on September 25, 1789. Boudinot and Sherman, who favored the Thanksgiving Proclamation, voted in favor of the adoption of the proposed amendments to the Constitution, including the Religion Clauses; Tucker, who opposed the Thanksgiving Proclamation, voted against the adoption of the amendments which became the Bill of Rights.

Within two weeks of this action by the House, George Washington responded to the Joint Resolution which by now had been changed to include the language that the President "recommend to the people of the United States a day of public thanksgiving and prayer, to be observed by acknowledging with grateful hearts the many and signal favors of Almighty God, especially by affording them an opportunity peaceably to establish a form of government for their safety and happiness." 1 J. Richardson, Messages and Papers of the Presidents, 1789–1897, p. 64 (1897). The Presidential Proclamation was couched in these words:

"Now, therefore, I do recommend and assign Thursday, the 26th day of November next, to be devoted by the people of these States to the service of that great and glorious Being who is the beneficent author of all the good that was, that is, or that will be; that we may then all unite in rendering unto Him our sincere and humble thanks for His kind care and protection of the people of this country previous to their becoming a nation; for the signal and manifold mercies and the favorable interpositions of His providence in the course and conclusion of the late war; for the great degree of tranquillity, union, and plenty which we have since enjoyed; for the peaceable and rational manner in which we have been enabled to establish constitutions of government for our safety and happiness, and particularly the national one now lately instituted; for the civil and religious liberty with which we are blessed, and the means we have of acquiring and diffusing useful knowledge; and, in general, for all the great and various favors which He has been pleased to confer upon us.

"And also that we may then unite in most humbly offering our prayers and supplications to the great Lord and Ruler of Nations, and beseech Him to pardon our national and other transgressions; to enable us all, whether in public or private stations, to perform our several and relative duties properly and punctually; to render our National Government a blessing to all the people by constantly being a Government of wise, just, and constitutional laws, discreetly and faithfully executed and obeyed; to protect and guide all sovereigns and nations (especially such as have shown kindness to us), and to bless them with good governments, peace, and concord; to promote the knowledge and practice of true religion and virtue, and the increase of science among them and us; and, generally, to grant unto all mankind such a degree of temporal prosperity as He alone knows to be best." Ibid.

George Washington, John Adams, and James Madison all issued Thanksgiving Proclamations; Thomas Jefferson did not, saying:

"Fasting and prayer are religious exercises; the enjoining them an act of discipline. Every religious society has a right to determine for itself the times for these exercises, and the objects proper for them, according to their own particular tenets; and this right can never be safer than in their own hands, where the Constitution has deposited it." 11 Writings of Thomas Jefferson 429 (A. Lipscomb ed. 1904).

As the United States moved from the 18th into the 19th century, Congress appropriated time and again public moneys in support of sectarian Indian education carried on by religious organizations. Typical of these was Jefferson's treaty with the Kaskaskia Indians, which provided annual cash support for the Tribe's Roman Catholic priest and church. (5) It was not until 1897, when aid to sectarian education for Indians had reached $500,000 annually, that Congress decided thereafter to cease appropriating money for education in sectarian schools. See Act of June 7, 1897, 30 Stat. 62, 79; cf. Quick Bear v. Leupp, 210 U.S. 50, 77–79, 28 S.Ct. 690, 694–696, 52L.Ed. 954 (1908); J. O'Neill, Religion and Education Under the Constitution 118–119 (1949). See generally R. Cord, Separation of Church and State 61–82 (1982). This history shows the fallacy of the notion found in Everson that "no tax in any amount" may be levied for religious activities in any form. 330 U.S., at 15–16, 67 S.Ct., at 511–512.

Joseph Story, a Member of this Court from 1811 to 1845, and during much of that time a professor at the Harvard Law School, published by far the most comprehensive treatise on the United States Constitution that had then appeared. Volume 2 of Story's Commentaries on the Constitution of the United States 630–632 (5th ed. 1891) discussed the meaning of the Establishment Clause of the First Amendment this way:

"Probably at the time of the adoption of the Constitution, and of the amendment to it now under consideration [First Amendment], the general if not the universal sentiment in America was, that Christianity ought to receive encouragement from the State so far as was not incompatible with the private rights of conscience and the freedom of religious worship. An attempt to level all religions, and to make it a matter of state policy to hold all in utter indifference, would have created universal disapprobation, if not universal indignation.

"The real object of the [First] [A]mendment was not to countenance, much less to advance, Mahometanism, or Judaism, or infidelity, by prostrating Christianity; but to exclude all rivalry among Christian sects, and to prevent any national ecclesiastical establishment which should give to a hierarchy the exclusive patronage of the national government. It thus cut off the means of religious persecution (the vice and pest of former ages), and of the subversion of the rights of conscience in matters of religion, which had been trampled upon almost from the days of the Apostles to the present age...." (Footnotes omitted.)

Thomas Cooley's eminence as a legal authority rivaled that of Story. Cooley stated in his treatise entitled Constitutional Limitations that aid to a particular religious sect was prohibited by the United States Constitution, but he went on to say:

"But while thus careful to establish, protect, and defend religious freedom and equality, the American constitutions contain no provisions which prohibit the authorities from such solemn recognition of a superintending Providence in public transactions and exercises as the general religious sentiment of mankind inspires, and as seems meet and proper in finite and dependent beings. Whatever may be the shades of religious belief, all must acknowledge the fitness of recognizing in important human affairs the superintending care and control of the Great Governor of the Universe, and of acknowledging with thanksgiving his boundless favors, or bowing in contrition when visited with the penalties of his broken laws. No principle of constitutional law is violated when thanksgiving or fast days are appointed; when chaplains are designated for the army and navy; when legislative sessions are opened with prayer or the reading of the Scriptures, or when religious teaching is encouraged by a general exemption of the houses of religious worship from taxation for the support of State government. Undoubtedly the spirit of the Constitution will require, in all these cases, that care be taken to avoid discrimination in favor of or against any one religious denomination or sect; but the power to do any of these things does not become unconstitutional simply because of its susceptibility to abuse...." Id., at * 470—* 471.

Cooley added that

"[t]his public recognition of religious worship, however, is not based entirely, perhaps not even mainly, upon a sense of what is due to the Supreme Being himself as the author of all good and of all law; but the same reasons of state policy which induce the government to aid institutions of charity and seminaries of instruction will incline it also to foster religious worship and religious institutions, as conservators of the public morals and valuable, if not indispensable, assistants to the preservation of the public order." Id., at *470.

It would seem from this evidence that the Establishment Clause of the First Amendment had acquired a well-accepted meaning: it forbade establishment of a national religion, and forbade preference among religious sects or denominations. Indeed, the first American dictionary defined the word "establishment" as "the act of establishing, founding, ratifying or ordaining," such as in "[t]he episcopal form of religion, so called, in England." 1 N. Webster, American Dictionary of the English Language (1st ed. 1828). The Establishment Clause did not require government neutrality between religion and irreligion nor did it prohibit the Federal Government from providing nondiscriminatory aid to religion. There is simply no historical foundation for the proposition that the Framers intended to build the "wall of separation" that was constitutionalized in Everson.

Notwithstanding the absence of a historical basis for this theory of rigid separation, the wall idea might well have served as a useful albeit misguided analytical concept, had it led this Court to unified and principled results in Establishment Clause cases. The opposite, unfortunately, has been true; in the 38 years since Everson our Establishment Clause cases have been neither principled nor unified. Our recent opinions, many of them hopelessly divided pluralities,(6) have with embarrassing candor conceded that the "wall of separation" is merely a "blurred, indistinct, and variable barrier," which "is not wholly accurate" and can only be "dimly perceived." Lemon v. Kurtzman, 403 U.S. 602, 614, 91 S.Ct. 2105, 2112, 29 L.Ed.2d 745 (1971); Tilton v. Richardson, 403 U.S. 672, 677–678, 91 S.Ct. 2091, 2095–2096, 29 L.Ed.2d 790 (1971); Wolman v. Walter, 433 U.S. 229, 236, 97 S.Ct. 2593, 2599, 53 L.Ed.2d 714 (1977); Lynch v. Donnelly, 465 U.S. 668, 673, 104 S.Ct. 1355, 1359, 79 L.Ed.2d 745 (1984).

Whether due to its lack of historical support or its practical unworkability, the Everson "wall" has proved all but useless as a guide to sound constitutional adjudication. It illustrates only too well the wisdom of Benjamin Cardozo's observation that "[m]etaphors in law are to be narrowly watched, for starting as devices to liberate thought, they end often by enslaving it." Berkey v. Third Avenue R. Co., 244 N.Y. 84, 94, 155 N.E. 58, 61 (1926).

But the greatest injury of the "wall" notion is its mischievous diversion of judges from the actual intentions of the drafters of the Bill of Rights. The "crucible of litigation," ante, at 2487, is well adapted to adjudicating factual disputes on the basis of testimony presented in court, but no amount of repetition of historical errors in judicial opinions can make the errors true. The "wall of separation between church and State" is a metaphor based on bad history, a metaphor which has proved useless as a guide to judging. It should be frankly and explicitly abandoned.

The Court has more recently attempted to add some mortar to Everson's wall through the three-part test of Lemon v. Kurtzman, supra, 403 U.S., at 614–615, 91 S.Ct., at 2112, which served at first to offer a more useful test for purposes of the Establishment Clause than did the "wall" metaphor. Generally stated, the Lemon test proscribes state action that has a sectarian purpose or effect, or causes an impermissible governmental entanglement with religion.

Lemon cited Board of Education v. Allen, 392 U.S. 236, 243, 88 S.Ct. 1923, 1926, 20 L.Ed.2d 1060 (1968), as the source of the "purpose" and "effect" prongs of the three-part test. The Allen opinion explains, however, how it inherited the purpose and effect elements from Schempp and Everson, both of which contain the historical errors described above. See Allen, supra, at 243, 88 S.Ct., at 1926. Thus the purpose and effect prongs have the same historical deficiencies as the wall concept itself: they are in no way based on either the language or intent of the drafters.

The secular purpose prong has proven mercurial in application because it has never been fully defined, and we have never fully stated how the test is to operate. If the purpose prong is intended to void those aids to sectarian institutions accompanied by a stated legislative purpose to aid religion, the prong will condemn nothing so long as the legislature utters a secular purpose and says nothing about aiding religion. Thus the constitutionality of a statute may depend upon what the legislators put into the legislative history and, more importantly, what they leave out. The purpose prong means little if it only requires the legislature to express any secular purpose and omit all sectarian references, because legislators might do just that. Faced with a valid legislative secular purpose, we could not properly ignore that purpose without a factual basis for doing so. Larson v. Valente, 456 U.S. 228, 262–263, 102 S.Ct. 1673, 1692–1693, 72 L.Ed.2d 33 (1982) (WHITE, J., dissenting).

However, if the purpose prong is aimed to void all statutes enacted with the intent to aid sectarian institutions, whether stated or not, then most statutes providing any aid, such as textbooks or bus rides for sectarian school children, will fail because one of the purposes behind every statute, whether stated or not, is to aid the target of its largesse. In other words, if the purpose prong requires an absence of any intent to aid sectarian institutions, whether or not expressed, few state laws in this area could pass the test, and we would be required to void some state aids to religion which we have already upheld. E.g., Allen, supra.

The entanglement prong of the Lemon test came from Walz v. Tax Comm'n, 397 U.S. 664, 674, 90 S.Ct. 1409, 1414, 25 L.Ed.2d 697 (1970). Walz involved a constitutional challenge to New York's time-honored practice of providing state property tax exemptions to church property used in worship. The Walz opinion refused to "undermine the ultimate constitutional objective [of the Establishment Clause] as illuminated by history," id., at 671, 90 S.Ct., at 1412, and upheld the tax exemption. The Court examined the historical relationship between the State and church when church property was in issue, and determined that the challenged tax exemption did not so entangle New York with the church as to cause an intrusion or interference with religion. Interferences with religion should arguably be dealt with under the Free Exercise Clause, but the entanglement inquiry in Walz was consistent with that case's broad survey of the relationship between state taxation and religious property.

We have not always followed Walz's reflective inquiry into entanglement, however. E.g., Wolman, supra, 433 U.S., at 254, 97 S.Ct., at 2608. One of the difficulties with the entanglement prong is that, when divorced from the logic of Walz, it creates an "insoluable paradox" in school aid cases: we have required aid to parochial schools to be closely watched lest it be put to sectarian use, yet this close supervision itself will create an entanglement. Roemer v. Maryland Bd. of Public Works, 426 U.S. 736, 768–769, 96 S.Ct. 2337, 2355–2356, 49 L.Ed.2d 179 (1976) (WHITE, J., concurring in judgment). For example, in Wolman, supra, the Court in part struck the State's nondiscriminatory provision of buses for parochial school field trips, because the state supervision of sectarian officials in charge of field trips would be too onerous. This type of self-defeating result is certainly not required to ensure that States do not establish religions.

The entanglement test as applied in cases like Wolman also ignores the myriad state administrative regulations properly placed upon sectarian institutions such as curriculum, attendance, and certification requirements for sectarian schools, or fire and safety regulations for churches. Avoiding entanglement between church and State may be an important consideration in a case like Walz, but if the entanglement prong were applied to all state and church relations in the automatic manner in which it has been applied to school aid cases, the State could hardly require anything of church-related institutions as a condition for receipt of financial assistance.

These difficulties arise because the Lemon test has no more grounding in the history of the First Amendment than does the wall theory upon which it rests. The three-part test represents a determined effort to craft a workable rule from a historically faulty doctrine; but the rule can only be as sound as the doctrine it attempts to service. The three-part test has simply not provided adequate standards for deciding Establishment Clause cases, as this Court has slowly come to realize. Even worse, the Lemon test has caused this Court to fracture into unworkable plurality opinions, see n. 6, supra, depending upon how each of the three factors applies to a certain state action. The results from our school services cases show the difficulty we have encountered in making the Lemon test yield principled results.

For example, a State may lend to parochial school children geography textbooks(7) that contain maps of the United States, but the State may not lend maps of the United States for use in geography class.(8) A State may lend textbooks on American colonial history, but it may not lend a film on George Washington, or a film projector to show it in history class. A State may lend classroom workbooks, but may not lend workbooks in which the parochial school children write, thus rendering them nonreusable.(9) A State may pay for bus transportation to religious schools(10) but may not pay for bus transportation from the parochial school to the public zoo or natural history museum for a field trip. (11) A State may pay for diagnostic services conducted in the parochial school but therapeutic services must be given in a different building; speech and hearing "services" conducted by the State inside the sectarian school are forbidden, Meek v. Pittenger, 421 U.S. 349, 367, 371, 95 S.Ct. 1753, 1764, 1766, 49 L.Ed.2d 179 (1975), but the State may conduct speech and hearing diagnostic testing inside the sectarian school. Wolman, 433 U.S., at 241, 97 S.Ct., at 2602. Exceptional parochial school students may receive counseling, but it must take place outside of the parochial school,(12) such as in a trailer parked down the street. Id., at 245, 97 S.Ct., at 2604. A State may give cash to a parochial school to pay for the administration of state-written tests and state-ordered reporting services,(13) but it may not provide funds for teacher-prepared tests on secular subjects.(14) Religious instruction may not be given in public school,(15) but the public school may release students during the day for religion classes elsewhere, and may enforce attendance at those classes with its truancy laws.(16)

These results violate the historically sound principle "that the Establishment Clause does not forbid governments . . . to [provide] general welfare under which benefits are distributed to private individuals, even though many of those individuals may elect to use those benefits in ways that 'aid' religious instruction or worship." Committee for Public Education & Religious Liberty v. Nyquist, 413 U.S. 756, 799, 93 S.Ct. 2955, 2989, 37 L.Ed.2d 948 (1973) (BURGER, C.J., concurring in part and dissenting in part). It is not surprising in the light of this record that our most recent opinions have expressed doubt on the usefulness of the Lemon test.

Although the test initially provided helpful assistance, e.g., Tilton v. Richardson, 403 U.S. 672, 91 S.Ct. 2091, 29 L.Ed.2d 790 (1971), we soon began describing the test as only a "guideline," Committee for Public Education & Religious Liberty v. Nyquist, supra, and lately we have described it as "no more than [a] useful signpos[t]." Mueller v. Allen, 463 U.S. 388, 394, 103 S.Ct. 3062, 3066, 77 L.Ed.2d 721 (1983), citing Hunt v. McNair, 413 U.S. 734, 741, 93 S.Ct. 2868, 2873, 37 L.Ed.2d 923 (1973); Larkin v. Grendel's Den, Inc., 459 U.S. 116, 103 S.Ct. 505, 74 L.Ed.2d 297 (1982). We have noted that the Lemon test is "not easily applied," Meek, supra, 421 U.S., at 358, 95 S.Ct., at 1759, and as Justice WHITE noted in Committee for Public Education v. Regan, 444 U.S. 646, 100 S.Ct. 840, 63 L.Ed.2d 94 (1980), under the Lemon test we have "sacrifice[d] clarity and predictability for flexibility." 444 U.S., at 662, 100 S.Ct., at 851. In Lynch we reiterated that the Lemon test has never been binding on the Court, and we cited two cases where we had declined to apply it. 465 U.S., at 679, 104 S.Ct., at 1362, citing Marsh v. Chambers, 463 U.S. 783, 103 S.Ct. 3330, 77 L.Ed.2d 1019 (1983); Larson v. Valente, 456 U.S. 228, 102 S.Ct. 1673, 72 L.Ed.2d 33 (1982).

If a constitutional theory has no basis in the history of the amendment it seeks to interpret, is difficult to apply and yields unprincipled results, I see little use in it. The "crucible of litigation," ante, at 2487, has produced only consistent unpredictability, and today's effort is just a continuation of "the sisyphean task of trying to patch together the 'blurred, indistinct and variable barrier' described in Lemon v. Kurtzman." Regan, supra, 444 U.S., at 671, 100 S.Ct., at 855 (STEVENS, J., dissenting). We have done much straining since 1947, but still we admit that we can only "dimly perceive" the Everson wall. Tilton, supra. Our perception has been clouded not by the Constitution but by the mists of an unnecessary metaphor.

The true meaning of the Establishment Clause can only be seen in its history. See Walz, 397 U.S., at 671–673, 90 S.Ct., at 1412–1413; see also Lynch, supra, at 673–678, 104 S.Ct., at 1359–1362. As drafters of our Bill of Rights, the Framers inscribed the principles that control today. Any deviation from their intentions frustrates the permanence of that Charter and will only lead to the type of unprincipled decision-making that has plagued our Establishment Clause cases since Everson.

The Framers intended the Establishment Clause to prohibit the designation of any church as a "national" one. The Clause was also designed to stop the Federal Government from asserting a preference for one religious denomination or sect over others. Given the "incorporation" of the Establishment Clause as against the States via the Fourteenth Amendment in Everson, States are prohibited as well from establishing a religion or discriminating between sects. As its history abundantly shows, however, nothing in the Establishment Clause requires government to be strictly neutral between religion and irreligion, nor does that Clause prohibit Congress or the States from pursuing legitimate secular ends through nondiscriminatory sectarian means.

The Court strikes down the Alabama statute because the State wished to "characterize prayer as a favored practice." Ante, at 2492. It would come as much of a shock to those who drafted the Bill of Rights as it will to a large number of thoughtful Americans today to learn that the Constitution, as construed by the majority, prohibits the Alabama Legislature from "endorsing" prayer. George Washington himself, at the request of the very Congress which passed the Bill of Rights, proclaimed a day of "public thanksgiving and prayer, to be observed by acknowledging with grateful hearts the many and signal favors of Almighty God." History must judge whether it was the Father of his Country in 1789, or a majority of the Court today, which has strayed from the meaning of the Establishment Clause.

The State surely has a secular interest in regulating the manner in which public schools are conducted. Nothing in the Establishment Clause of the First Amendment, properly understood, prohibits any such generalized "endorsement" of prayer. I would therefore reverse the judgment of the Court of Appeals.

1. Reynolds is the only authority cited as direct precedent for the "wall of separation theory." 330 U.S., at 16, 67 S.Ct., at 512. Reynolds is truly inapt; it dealt with a Mormon's Free Exercise Clause challenge to a federal polygamy law.

2. The New York and Rhode Island proposals were quite similar. They stated that no particular "religious sect or society ought to be favored or established by law in preference to others." 1 Elliot's Debates, at 328; id., at 334.

3. In a letter he sent to Jefferson in France, Madison stated that he did not see much importance in a Bill

of Rights but he planned to support it because it was "anxiously desired by others . . . [and] it might be of use, and if properly executed could not be of disservice." 5 Writings of James Madison, 271 (G. Hunt ed. 1904).

4. State establishments were prevalent throughout the late 18th and early 19th centuries. See Mass. Const. of 1780, Part I, Art. III; N. H. Const. of 1784, Art.VI; Md. Declaration of Rights of 1776, Art.XXXIII; R. I. Charter of 1633 (superseded 1842).

5. The treaty stated in part:

"And whereas, the greater part of said Tribe have been baptized and received into the Catholic church, to which they are much attached, the United States will give annually for seven years one hundred dollars towards the support of a priest of that religion . . . [a]nd . . . three hundred dollars, to assist the said Tribe in the erection of a church." 7 Stat. 79.

From 1789 to 1823 the United States Congress had provided a trust endowment of up to 12,000 acres of land "for the Society of the United Brethren, for propagating the Gospel among the Heathen." See, e.g., ch. 46, 1 Stat. 490. The Act creating this endowment was renewed periodically and the renewals were signed into law by Washington, Adams, and Jefferson.

Congressional grants for the aid of religion were not limited to Indians. In 1787 Congress provided land to the Ohio Company, including acreage for the support of religion. This grant was reauthorized in 1792. See 1 Stat. 257. In 1833 Congress authorized the State of Ohio to sell the land set aside for religion and use the proceeds "for the support of religion . . . and for no other use or purpose whatsoever. . . ." 4 Stat. 618–619.

6. Tilton v. Richardson, 403 U.S. 672, 677, 91 S.Ct. 2091, 2095, 29 L.Ed.2d 790 (1971); Meek v. Pittenger, 421 U.S. 349, 95 S.Ct. 1753, 44 L.Ed.2d 217 (1975) (partial); Roemer v. Maryland Bd. of Public Works, 426 U.S. 736, 96 S.Ct. 2337, 49 L.Ed.2d 179 (1976); Wolman v. Walter, 433 U.S. 229, 97 S.Ct. 2593, 53 L.Ed.2d 714 (1977).

Many of our other Establishment Clause cases have been decided by bare 5–4 majorities. Committee for Public Education & Religious Liberty v. Regan, 444 U.S. 646, 100 S.Ct. 840, 63 L.Ed.2d 94 (1980); Larson v. Valente, 456 U.S. 228, 102 S.Ct. 1673, 72 L.Ed.2d 33 (1982); Mueller v. Allen, 463 U.S. 388, 103 S.Ct. 3062, 77 L.Ed.2d 721 (1983); Lynch v. Donnelly, 465 U.S. 668, 104 S.Ct. 1355, 29 L.Ed.2d 745 (1984); cf. Levitt v. Committee for Public Education & Religious Liberty, 413 U.S. 472, 93 S.Ct. 2814, 37 L.Ed.2d 736 (1973).

7. Board of Education v. Allen, 392 U.S. 236, 88 S.Ct. 1923, 20 L.Ed.2d 1060 (1968).

8. Meek, 421 U.S., at 362–366, 95 S.Ct., at 1761–1763. A science book is permissible, a science kit is not. See Wolman, 433 U.S., at 249, 97 S.Ct., at 2606.

9. See Meek, supra, at 354–355, nn. 3, 4, 362–366, 95 S.Ct., at 1761–1763.

10. Everson v. Board of Education, 330 U.S. 1, 67 S.Ct. 504, 91 L.Ed. 711 (1947).

11. Wolman, supra, 433 U.S., at 252–255, 97 S.Ct., at 2608–2609.

12. Wolman, supra, at 241–248, 97 S.Ct., at 2602–2605; Meek, supra, at 352, n. 2, 367–373, 95 S.Ct., at 1756, n. 2, 1764–1767.

13. Regan, 444 U.S., at 648, 657–659, 100 S.Ct., at 844, 848–849.

14. Levitt, 413 U.S., at 479–482, 93 S.Ct., at 2818–2820.

15. Illinois ex rel. McCollum v. Board of Education, 333 U.S. 203, 68 S.Ct. 461, 92 L.Ed. 649 (1948).

16. Zorach v. Clauson, 343 U.S. 306, 72 S.Ct. 679, 96 L.Ed. 954 (1952).

QUESTIONS

1. According to John Jay, who would later become the first Chief Justice of the Supreme Court, what document first created us as a nation of one people?

2. What was Representative Gerry's opposition to the word "national" in Madison's proposal for the no establishment clause? What was Madison's reason for having included the word "national?"

3. Why did Madison and Hamilton not see a need for the Bill of Rights?

4. What was Rep. Huntington's concerns about the latitude that could be taken with the 1st Amendment and how it could then be incorrectly used?

Chapter 9

CONSTITUTIONAL REPUBLIC

Original Sources:
1. FEDERALIST PAPER No. 10, James Madison, 1787
2. LEX REX, Samuel Rutherford, 1644

To open this discussion, let's revisit the conversation between Mrs. Powel and Benjamin Franklin that was presented in the Introduction. At the close of the Constitutional Convention Benjamin Franklin was asked by a Mrs. Powel of Philadelphia,

> "Well Doctor, what have we got, a republic or a monarchy?"

Benjamin Franklin's famous response to Mrs. Powel's question was simply,

> "A republic, if YOU can keep it."

Benjamin Franklin © yurchello108/Shutterstock.com

It is meaningful to note that Mrs. Powel did not ask if we had been given a Democracy. That is because a Democracy was not even considered as a viable option. The Founding Fathers expressed great respect and admiration for republics, and strong dislike for democracies and their inherent weaknesses.

> "[W]e are confirmed in the opinion, that the present age would be deficient in their duty to God, their posterity and themselves, if they do not establish an American republic. This is the only form of government we wish to see established; for we can never be willingly subject to any other King than He who, being possessed of infinite wisdom, goodness and rectitude, is alone fit to possess unlimited power."
>
> Instructions of Malden, Massachusetts, for a Declaration of Independence, May 27, 1776

> "A pure democracy is generally a very bad government, It is often the most tyrannical government on earth; for a multitude is often rash, and will not hear reason."
>
> —Noah Webster, The Original Blue Back Speller

> "Democracy is two wolves and a lamb voting on what to have for lunch. Liberty is a well-armed lamb contesting the vote."
>
> ~Benjamin Franklin

> "Remember, democracy never lasts long. It soon wastes, exhausts, and murders itself. There never was a democracy yet that did not commit suicide. It is in vain to say that democracy is less vain, less proud, less selfish, less ambitious, or less avaricious than aristocracy or monarchy. It is not true, in fact, and nowhere appears in history. Those passions are the same in all men, under all forms of simple government, and when unchecked, produce the same effects of fraud, violence, and cruelty. When clear

prospects are opened before vanity, pride, avarice, or ambition, for their easy gratification, it is hard for the most considerate philosophers and the most conscientious moralists to resist the temptation. Individuals have conquered themselves. Nations and large bodies of men, never."

John Adams, letter to John Taylor, April 15, 1814

Our Founding Fathers established us as a Republic because that was the form of government they believed to be most protective of liberty. Democracy, being a form of government that directly reflected the will of the people they saw as a government of men, not of laws. They preferred instead to create us as a government of laws, not of men, because laws were more stable and less selfish and fickle than men.

". . . there is no good government but what is republican. That the only valuable part of the British constitution is so; because the very definition of a republic is "an empire of laws, and not of men." That, as a republic is the best of governments, so that particular arrangement of the powers of society, or, in other words, that form of government which is best contrived to secure an impartial and exact execution of the laws, is the best of republics.

John Adams, Thoughts on Government, April 1776

The concerns of the Founders were that with a democracy majority opinion establishes law. On the other hand, with a Republic, law was the ultimate standard whereby both the majority and the minority were equally governed. The Founders did not want a government where the will of the minority could trample on the majority, but neither did they want a government where the will of the majority could trample upon the minority. They desired a government where the Law was King, rather than a government where the King, or a man, or any group of men for that matter, were Law. It was this belief in **Lex Rex** (Law is King) over **Rex Lex** (King is Law) that fueled their passion for a Republican form of government.

Madison was an extremely outspoken opponent of rule by **factions** of any type; he believed that they were a threat to liberty. The thought was that to allow the minority to rule was an improper form of governance that threatened the freedoms and rights of the majority. However, he did not find it any more acceptable to allow majority factions to threaten the freedoms and rights of the minority. That is what would happen within a Democracy where laws could be created upon the simple rationale of majority opinion, and that is why Madison, along with the other Founding Fathers, so strongly opposed a democratic form of government. He believed the greatest comfort to the fear of controlling factions could not be found in Democracy since it placed control in the hands of majority factions, but rather the representation of Republicanism.

From this view of the subject it may be concluded that a pure democracy, by which I mean a society consisting of a small number of citizens, who assemble and administer the government in person, can admit of no cure for the mischiefs of faction. A common passion or interest will, in almost every case, be felt by a majority of the whole; a communication and concert result from the form of government itself; and there is nothing to check the inducements to sacrifice the weaker party or an obnoxious individual. Hence it is that such democracies have ever been spectacles of turbulence and contention; have ever been found incompatible with personal security or the rights of property; and have in general been as short in their lives as they have been violent in their deaths. Theoretic politicians, who have patronized this species of government, have erroneously supposed that by reducing mankind to a perfect equality in their political rights, they would, at the same time, be perfectly equalized and assimilated in their possessions, their opinions, and their passions.

A republic, by which I mean a government in which the scheme of representation takes place, opens a different prospect, and promises the cure for which we are seeking.

James Madison,
Federalist Paper #10

Our Founders used the term Republic to mean a representative government tied to the Rule of Law. Our Rule of Law is found within our Constitution. It is for this reason that our form of government is most accurately defined as a **Constitutional Republic**- a representative government whose representatives serve for an established tenure and are sworn to uphold the Constitution. Part of the beauty that Madison felt protected this Constitutional Republic from the diseases of factions was to be found within the principles of federalism injected throughout our governmental structure. The Constitution, with its 10th Amendment, created coexisting sovereigns, the general government and the states. This structure effectively prevented the creation of one national ruling authority. This was viewed as a **vertical distribution of powers** between sovereigns.

Likewise, within the general government, coexisting sovereigns were created in the form of the three branches. The checks and balances between these branches effectively prevented the creation of one national ruling authority becoming supreme by uniting several of the powers in one branch. The goal of placing competing interests within various factions: the states v the general government and the legislative v the executive v the judicial, was to prevent the likelihood of majority consensus, and thereby prevent the creation of a single ruling class.

The question of how to balance this tension between factions continues to this day. The Founding Fathers believed the answer was to create a government that would remain fairly weak through its structure, which would ultimately serve to oppose a strong centralized government. Many of those safeguards have been erased through subsequent changes implemented by Presidents, Congressmen and Supreme Court Rulings. However, nothing has been done that cannot be corrected by the highest ruling authority in our nation, our Constitution, which is to be carefully safeguarded by "We the People."[1] It is up to us to know who we are as Americans, to value the Constitutional Republic that has been given to us, and to fight for its preservation against attacks from within. It has been said that, "knowledge is power, knowledge is safety and knowledge is happiness."[2] You now have the knowledge, which means you now have the power to preserve our Republic's safety and ensure its continued happiness.

---

1 Preamble, The Constitution of the United States, September 17, 1787
2 Thomas Jefferson to George Ticknor, 25 November 1817[2]

The Federalist Papers: No. 10
The Union as a Safeguard Against Domestic Faction and Insurrection

Friday, November 23, 1787

James Madison

To the People of the State of New York:

AMONG the numerous advantages promised by a wellconstructed Union, none deserves to be more accurately developed than its tendency to break and control the violence of faction. The friend of popular governments never finds himself so much alarmed for their character and fate, as when he contemplates their propensity to this dangerous vice. He will not fail, therefore, to set a due value on any plan which, without violating the principles to which he is attached, provides a proper cure for it. The instability, injustice, and confusion introduced into the public councils, have, in truth, been the mortal diseases under which popular governments have everywhere perished; as they continue to be the favorite and fruitful topics from which the adversaries to liberty derive their most specious declamations. The valuable improvements made by the American constitutions on the popular models, both ancient and modern, cannot certainly be too much admired; but it would be an unwarrantable partiality, to contend that they have as effectually obviated the danger on this side, as was wished and expected. Complaints are everywhere heard from our most considerate and virtuous citizens, equally the friends of public and private faith, and of public and personal liberty, that our governments are too unstable, that the public good is disregarded in the conflicts of rival parties, and that measures are too often decided, not according to the rules of justice and the rights of the minor party, but by the superior force of an interested and overbearing majority. However anxiously we may wish that these complaints had no foundation, the evidence, of known facts will not permit us to deny that they are in some degree true. It will be found, indeed, on a candid review of our situation, that some of the distresses under which we labor have been erroneously charged on the operation of our governments; but it will be found, at the same time, that other causes will not alone account for many of our heaviest misfortunes; and, particularly, for that prevailing and increasing distrust of public engagements, and alarm for private rights, which are echoed from one end of the continent to the other. These must be chiefly, if not wholly, effects of the unsteadiness and injustice with which a factious spirit has tainted our public administrations.

By a faction, I understand a number of citizens, whether amounting to a majority or a minority of the whole, who are united and actuated by some common impulse of passion, or of interest, adversed to the rights of other citizens, or to the permanent and aggregate interests of the community.

There are two methods of curing the mischiefs of faction: the one, by removing its causes; the other, by controlling its effects.

There are again two methods of removing the causes of faction: the one, by destroying the liberty which is essential to its existence; the other, by giving to every citizen the same opinions, the same passions, and the same interests.

It could never be more truly said than of the first remedy, that it was worse than the disease. Liberty is to faction what air is to fire, an aliment without which it instantly expires. But it could not be less folly to abolish liberty, which is essential to political life, because it nourishes faction, than it would be to wish the annihilation of air, which is essential to animal life, because it imparts to fire its destructive agency.

The second expedient is as impracticable as the first would be unwise. As long as the reason of man continues fallible, and he is at liberty to exercise it, different opinions will be formed. As long as the connection subsists between his reason and his self-love, his opinions and his passions will have a reciprocal influence on each other; and the former will be objects to which the latter will attach themselves. The diversity in the faculties of men, from which the rights of property originate, is not less an insuperable obstacle to a uniformity of interests. The protection of these faculties is the first object of government. From the protection of different and unequal faculties of acquiring property, the possession of different degrees and kinds of property immediately results; and from the influence of these on the sentiments and views of the respective proprietors, ensues a division of the society into different interests and parties.

The latent causes of faction are thus sown in the nature of man; and we see them everywhere brought into different degrees of activity, according to the different circumstances of civil society. A zeal for different opinions concerning religion, concerning government, and many other points, as well of speculation as of practice; an attachment to different leaders ambitiously contending for pre-eminence and power; or to persons of other descriptions whose fortunes have been interesting to the human passions, have, in turn, divided mankind into parties, inflamed them with mutual animosity, and rendered them much more disposed to vex and oppress each other than to co-operate for their common good. So strong is this propensity of mankind to fall into mutual animosities, that where no substantial occasion presents itself, the most frivolous and fanciful distinctions have been sufficient to kindle their unfriendly passions and excite their most violent conflicts. But the most common and durable source of factions has been the various and unequal distribution of property. Those who hold and those who are without property have ever formed distinct interests in society. Those who are creditors, and those who are debtors, fall under a like discrimination. A landed interest, a manufacturing interest, a mercantile interest, a moneyed interest, with many lesser interests, grow up of necessity in civilized nations, and divide them into different classes, actuated by different sentiments and views. The regulation of these various and interfering interests forms the principal task of modern legislation, and involves the spirit of party and faction in the necessary and ordinary operations of the government.

No man is allowed to be a judge in his own cause, because his interest would certainly bias his judgment, and, not improbably, corrupt his integrity. With equal, nay with greater reason, a body of men are unfit to be both judges and parties at the same time; yet what are many of the most important acts of legislation, but so many judicial determinations, not indeed concerning the rights of single persons, but concerning the rights of large bodies of citizens? And what are the different classes of legislators but advocates and parties to the causes which they determine? Is a law proposed concerning private debts? It is a question to which the creditors are parties on one side and the debtors on the other. Justice ought to hold the balance between them. Yet the parties are, and must be, themselves the judges; and the most numerous party, or, in other words, the most powerful faction must be expected to prevail. Shall domestic manufactures be encouraged, and in what degree, by restrictions on foreign manufactures are questions which would be differently decided by the landed and the manufacturing classes, and probably by neither with a sole regard to justice and the public good. The apportionment of taxes on the various descriptions of property is an act which seems to require the most exact impartiality; yet there is, perhaps, no legislative act in which greater opportunity and temptation are given to a predominant party to trample on the rules of justice. Every shilling with which they overburden the inferior number, is a shilling saved to their own pockets.

It is in vain to say that enlightened statesmen will be able to adjust these clashing interests, and render them all subservient to the public good. Enlightened statesmen will not always be at the helm. Nor, in many cases, can such an adjustment be made at all without taking into view indirect and remote considerations, which will rarely prevail over the immediate interest which one party may find in disregarding the rights of another or the good of the whole.

The inference to which we are brought is, that the CAUSES of faction cannot be removed, and that relief is only to be sought in the means of controlling its EFFECTS.

If a faction consists of less than a majority, relief is supplied by the republican principle, which enables the majority to defeat its sinister views by regular vote. It may clog the administration, it may convulse the society; but it will be unable to execute and mask its violence under the forms of the Constitution. When a majority is included in a faction, the form of popular government, on the other hand, enables it to sacrifice to its ruling passion or interest both the public good and the rights of other citizens. To secure the public good and private rights against the danger of such a faction, and at the same time to preserve the spirit and the form of popular government, is then the great object to which our inquiries are directed. Let me add that it is the great desideratum by which this form of government can be rescued from the opprobrium under which it has so long labored, and be recommended to the esteem and adoption of mankind.

By what means is this object attainable? Evidently by one of two only. Either the existence of the same passion or interest in a majority at the same time must be prevented, or the majority, having such coexistent passion or interest, must be rendered, by their number and local situation, unable to concert and carry into effect schemes of oppression. If the impulse and the opportunity be suffered to coincide, we well know that neither moral nor religious motives can be relied on as an adequate control. They are not found to be such on the injustice and violence of individuals, and lose their efficacy in proportion to the number combined together, that is, in proportion as their efficacy becomes needful.

From this view of the subject it may be concluded that a pure democracy, by which I mean a society consisting of a small number of citizens, who assemble and administer the government in person, can admit of no cure for the mischiefs of faction. A common passion or interest will, in almost every case, be felt by a majority of the whole; a communication and concert result from the form of government itself; and there is nothing to check the inducements to sacrifice the weaker party or an obnoxious individual. Hence it is that such democracies have ever been spectacles of turbulence and contention; have ever been found incompatible with personal security or the rights of property; and have in general been as short in their lives as they have been violent in their deaths. Theoretic politicians, who have patronized this species of government, have erroneously supposed that by reducing mankind to a perfect equality in their political rights, they would, at the same time, be perfectly equalized and assimilated in their possessions, their opinions, and their passions.

A republic, by which I mean a government in which the scheme of representation takes place, opens a different prospect, and promises the cure for which we are seeking. Let us examine the points in which it varies from pure democracy, and we shall comprehend both the nature of the cure and the efficacy which it must derive from the Union.

The two great points of difference between a democracy and a republic are: first, the delegation of the government, in the latter, to a small number of citizens elected by the rest; secondly, the greater number of citizens, and greater sphere of country, over which the latter may be extended.

The effect of the first difference is, on the one hand, to refine and enlarge the public views, by passing them through the medium of a chosen body of citizens, whose wisdom may best discern the true interest of their country, and whose patriotism and love of justice will be least likely to sacrifice it to temporary or partial considerations. Under such a regulation, it may well happen that the public voice, pronounced by the representatives of the people, will be more consonant to the public good than if pronounced by the people themselves, convened for the purpose. On the other hand, the effect may be inverted. Men of factious tempers, of local prejudices, or of sinister designs, may, by intrigue, by corruption, or by other means, first obtain the suffrages, and then betray the interests, of the people. The question resulting is, whether small or extensive republics are more favorable to the election of proper guardians of the public weal; and it is clearly decided in favor of the latter by two obvious considerations:

In the first place, it is to be remarked that, however small the republic may be, the representatives must be raised to a certain number, in order to guard against the cabals of a few; and that, however large it may be, they must be limited to a certain number, in order to guard against the confusion of a multitude. Hence, the number of representatives in the two cases not being in proportion to that of the two constituents, and being proportionally greater in the small republic, it follows that, if the proportion of fit characters be not less in the large than in the small republic, the former will present a greater option, and consequently a greater probability of a fit choice.

In the next place, as each representative will be chosen by a greater number of citizens in the large than in the small republic, it will be more difficult for unworthy candidates to practice with success the vicious arts by which elections are too often carried; and the suffrages of the people being more free, will be more likely to centre in men who possess the most attractive merit and the most diffusive and established characters.

It must be confessed that in this, as in most other cases, there is a mean, on both sides of which inconveniences will be found to lie. By enlarging too much the number of electors, you render the representatives too little acquainted with all their local circumstances and lesser interests; as by reducing it too much, you render him unduly attached to these, and too little fit to comprehend and pursue great and national objects. The federal Constitution forms a happy combination in this respect; the great and aggregate interests being referred to the national, the local and particular to the State legislatures.

The other point of difference is, the greater number of citizens and extent of territory which may be brought within the compass of republican than of democratic government; and it is this circumstance principally which renders factious combinations less to be dreaded in the former than in the latter. The smaller the society, the fewer probably will be the distinct parties and interests composing it; the fewer the distinct parties and interests, the more frequently will a majority be found of the same party; and the smaller the number of individuals composing a majority, and the smaller the compass within which they are placed, the more easily will they concert and execute their plans of oppression. Extend the sphere, and you take in a greater variety of parties and interests; you make it less probable that a majority of the whole will have a common motive to invade the rights of other citizens; or if such a common motive exists, it will be more difficult for all who feel it to discover their own strength, and to act in unison with each other. Besides other impediments, it may be remarked that, where there is a consciousness of unjust or dishonorable purposes, communication is always checked by distrust in proportion to the number whose concurrence is necessary.

Hence, it clearly appears, that the same advantage which a republic has over a democracy, in controlling the effects of faction, is enjoyed by a large over a small republic,—is enjoyed by the Union over the States composing it. Does the advantage consist in the substitution of representatives whose enlightened views and virtuous sentiments render them superior to local prejudices and schemes of injustice? It will not be denied that the representation of the Union will be most likely to possess these requisite endowments. Does it consist in the greater security afforded by a greater variety of parties, against the event of any one party being able to outnumber and oppress the rest? In an equal degree does the increased variety of parties comprised within the Union, increase this security. Does it, in fine, consist in the greater obstacles opposed to the concert and accomplishment of the secret wishes of an unjust and interested majority? Here, again, the extent of the Union gives it the most palpable advantage.

The influence of factious leaders may kindle a flame within their particular States, but will be unable to spread a general conflagration through the other States. A religious sect may degenerate into a political faction in a part of the Confederacy; but the variety of sects dispersed over the entire face of it must secure the national councils against any danger from that source. A rage for paper money, for an abolition of debts, for an equal division of property, or for any other improper or wicked project, will be less apt to pervade the whole body of the Union than a particular member of it; in the same proportion as such a malady is more likely to taint a particular county or district, than an entire State.

In the extent and proper structure of the Union, therefore, we behold a republican remedy for the diseases most incident to republican government. And according to the degree of pleasure and pride we feel in being republicans, ought to be our zeal in cherishing the spirit and supporting the character of Federalists.

PUBLIUS.

Lex Rex
The Law and the Prince
Samuel Rutheford
1644

Power and absolute monarchy is tyranny; unmixed democracy is confusion; untempered aristocracy is factious dominion; and a limited monarchy hath from democracy respect to public good, without confusion. From aristocracy safety in multitude of counsels without factious emulation, and so a bar laid on tyranny by joint powers of many; and from sovereignty union of many children in one father; and all the three thus contempered have their own sweet fruits through God's blessing, and their own diseases by accident, and through men's corruption; and neither reason nor Scripture shall warrant any one in its rigid purity without mixture. And God having chosen the best government to bring men fallen in sin to happiness, must warrant in any one a mixture of all three . . .

Hence all the three forms are from God; but let no man say, if they be all indifferent, and equally of God, societies and kingdoms are left in the dark, and know not which of the three they shall pitch upon, because God hath given to them no special direction for one rather than for another. But this is easily answered. 1st, That a republic appoint rulers to govern them is not an indifferent, but a moral action, because to set no rulers over themselves I conceive were a breach of the fifth commandment, which commandeth government to be one or other. 2nd, It is not in men's free will that they have government or no government, because it is not in their free will to obey or not to obey the acts of the court of nature, which is God's court; and this court enacteth that societies suffer not mankind to perish, which must necessarily follow if they appoint no government; also it is proved elsewhere, that no moral acts, in their exercises and use, are left indifferent to us; so then, the aptitude and temper of every commonwealth to monarchy, rather than to democracy or aristocracy, is God's warrant and nearest call to determine the wills and liberty of people to pitch upon a monarchy, hic et nunc, rather than any other form of government, though all the three be from God, even as single life and marriage are both the lawful ordinances of God, and the constitution and temper of the body is a calling to either of the two; nor are we to think that aristocracy and democracy are either unlawful ordinances, or men's inventions, or that those societies whichthat want monarchy do therefore live in sins.

Very well; for the surrender is so voluntary, that it is also natural, and founded on the law of nature, that men must have governors, either many, or one supreme ruler. And it is voluntary, and dependeth on a positive institution of God, whether the government be by one supreme ruler, as in a monarchy, or in many, as in an aristocracy, according as the necessity and temper of the commonwealth do most require. This constitution is so voluntary, as it hath below it the law of nature for its general foundation, and above it, the supervenient institution of God, ordaining that there should be such inagistrates, both kings and other judges, because without such, all human societies should be dissolved. Individual persons, in creating a magistrate, doth not properly surrender their right, which can be called a right; for they do but surrender their power of doing violence to those of their fellows in that same community, so as they shall not now have moral power to do injuries without punishment; and this is not right or liberty properly, but servitude, for a power to do violence and injuries is not liberty, but servitude and bondage.

QUESTIONS

1. To what was Madison referring when he said they have always been, "spectacles of turbulence and contention; have ever been found incompatible with personal security or the rights of property; and have in general been as short in their lives as they have been violent in their deaths?"

2. How did Franklin, Adams and Webster feel about democracies?

3. Which form of government could be deemed an empire of men, and which an empire of laws?

4. Did Madison perceive any less threat to liberty from control by a majority faction than from control by a minority faction? Explain.

Glossary of Terms

A

Adjournment—An adjournment formally ends a meeting or session in Congress. An adjournment "sine die" ("without day") means that congress has adjourned without setting a day to reassemble, and will not resume meeting until the first day of the next session. The Constitution requires both chambers to agree for an adjournment sine die to take place unless the next session is about to convene. This is adopted through a concurrent resolution, and allows if necessary for leaders of either chamber to call members to reconvene.

Adjudicate—To determine in a court of law.

Agrarian—Of or relating to farming or agriculture.

Amendment—An amendment is a suggested change to a bill or text. There are twenty-seven constitutional amendments. The first ten of these are called the Bill of Rights.

Anarchy—Anarchy is chaos caused by the absence of laws or government.

Anti-Federalists—Anti-federalists opposed the expansion of the federal government and fought for many of the checks and balances now in the constitution. They championed state's rights, and small government. Notable anti-federalists include Patrick Henry, William Penn, and James Winthrop, among others.

Appellate Jurisdiction—Appellate jurisdiction is generally legislated, and allows the court to review and change the decisions made in lower courts.

Appropriations—An appropriation bill sets money aside for purposed spending.

Articles of Confederation—After the creation of the United States by the Declaration of Independence, the Articles of Confederation loosely governed the thirteen states from 1781–1789 until the U.S. Constitution was ratified.

B

Bicameral Legislature—This literally means "two chambers." Congress is the legislative, or law making body, and is composed of two chambers, the House of Representatives, and the Senate.

Bill—The primary method used by congress to propose a new law.

Blackstone, Sir William—An eighteenth-century political philosopher from England who wrote the Commentaries on the Laws of England. He was the second most-quoted political philosopher by America's Founding Fathers.

Bylaws—The set of rules by which an entity is to be governed.

C

Case or Controversy—This sets the boundaries for judicial authority in that they may only address actual conflicts between individuals or parties that involve the parties' legal rights. The disputes must not be moot (already resolved); they must be ripe (dispute currently exists and is not some potential issue in the future). The judicial branch, therefore, only has authority over cases or controversies, not legislating general legal principles for society as a whole; that is the role of the legislative branch.

Civil Disobedience—The taking of action to oppose positive laws that have been enacted that are contrary to just laws.

Common Law—This is the part of the law taken from England and derived through custom and judicial precedent; it was derived from that which was accepted as preexisting law. This is different than statutory law.

Concurrent Resolution—Legislation that regulates business in both chambers of congress. It does not propose changes to law.

Constitutional Convention of 1787—55 delegates from 12 different states met in Philadelphia and constructed and ratified the Constitution of the United States.

Constitutional Republic—A representative government, whose representatives serve for an established tenure, and who are sworn to uphold the Constitution. The representatives are generally elected by the people, but are sworn to uphold the Constitution, rather than the majority opinion of their constituency. It is, therefore, an empire of laws, not of men, with the supreme law of the land being the Constitution.

D

Despotic or Tyrannical rule—The exercise of absolute power in an oppressive manner.

Democracy—A system of government where majority will of the people governs.

E

Electoral College—The Electoral College consists of 538 electors. A majority of 270 electoral votes is required to elect the President. Each state has the same number of electors as they do in congress. They have one for every member of the House of Representatives plus two for each Senator. Each state has the freedom to decide how their electoral votes are cast.

Engrossed—A bill that has already been passed by one chamber of congress.

Enumerated Powers—The specifically listed areas over which Congress may legislate listed in Article 1, Section 8. Congress has no authority to make laws governing a specific area unless permission for that area is expressly found in the Constitution.

Executive Branch—Created by Article II of the U.S. Constitution. This branch is charged with the enforcement and execution of laws and polices.

F

Factions—Groups with opposing views, or discord between various groups of people.

Federalism—A system of government where the same geographic region is simultaneously governed by two different levels of governmental authority.

Federalists—Those who supported Federalism.

Federalist Papers—A series of papers written to encourage ratification of the Constitution. They were composed by three authors: Alexander Hamilton authored fifty-two, James Madison authored twenty-eight, and John Jay authored five.

G

Germane—This requires an amendment to be related to the subject matter it proposes to amend.

General Government—Name given to the Federal government by Thomas Jefferson.

General Welfare—Language that prohibits congress from enacting legislation that only benefits special interest groups, or special welfare, rather than generally for the welfare of all. This clause only enabled Congress to spend money for the general welfare of the people on those powers specifically enumerated in Article I, Section 8.

H

Horizontal Distribution of Power—Enacted by the founders to act as checks and balances upon the branches of government. This required power to be distributed between the Legislative, Executive, and Judicial branches of government.

J

Jay, John—The First Chief Justice of the Supreme Court of the United States. He was one of the three authors of the Federalist Papers.

Joint Resolution—This is a legislative method used to propose changes in law, or to propose an amendment to the U.S. Constitution.

Judiciary—This is one of the three branches of the Federal government created by Article III of the U.S. Constitution. The judiciary is to take laws passed by Congress and apply them to a given set of facts, otherwise known as a case or controversy.

L

Law of Nature and Nature's God—The will of The Maker revealed through the Holy Scriptures.

Legislative Power—This is the power to make or implement law, statutes, and policies that are applicable to every member of society as a whole. Article I of the U.S. Constitution grants this power solely to Congress as part of the horizontal distribution of power.

Lex Rex—This is the principle that the Law is King.

Licentiousness—The freedom to have full license to do whatever one wants, without restraint from either law or what is deemed morally acceptable.

Locke, John—A seventeenth-century political philosopher from England who wrote Two Treatises on Government; he was the third most-quoted political philosopher by America's Founding Fathers.

M

Madison, James—The 4th U.S. president also called "the Father of the Constitution" for his instrumental role in the construction of the U.S. Constitution. He was one of the three authors of the Federalist Papers.

Montesquieu, Charles-Louis de Secondat, Baron de—An eighteenth-century political philosopher who championed the preexistence of law. His writings influenced both the American and French revolutions. He was the most-quoted political philosopher by America's founding fathers.

N

Nationalists—Those who propose diminishing the power of the states, and establishing a strong centralized national government.

Necessary and Proper—This defines the power vested in congress to create legislation needed to execute the enumerated powers previously listed in Article I, Section 8.

Non-Acquiescence—This is the purposed refusal of one branch of the government to acquiesce to the exertion of power by another branch.

Nullification—Each individual state has the right to reject laws or actions passed by the federal government not granted by the enumerated powers.

P

Positive Laws—Man-made laws.

Providential—Guided by providence, or the hand of a higher power.

Pursuit of Happiness—To pursue doing only those things that lead to our ultimate good and, therefore, our true felicity.

Q

Quorum—This is the minimum number of House or Senate members required to vote or conduct business.

R

Republic—A representative form of government.

Rex Lex—The principle that the King is Law.

Right to Petition—The Constitutional right to directly request a remedy from the general government.

Rule of Law—The principle that only formally established laws govern; this opposes arbitrary rule.

S

Simple Resolution—Legislation presented and potentially implemented by only one congressional chamber and used for the regulation of business only within that chamber.

Story, Justice Joseph—A renowned Jurist who was a Harvard Law Professor and U.S. Supreme Court Justice who served under Chief Justice John Marshall. He wrote the Commentaries on the Constitution of the United States.

U

Unalienable Right—Specific rights that all men have that cannot be alienated, sold, or given away, not even by the individuals themselves.

V

Vertical Distribution of Power—The distribution of power between the federal government and that of the states.

Veto—Action taken by the President to either actively refuse or fail to timely sign into law a bill that has been approved by both chambers of Congress.

W

Writ of Certiorari—A request from a higher court to a lower court for documents on a case in order that the higher court may review the case. This writ is most frequently used regarding the consent of the U.S. Supreme Court to hear a specific case or controversy.

CPSIA information can be obtained at www.ICGtesting.com
Printed in the USA
LVOW02s2123290815

451826LV00002B/2/P